BROWNING'S
PARLEYINGS

BROWNING'S PARLEYINGS

THE AUTOBIOGRAPHY
OF A MIND

BY

WILLIAM CLYDE DeVANE

PROFESSOR OF ENGLISH IN YALE UNIVERSITY

NEW YORK

RUSSELL & RUSSELL · INC

1964

THE AUTHOR'S PREFACE
TO THE SECOND EDITION

THIS book was written almost forty years ago, and was first published in 1927. Except for a change of rank in the author's standing on the title-page, the name of the press which first published the book, early acknowledgements, and the addition of the present preface the work is now republished without change. It will be apparent to the new reader that the book is the product of a youthful scholar and reflects the time and manner of the scholarship of the decade in which it was written. At the same time, it will be evident, I think, that the book, though deficient in some respects, was well done, was the product of discovery and excitement, and opened new vistas in the serious study of Browning's poetry and biography. Literary fashions change, but honest and valuable work seldom goes out of fashion. If I were rewriting the book now it would be done differently. Possibly it might be wiser and more perceptive. It would avoid a number of petty mistakes. But I am not sure that I could still capture the "first fine careless rapture" of discovery—which is, after all, the essence of scholarship.

In the forty years which have intervened since the book was written a good deal of new information upon the poet and his poetry has come to light, some of which I have been able to contribute. An example of the new biographical evidence which we now possess may be seen in the Lady Louisa Ashburton episode in Browning's life. When I wrote the chapter upon the *Parleying with Daniel Bartoli* I deduced from internal evidence, and with the help of some veiled references in his other poems, that Browning was in this poem recording an event in his life, an affair with a dark "bold she-shape," and his consequent fierce self-reproach that he had been "false to Love"—that is, to the memory of Elizabeth Barrett Browning. I was convinced of the fact, but I had the wrong date, and when I appealed to England for confirmation the fact was admitted, but I was requested to withhold the name of the lady. In 1933, however, Professor Thurman L. Hood edited a volume of Browning letters in which he included an appendix clearly showing that the person to whom the poet proposed marriage was Lady Louisa Ashburton, and that the proper date of the episode was 1869-71. In itself, the biographical fact is of no great consequence except that the disclosure shed much new light on many of Browning's later poems which, like the *Parleying with Daniel Bartoli* itself, had been enigmas. The new interpretations, together with the proper credits, may be seen in the 1955 edition of my *Browning Handbook*.

In the work of forty years ago one may detect a number of errors and inadequacies, and it may be useful to point out a few typical ones. The occasional small errors of fact are immediately apparent and easily corrected. Beyond these, there are instances of youthful writing, painful now to me at least—flat, unmodified statements exhibiting an unwarranted assurance; labored writing, full of enthusiasm, to prove an inconsequential point; and a tendency occasionally to forget that it is Browning's characters who are speaking and not the poet himself—a common mistake.

There are too, inevitably, critical misjudgments. One particular error in judgment may be seen in my treatment of the *Prologue* and the *Epilogue* to the *Parleyings*. In 1927 I was inclined to dismiss them as having little direct connection with the seven *Parleyings*, when in fact they are intimate and important parts of Browning's whole purpose in his poem. Not only does each of them reinforce the preachments which are major themes throughout all the *Parleyings*, but in celebrating the birth of imagination in *Apollo and the*

Fates and the invention of printing in *Fust and his Friends*, Browning was thus recording the process of poetry from its origin in the poet's imagination to its dissemination in the modern world. This was, in little, Browning's career, and was thus properly recorded in his autobiographical work.

Moreover, the content of the *Prologue*—Apollo tricking the Fates to allow his friend Admetus to live if a substitute for him can be found—would have been an appropriate prelude to Browning's poem, *Balaustion's Adventure,* in which he transcribed Euripides' *Alcestis*. One remembers that *Balaustion's Adventure* (1871) has special reference to Elizabeth Barrett Browning ten years after her death. I think, too, that it was written in a spirit of revulsion from the recent Ashburton affair. The *Prologue*, therefore, touched upon a most intimate part of Browning's biography in this veiled manner, and referred at once to a biographical event as well as one of his most significant later poems.

One further comment may be useful to the new reader. Throughout my book of 1927 references were made in the footnotes to two different collections of Browning's letters which since that time have been re-edited and published in better and more accessible works. In the present book the older references still stand, but the reader is reminded of the following facts:

1) *Letters of Robert Browning to Various Correspondents*, ed. T. J. Wise, were published in London in two series of two small volumes each; the first series in 1895-1896, the second series in 1907-1908. These letters, with others, were included in *The Letters of Robert Browning, Collected by T. J. Wise*, ed. with Introduction and Notes by Thurman L. Hood, New Haven, 1933.

2) *Letters of Robert Browning to Miss Isa Blagden*, Arranged for publication by A. Joseph Armstrong, Waco, 1923. These letters were republished as a volume called *Dearest Isa: Robert Browning's Letters to Isabella*

viii   PREFACE TO THE SECOND EDITION

Blagden, ed. Edward C. McAleer, Austin, 1951.
The reader of the present volume should have little trouble
in transposing the references to the newer volumes.

Finally, I should like to record my gratification that my
early work has proved so useful to scholars that after all
these years a second edition is called for.

W. C. DeVane

July 24, 1964.

PREFACE

"So much misconception at best, ignorance at middling, and malice at worst, in those old slaps on my face in order apparently to keep some fellow's critical hands warm!"

BROWNING'S experience at the hands of his critics was not a happy one, and it is with some trepidation that a new critic adds himself to the list. Therefore, it would perhaps be both wise and gracious to propitiate the spirit of the poet by putting him first on the list of those to whom thanks are due. For it is he, more than anyone else, "without whose aid this book could not have been written"; and I trust that he (and not malice, misconception, or ignorance) is the onlie begetter of the ideas herein attributed to him. In so far as it has been possible I have let Browning speak for himself, though this is not always safe. Pursuing the poet through the mazy tracts of his thought has done, or should have done, much in helping me to keep my critical hand in, and for this too I am duly grateful.

My further indebtednesses are indeed numerous, and I take this occasion to express my thanks. To the editors and critics who have aided this study by their work in Browning criticism, I have recorded my debt in the Introduction; and I have faithfully detailed all such indebtednesses in my notes. Those upon whom I have leaned most heavily are listed in a bibliographical notice, which also serves as a key to abbreviated references, at the end of the volume.

To the staff of the Yale University Library, and especially to my friend, Miss Emily Hall, I hereby render gratitude which, though great, is still insufficient return for their kindness. To Professors Paul de Reul, J. E. Shaw, Mr. H. C. Minchin, and the Hon. J. M. Robertson, I wish to express my thanks for a number of favors. To the late Professor Albert Stanburrough Cook, and to Professors Chauncey Brewster Tinker and William Lyon Phelps I am grateful for

x   PREFACE

allowing me the use of books otherwise inaccessible, and for greater gifts which may not be mentioned here. For advice and counsel I wish to thank Professors Karl Young and William Lyon Phelps, though I absolve them entirely from responsibility for the matter and manner of the book. For permission to print the work, I thank the Kingsley Trust Association, donors of the John Addison Porter prize. To Mr. George Parmly Day and The Yale University Press I am happy to have this chance of expressing my appreciation of their generosity and unfailing consideration. And finally, all thanks must go to her who is first in the realms of help.

W. C. D.

September 3, 1927.

CONTENTS

INTRODUCTION

The History and Significance of Browning's "Parleyings With Certain People of Importance"

ADMIRERS of Browning, from his own time to this, have neglected his later work, preferring to remember him as the author of *Men and Women, Dramatis Personae,* and *The Ring and the Book.* Inspiration had departed after *Balaustion's Adventure,* in 1871, and only argument was left to fill its place. The judgment which he had made in 1855 against the author of *"Transcendentalism: A Poem in Twelve Books,"* is the most apt and just criticism of Robert Browning himself in the last two decades of his life.

> Stop playing, poet! May a brother speak?
> 'T is you speak, that's your error. Song's our art . . .

For Browning, a philosophical poet in the best of his time, finally took philosophy as his main business in life. As his poetic inspiration declined, and the earnestness of his moral purpose increased, he came into the lists as a philosopher armed cap-a-pie. In the heat of the conflict all the personal qualities of his later years—perverse ingenuity, capriciousness, self-will, crabbed independence, and sometimes bad temper—qualities which were really the darker sides of his virtues—often appeared too plainly. Consequently his poetry had in it more and more of the ingenuity of the metaphysician, and less and less of the spontaneous wedding of idea and music.

The change brought another deplorable loss. Creation of character, which had been the crowning glory of Browning's art, ceased almost entirely. In the full years before 1871 Browning's *dramatis personae* had been genuine personalities, speaking for the most part their own thoughts. After that year, no matter by what name he called the character, the voice was the voice of Browning. Finally he threw aside all disguise, and in the last volume published in his lifetime, *Parleyings With Certain People of Importance in Their Day*, he spoke openly in his own person. The form used in this volume is, ironically and significantly enough, the dramatic monologue which he had made famous in the creation of other characters; but here it is Browning who does all the talking. The seven men whom he calls before him appear only that Browning may give to the world his own opinions, through his comment upon them. It is in point, in this connection, to recall that the poet in his later years had no knack for conversation, though he was an excellent talker upon any subject which aroused his interest;[1] for the *Parleyings* are conversations only in name. Actually they are a series of expositions of the poet's favorite doctrines.

Browning had ceased to draw the portraits of imaginary men in order to draw at full length the portrait of himself. The habit had been growing upon him, until in the *Parleyings* he did this not unconsciously, but painstakingly and deliberately. That volume was to be his autobiography, in a new and better sense of the word.

Great pressure had been brought to bear upon Browning to write or to supply material for a biography of himself. With the establishment of a society in his honor he had become a public character. Honorary degrees had been conferred upon him. He was a social lion, seen everywhere. Naturally there was a curiosity in the literary world, concerning his life. Biographies of his contemporaries were appearing, in which, it may be said, Browning himself took a very great interest.[2] But he was deaf to all appeals for information about himself and his family. Many men, Furnivall, Wise, Gosse, and Ingram among them, requested biographical data;[3] but Browning never went further than to agree, courteously but cautiously, to correct any misstatements in the accounts that they might write. His anger

---

[1] See Orr, *Life,* pp. 364–365.

[2] See Orr, *Life,* p. 363.

[3] See *Letters from R. B. to Various Correspondents,* 1st Series, I, 50, 60; II, 9, 40, etc.

INTRODUCTION

XV

against those who presumed to pry into his life without permission, was fierce: "Think of the beast working away, not
deeming my feelings, or those of her family, worthy of notice.
It shall not be done if I can stop the scamp's knavery along
with his breath."[4] Furthermore, he destroyed all his own letters
that he could get possession of, save those between himself and
Elizabeth Barrett. His life was to be protected from any such
treatment as Froude had recently dealt out to Carlyle.

Despising the reminiscence and gossip of ordinary biography, he simply referred people to his poetry:

> Outside should suffice for evidence,
> And whoso desires to penetrate
> Deeper, must dive by the spirit sense.[5]

And in a very real way Browning was to be found in his poetry.
Through it he had expressed in pure art, in the vigorous middle
years, his philosophy of optimism. So in the later years, in a
different way but to a greater degree, he was to be found in his
poetry. His philosophy, from the necessity of his nature, still
demanded expression, though the poetical inspiration had fled.
No longer able to put his principles into action in character, he
had to explain them, justify them, defend them. But, as it has
been so aptly said, Browning was a better physician than a
metaphysician. His argument begot more argument. After finishing *Ferishtah's Fancies* he wrote to his friend Furnivall that
he did not know how people would like the volume, but he had
said a thing or two in it that he had wanted to say.[6] In the next
volume, the *Parleyings*, he said everything that he wanted to
say. Resisting the external pressure, Browning could not resist
this necessity of his own nature to explain himself fully in his
poetry.

He would write an autobiographical poem—but it was to be
autobiography of a distinct and unusual sort. There would be

[4] Chesterton, *Robert Browning*, New York, 1904, p. 116.
[5] *House*, ll. 33-35.
[6] See *Letters from R. B. to Various Correspondents*, 1st Series, II, 38.

no gossip, no reminiscence for its own sake. It would follow a new plan. He would call before him the men whose works had played an important part in his early education. They would be, each of them, representative of a different art; and, parleying with each in turn, he would describe the origin of his ideas, his development, and finally his mature opinion upon the art for which each stood. The volume, when completed, would be actually a biography of his mental life, from youth to old age.

The plan was truly an ambitious one, and the execution of it was difficult. His friend Mrs. Orr says that

. . . the revision of the work caused him considerable trouble. The subjects he had chosen strained his powers of exposition; and I think he often tried to remedy by mere verbal correction, what was a defect in the logical arrangement of his ideas. They would slide into each other where a visible dividing line was required.[7]

He worked longer on the volume than was his custom for a poem of that length. It was begun in September of 1885[8] as he was passing over the Italian Alps in his journey to Venice, a fact which accounts, perhaps, for several splendid descriptions of mountain scenery in the volume. On January 28, nearly a year and a half later, the book was published. It had an impressive, though somewhat ponderous, title-page:[9]

[7] Orr, *Life*, p. 347.

[8] See *Letters from R. B. to Various Correspondents*, 1st Series, II, 42. *Ferishtah's Fancies* had been published in the autumn of 1884. The poem Browning speaks of in his letter could have been only his *Parleyings*.

[9] Browning probably got his title, as well as the general idea for the form of the poem, from Dante's *Vita Nuova*, xxxv. He had previously used the same incident from Dante's life in *One Word More*, ll. 32-49.

PARLEYINGS WITH CERTAIN PEOPLE
OF IMPORTANCE IN THEIR DAY:

To wit: BERNARD DE MANDEVILLE,
DANIEL BARTOLI,
CHRISTOPHER SMART,
GEORGE BUBB DODINGTON,
FRANCIS FURINI,
GERARD DE LAIRESSE,
and CHARLES AVISON,

Introduced by
A DIALOGUE BETWEEN APOLLO AND THE FATES

Concluded by
ANOTHER BETWEEN JOHN FUST AND HIS FRIENDS.

BY ROBERT BROWNING.

London;
Smith, Elder, & Co., 15 Waterloo Place.
1887.

To the general public of Browning's day, as to ours, the
names of the men with whom he parleyed conveyed little. To his
friends the volume was another of the poet's whimsicalities. To
the hostile it was a parade of curious and obsolete learning.
But readers of to-day, with their knowledge of what books were
in the library of the poet's father, know that such men as Gerard de Lairesse and Daniel Bartoli were chosen neither casually
nor pedantically, but with a wise economy. All the men with
whom Browning parleyed, save one, were men whose books he
had read as a boy; their books had been the tutors of his very
irregular education. They were in short "with one exception his
old familiar friends: men whose works connect themselves with
the intellectual sympathies and the imaginative pleasures of
his very earliest youth."[10] They were, moreover, representative
men. Browning selected a philosopher, an historian, a poet, a

[10] Orr, *Handbook,* p. 339.

politician, a priest, a painter, and a musician. By parleying
with each in turn, he attempted to give a history of the origin,
growth, and final maturity of his opinions upon seven major
interests of his life. But, commending or condemning these
"people of importance in their day," Browning felt it necessary
to contrast his mature opinions upon each subject under discussion, with those of some eminent man of his own day. Thus
the volume, from a recounting of the poet's "boyhood loves,"[11]
became finally the expression of "the accumulated convictions
of a lifetime."[12]

Pregnant with meaning as Browning meant his poem to be,
he offered no immediate explanations concerning it, either to
his friends or the critics. This was in accordance with his custom, for he considered it unfair to give one reviewer the advantage over another either by giving information that would aid
judgments on his work, or by sending out early proof-sheets.
In this case, however, he was prevailed upon by his publishers,
who felt that a review was needed to appear simultaneously
with the book, to overlook some of his scruples. Reluctantly he
allowed the proof-sheets to be sent to his friend George Barnett
Smith,[13] the reviewer for the *Times.* Clearly, however, he gave
Smith no further aid; for when the review appeared on the day
of publication, Smith, who had heard the rumor that this volume contained Browning's long-expected reminiscences,[14] missed
entirely the point of the book. "The supposition that Mr.
Browning's new work was to be of an autobiographical character," the review began, "is entirely erroneous."[15]

In fact, the astonishment, chagrin, and genuine bewilderment
of most of the reviewers makes rather ludicrous reading now.
The biographical intention of the poem entirely escaped them.

[11] Orr, *Life,* p. 348.
[12] Orr, *Handbook,* p. 339.
[13] See *Letters from R. B. to Various Correspondents,* 1st Series, II, 92;
2d Series, I, 71-72.
[14] See *idem,* 1st Series, II, 82.
[15] The *Times,* January 28, 1887.

INTRODUCTION xix

General opinion is well represented by the criticism which appeared in the *Saturday Review:*

Mr. Browning, who often amuses himself by writing in a cipher to which he alone has the key, has seldom propounded to his disciples a more hopeless puzzle . . .[16]

Another critic was filled with sympathy for the poor scholar who might some day be called upon to translate the poem:

Mr. Browning's translator, if this work should ever be translated into any foreign language, will come upon difficulties to which even the difficulties of translators of a corrupt chorus of the Agamemnon will be trivial.[17]

Most of the reviewers could make nothing of it, and gave up the whole problem in complete despair, the only notable exception being an able, though very brief, review in the *Academy*.[18] In short, the critics made little of the *Parleyings*, and the general public nothing at all. Only the members of the Browning Society, and not all of them, pretended to understand it.[19] The volume, had it not been for Browning's reputation, would have been still-born. The poem has, of course, been published in all editions of Browning's complete works, but no separate edition has been called for since the first.

The *Parleyings* are written in the characteristically metaphysical manner of Browning's later poems. To him the volume seemed, as in accordance with his theory of progress each new volume always seemed, his best work thus far.[20] But the first fine careless rapture of his halcyon days was not to be stalked intellectually, however ingenious the hunter might be. Occasionally he achieves a rare strain of wild beauty in the manner of *Pauline;* here and there one finds a suggestion of his former power. But for the most part the book is "mere gray argu-

16 The *Saturday Review,* February 26, 1887.
17 The *Spectator,* February 5, 1887.
18 On February 12, 1887.
19 See the amusing discussion reported in the *Browning Society Papers* (London), II, 211-212. Mr. Bernard Shaw is present.
20 See Orr, *Life,* p. 360.

ment," in terminology which is often grotesque, and always arbitrarily Browningesque; and the fact that the argument concerns itself chiefly with the eternal and great questions asked by mankind does not compensate for these faults.

It was the very complexity and abstruseness of the plan which doomed it to failure. As we have seen, the subjects he had chosen strained his powers of exposition, and the revision caused him considerable trouble. The poem is difficult reading, and without the knowledge of Browning's autobiographical intention, or without cognizance of the biographical significance of his interlocutors as a key, it is almost unintelligible. There is a tragic irony in the fact that this volume, in which Browning tried to set forth his most cherished opinions, should have been one of the least understood of his works.

We to-day have the advantage of the public of 1887. In the first place, we are able to see Browning's work in its proper perspective, and thus to view the *Parleyings* as the inevitable culmination of his poetic career. The *Parleyings* are more unintelligible than "the entirely unintelligible *Sordello*" unless they are studied in relation to all of Browning's work. In the second place, much more of the evidence is in. Each of the few commentators on the *Parleyings* has made his contribution, and it has remained for the present writer, in the first study that has attempted to be complete or exhaustive, to put the evidence together, to seek out new, and thus to demonstrate Browning's autobiographical purpose in the poem.

Of the commentators, one of the first in importance is Mrs. Sutherland Orr. She was a personal friend, as well as a biographer of the poet (after his death), and gained considerable information by word of mouth from him. Her *Handbook* has the additional advantage of having been corrected by Browning himself.[21] She knew—what the critics could not know—that the men with whom the poet parleyed were his "boyhood loves,"[22] "men whose works connect themselves with the intellectual sym-

[21] See Orr, *Handbook,* pp. vi-vii.
[22] Orr, *Life,* p. 348.

pathies and the imaginative pleasures of his very earliest youth."[23] She saw that the volume held the "accumulated convictions"[24] of his life. She knew, too, something of Browning's allusions to his contemporaries, for she suggested hesitantly, as if Browning had told her and she knew not how to take it, that the *Parleying With Bernard de Mandeville* contained an attack on Carlyle, and the *George Bubb Dodington,* one on Disraeli. She made little of these hints, however, and her remarks upon the poems run off into a faulty and inadequate condensation of each *Parleying.*

W. Hall Griffin and Harry Christopher Minchin, Browning's most trustworthy and adequate biographers, came nearer to a just estimate of the *Parleyings.* Griffin had access to the Browning library in 1908-1909 when he was preparing the biography, and was therefore able to write some very illuminating chapters upon the books which played their part in the irregular education of the poet.[25] The works of the men with whom Browning parleyed, and many more of his favorite books in the strange collection of six thousand volumes, were inspected and commented upon. Griffin died before he could reap the full harvest of his labors. While he saw the *Parleyings* as an account of the influence of the poet's boyish reading, he missed the wider biographical significance of the volume.

Beyond these, three works deserve mention. The essay upon the *Parleyings* by Arthur Symons,[26] delivered before the Browning Society at London on April 29, 1887, is the best appreciation of the literary merits of the volume. J. T. Nettleship in his *Essays and Thoughts*[27] is particularly good in suggesting the occurrence of similar ideas elsewhere in Browning's works. The Florentine edition[28] of the poet's works contains, be-

---

[23] Orr, *Handbook,* p. 339.
[24] *Ibid.*
[25] See Griffin and Minchin, pp. 1-41.
[26] See *Notes Upon Mr. Browning's Latest Volume,* Browning Society Papers (London), II, 169 ff.
[27] Published in London, 1890. See pp. 397-452.
[28] See the bibliographical note to this volume.

sides excellent introductory essays, the only annotation that
has been done upon the *Parleyings*, but its notes do not pretend
to completeness.

Proceeding upon the hints supplied by Griffin and Mrs. Orr,
the present writer has been able to show that not only were the
poet's interlocutors important educational influences, but that
they often supplied ideas or material which he later used in his
poetry. Much of the study has necessarily concerned itself directly with the men with whom Browning parleyed, in an effort
to discover the true personality of each man, his influence on
Browning, exactly the works of the man which the poet knew,
and their influence on his work. In this connection the work of
Griffin has been of great assistance, as also has been the descriptive catalogue of the books and pictures in the Browning
library published by Sotheby, Wilkinson and Hodge[29] upon the
dispersal of the library in 1913.

The educational significance of the poem is, however, only
the starting-point. Embodying as they do Browning's mature
philosophy, the *Parleyings* must be studied as the culmination
of his opinions; wherefore the whole body of his poetry, and all
the biographical documents, have been considered as evidence.
Further than this, because of Browning's allusions to his contemporaries, it has been necessary to investigate his connection
with certain nineteenth-century men and movements. Browning's references to his contemporaries, it may here be stated, are
of two sorts. First, he frequently calls in some contemporary
with whom he differs on some great philosophical question, in
order to refute him; as, for example, he summons Carlyle to be
refuted by the sage De Mandeville. Second, there are other local
and contemporaneous allusions of a more incidental nature, as,
in *Furini*, the startling invective against prudish critics of art.
Through the investigation of these things the study contributes
new information on Browning's attitude to certain tendencies of
his time, and to the individual exponents of these tendencies.

[29] See the bibliographical note to this volume.

Finally, it attempts to make clear in a more general way the relation between Browning's thought and that of his age.

The study of each *Parleying* has naturally divided itself into three main parts. The first part contains the account of Browning's relation to the man who gives his name to the *Parleying*, and of Browning's development in the art which that man represents. There is next a section which deals with the relation of the ideas expressed in the particular *Parleying* to the whole of Browning's philosophy. The third part contains an exegesis of the poem under study. Naturally these arbitrary divisions are subject to the demands of circumstances, and the divisions shrink or expand accordingly. The plan, however, has been followed throughout except in the chapter on Bartoli, where the problem was so distinctly different as to require an exegesis of the poem before its significance as a part of Browning's thought could be considered. The *Prologue* and *Epilogue*, being unlike the *Parleyings*, are treated together in a separate chapter at the end.

The study, concerning itself in the presentation of new material, in the evaluation of evidence, and in the tracing of ideas, is necessarily detailed. Yet out of the detail should emerge, finally, the picture of Robert Browning in the year 1887. He intended the *Parleyings* to be precisely that. It is unfortunate that so significant a work should need so much explanation, and should have lacked it for so long; but the very need of explanation is the reason for its failure. It is the hope of the present writer that this study, through its explanation, may serve to show forth the poem for what Browning intended it to be, the autobiography of his mind.

BROWNING'S PARLEYINGS

CHAPTER I

THE PARLEYING WITH
BERNARD DE MANDEVILLE

I

IT is highly significant that Browning should have chosen
a philosopher, Bernard de Mandeville, as the first of the
seven people of importance with whom he was to parley. For
philosophy, ever a vital factor in Browning's thought, had in
his later years usurped the place of chief importance, until
at last it almost drove out his poetic art altogether. The conviction that God was in his heaven and all was right with the
world came to be supported by an ever-increasing weight of
logic in Browning's mind; and here, in the *Parleying With
Bernard de Mandeville*, the philosophy which has been striving for utterance in almost every poem since *Paracelsus* finds
its fullest and most explicit expression. Browning, casting
aside all disguise, delivers a summary of his philosophy in
his own person.

He calls upon Bernard de Mandeville, whose *Fable of the
Bees* he had read in his early years, to listen to this philosophy and to confirm his arguments. But the poet had taken
the clever and paradoxical Mandeville at his word, and had
in consequence completely misunderstood his doctrines. The
Parleying is not nearly so much concerned with Mandeville,
however, as it is with Browning's twin literary philosopher
of the nineteenth century, Thomas Carlyle. For Mandeville
is summoned chiefly that he may help Browning confute
Carlyle's gloomy and despairing attitude toward God and
the problem of evil in the world. In preparation for an exegesis of the poem this chapter, therefore, first concerns itself
with Browning's knowledge and understanding of the two
philosophers whose ghostly figures appear before him; one,

2 BROWNING'S PARLEYINGS

Mandeville, dead long since—the other, Thomas Carlyle, dead only yesterday.

Browning's knowledge of Bernard de Mandeville dates back at least as far as the early part of the year 1833. The celebrated Dutch philosopher, who had made his home in London for many years, died there on January 21, 1732/3 (O. S.); and it was probably in commemoration of the hundredth anniversary of this event that Robert Browning, senior, gave to his son a copy of Mandeville's *Fable of the Bees*. The date of the gift was inscribed on the title-page, "Friday 1 February, 1833"; and the book had been annotated by the elder Browning as was his custom.[1] The volume was not a first edition as Mrs. Orr implies,[2] nor even a very rare one, but was the edition of 1795, which combined the former two volumes of the *Fable* into one.[3] It is this edition, therefore, which was consulted for this study, and from which my quotations will be made.

The Fable of the Bees was a product of long and gradual growth. Its author, Bernard de Mandeville (1670-1733), was a Dutch physician and student of philosophy who had gone to England in his young manhood and soon decided to make his home there. He became prosperous and honored,[4] and was a favorite with the Earl of Macclesfield. There was apparently a great deal of strong-minded boldness about Mandeville, and an independence of judgment which is illustrated in the story of his encounter with Addison:

Lord Macclesfield, when chief-justice, was used often to have him at his house, and was pleased with his conversation. He once

[1] Most of the facts concerning Browning's copy of *The Fable of the Bees* are given by Griffin and Minchin, p. 19. The suggestion that the book was given to the poet in commemoration of the anniversary of Mandeville's death is my own. It will be noticed when the correction to the new style of dates is made, that February 1 is the exact anniversary.

[2] See Orr, *Life*, p. 30.

[3] See Sotheby, *Catalogue*, item no. 898.

[4] This is proved conclusively by F. B. Kaye in his edition of *The Fable of the Bees* . . ., Oxford, 1924, 2 vols. See *Life of Mandeville*, in *Introduction*, I, xvii-xxx.

got Mr. Addison to meet him, of whom, being asked his opinion by his lordship, Mandeville answered, he thought him a parson in a tye-wig.[5]

Mandeville was a keen observer of economic conditions, and went into an analysis of causes with the attitude of a modern scientist. *The Fable of the Bees* is largely an outgrowth of that observation, coupled with his perception that the commercial ideals of the English were decidedly inconsistent with the type of Christianity that they professed.

This philosophy was first put forward in a small pamphlet called *The Grumbling Hive: Or, Knaves turn'd Honest*, which was published in 1705. As the later title indicates, and as this one suggests, the argument was set forth in the form of a fable. A hive of bees conducted its affairs, the story goes, much as men conduct theirs, and the group was busy and prosperous. But condemnation of fraud and dishonesty was often heard among them, until at last Jupiter in indignation swore that he would rid them of the sins that they complained of. From that moment everyone paid his debts, those who were in the wrong ceased to complain of others, and the business of the lawyers was gone. The business of doctors was considerably lessened because no disease was complicated by the practices of quacks. The clergy had very little to do. There was no self-seeking at court, and business could be done there by a few honest bees. Trade languished because all vain desires had disappeared. Arts and crafts were neglected because content, the bane of industry, had come among them. Finally, the fable says, the bees flew away from their hive in a last protest against extravagance, and took up their dwelling in a hollow tree.

In 1714 the verse-fable was printed, again anonymously, as part of a book called *The Fable of the Bees: or, Private Vices, Publick Benefits*. In this work Mandeville's views were

[5] Hawkins, *Life of Johnson*, London, 1787, p. 264. Johnson had told the same story in his *Life of Addison;* see *Johnson's Works,* ed. Hawkins, London, 1787, III, 71, 72.

definitely set forth by means of notes to the poem, and an
essay called *An Enquiry into the Origin of Moral Virtue*. In
the edition of 1723 his philosophy was still further elaborated in two additional essays, *An Essay on Charity and
Charity-Schools* and *A Search into the Nature of Society*. In
this year the views of Mandeville began to attract attention,
and the work was condemned by the Grand Jury of Middlesex and attacked in a letter published in one of the London
newspapers. The next edition of the *Fable*, in 1724, and all
succeeding editions, contained an answer or *Vindication*,
which we shall have occasion to discuss later. Further editions of the work continued to appear, and in 1729 Mandeville issued a second part, which also went through many editions. It was a book much read all through the century. In
1795 the two parts were published in one volume; and, as we
have seen, it was this edition which Robert Browning read.

If we come now to search for the true meaning of Mandeville's philosophy, we shall find it expressed in the terms of a
brilliant and devastating paradox. Mandeville took the ascetic creed from contemporary philosophy, chiefly from the
divines, and defined virtue in their terms. Without self-denial
there could be no virtue, and those acts alone were virtuous

. . . by which man, contrary to the impulse of nature, should
endeavour the benefit of others, or the conquest of his own passions, out of a rational ambition of being good.[6]

Thus all things that were in the least tainted with self were
essentially vicious. Equipped with this definition of virtue,
Mandeville found that the affairs of the world were conducted on an altogether different moral plane. More than
that, it was the selfish qualities in man—pride, envy, jeal-
ousy, love of money—that made business and trade flourish
and made a prosperous society possible. Thus trade, rising
from vice and therefore vicious, was nevertheless a benefit to
society. Mandeville's paradoxical title, *Private Vices, Pub-*

---

[6] *The Fable of the Bees*, London, 1795, p. 17.

lick Benefits, is due to his application of this rigorous definition of virtue, by which all the prosperity of nations stands condemned. If daily life were conducted in accordance with this ideal, all trade would cease, for arts and crafts exist to supply purely mundane wants. When Jove, tired of listening to the grumbling of the bees, made them honest, he ruined at once the greatness of the hive.

Mandeville was of course insisting upon the incompatibility of ascetic virtue and a prosperous society. His position is stated clearly in the *Vindication:*

> After this, I flatter myself to have demonstrated, that neither the friendly qualities and kind affections that are natural to man, nor the real virtues he is capable of acquiring by reason and self-denial, are the foundation of society; but that what we call evil in this world, moral as well as natural, is the grand principle that makes us sociable creatures; the solid basis, the life and support of all trades and employments without exception: That there we must look for the true origin of all arts and sciences; and that the moment evil ceases, the society must be spoiled, if not totally dissolved.[7]

This paradox is achieved, as Kaye has admirably demonstrated,[8] by the use of two different standards. Private actions are judged by an ascetic standard, conduct being evaluated not by its consequences but by the motives that induced it. But the effects of the actions are judged by utilitarian standards, and thus anything productive of national happiness and prosperity becomes a benefit. Mandeville, by the statement of his paradox, put his readers in a dilemma. They had either to renounce prosperity or to deny their ascetic creed—neither of which they were willing to do. No wonder the divines of the time were driven into impotent frothings of rage by Mandeville's book. No wonder, too, that the Grand Jury of Middlesex brought against the *Fable* the charge that it had

7 *The Fable of the Bees,* London, 1795, p. 251.
8 See *The Fable of the Bees,* I, xxxviii-lxxvi.

. . . a direct tendency to the subversion of all religion and civil government, our duty to the Almighty, our love to our country, and regard to our oaths . . .[9]

A complete condemnation of the *Fable* was the only answer that could be made to it: to attempt to answer the argument was to be forced to choose between the two unwelcome alternatives.

The attacks upon the book prompted Mandeville's *Vindication*, which is conciliatory in tone compared to the body of the book itself. For Mandeville had to defend his position without betraying the secret of his paradox. This meant that he had himself to state his position in regard to the whole question. Should mankind cease to strive for prosperity since such striving is selfish and wicked? Or should man declare the rigorous ascetic creed which condemns prosperity absurd? Ostensibly Mandeville chose the way of virtue. In a passage that he was careful to quote in the *Vindication* he had said:

. . . if I have shown the way to worldly greatness, I have always, without hesitation, preferred the road that leads to virtue.[10]

And again in the *Vindication* he took pains to point to a passage in his original *Remarks:*

When I say that societies cannot be raised to wealth and power, and the top of earthly glory, without vices, I do not think that, by so saying, I bid men be vicious, any more than I bid them be quarrelsome or covetous, when I affirm that the profession of the law could not be maintained in such numbers and splendor, if there was not abundance of too selfish and litigious people.[11]

[9] *The Fable of the Bees,* 1795, p. 240. This charge is quoted in the *Vindication.*
[10] *Idem,* pp. 138-139; quoted in *Vindication,* pp. 254-255.
[11] *Idem,* p. 138. The sense of the passage is quoted in p. 254 of the *Vindication.*

The *Vindication,* by its conciliatory tone and by its ostensible position on the side of virtue, softens to a considerable extent the true strength and daring of the book as a whole.

But no one who has comprehended Mandeville's ideas can doubt for a moment that though he chose the side of ascetic virtue, the choice was anything more than a formal one. His whole sympathy, it may be seen on every page, is with the cause of earthly glory. At heart he is utilitarian. He is trying to undermine subtly the ascetic formula of virtue by showing its absurdity. Mandeville's real position is that man has been deceiving himself by pretending to follow these standards, and that the more honest thing to do would be to be candidly "vicious."

It is obvious from every bit of evidence in the case that Browning did not understand the true purport of Mandeville's teaching. He read Mandeville—unless perchance he had read him before the gift of the *Fable*—[12] at an extremely critical period of his life. He was returning from atheism to orthodoxy, and the tendency of the reaction was to make him read orthodoxy into all things. He had begun his search, a search that was to continue the rest of his life, for evidence of a loving and gracious God who utilized evil in this life to make it bring forth moral good. The quest for good in the earth became the dominating force in Browning's life, especially in the latter years:

Peter has the secret! Fair and Good are products
(So he said) of Foul and Evil: one must bring to pass the other.[13]

It was just at the period when he had decided that he believed in light and truth, that the poet's attention was caught by Mandeville's paradoxical and striking sub-title, *Private Vices, Public Benefits.* Here was more evidence that a benevolent God turned evil to good. It is as one who like himself has

---

[12] This is extremely unlikely, and there is no evidence to support it.
[13] *Pietro of Albano,* ll. 185-186.

. . . recognized harmoniously combine
Evil with good . . .[14]

that Browning summons Mandeville to the *Parleying*.

The question naturally arises, how could so keen-witted a reader as Browning, who had just passed through a period of interest in radical views, have failed to grasp the true meaning of Mandeville's doctrines? In the first place, as we have seen, Browning had a preconceived notion of Mandeville, gained from the sub-title of the book. In the second place, there were passages in the book which would tend to confirm Browning in his notion. For example, Mandeville says:

The short-sighted vulgar, in the chain of causes, seldom can see farther than one link; but those who can enlarge their view, and will give themselves leisure of gazing on the prospect of concatenated events, may, in a hundred places, see good spring up, and pullulate from evil, as naturally as chickens do from eggs.[15]

But as we have seen, Mandeville based his whole paradox on an inconsistent definition of the terms good and evil, and meant something entirely different, by this passage, from Browning's optimistic philosophy. But the chief explanation of Browning's misunderstanding of the eighteenth-century philosopher lies in the fact that he took as literally true all of Mandeville's protestations of his love of ascetic virtue. That is, if Browning was at all puzzled by Mandeville's statements, he was completely reassured by the *Vindication*, which, as we have seen, tends to give an erroneous impression of the book as a whole.[16]

The validity of this explanation is verified by Mrs. Orr, whose book, it will be remembered, had the advantage of Browning's suggestions and corrections. Apparently puzzled by Browning's identification of himself with such a radical

14 *With Bernard de Mandeville*, ll. 8-9.
15 *The Fable of the Bees*, 1795, p. 252.
16 See above, pp. 6-7.

figure as Mandeville, Mrs. Orr seems to have questioned him on the subject:

> Mr. Browning fully accepts the vindication and even regards it as superfluous. He sees nothing, either in the fable itself or the commentary first attached to it, which may not equally be covered by the Christian doctrine of original sin, or the philosophic acceptance of evil as a necessary concomitant, or condition, of good: and finds fresh guarantees for a sound moral intention in the bright humour and sound practical sense in which the book abounds. This judgment was formed (as I have already implied) very early in Mr. Browning's life, even before the appearance of "Pauline," and supplies a curious comment on any impression of mental immaturity which his own work of that period may have produced.[17]

From this passage it is quite clear that Browning held one consistent opinion of Mandeville throughout his life, but an opinion that was almost unique.

The passage helps also to establish two other significant facts concerning Browning's knowledge of Mandeville. In the first place, it tends to connect Browning's reading of the *Fable* with a date close to that February 1 on which his father gave him a copy of the book. For *Pauline* was published in March, 1833, and Mrs. Orr says that Browning had formed his opinion of Mandeville even before the appearance of that work. It is likely that the poet connected the two in his mind, since he received the *Fable* just after finishing his poem,[18] and in all likelihood read it during the interval between that date and the publication of *Pauline*. Mandeville was still in his mind at the end of March. Writing to W. Johnson Fox, who had given ten pages in *The Monthly Repository* to a criticism of *Pauline*, Browning uttered these thanks for the review:

> . . . all things considered, I think you are almost repaid, if you imagine what I must feel—and it will have been worth while to

---

[17] Orr, *Handbook*, p. 345.
[18] Browning finished *Pauline* in January, 1833.

have made a fool of myself, only to have obtained a "case" which leaves my fine fellow Mandeville at a dead lock.[19]

In short, all the evidence points to the fact that Browning read Mandeville for the first time after his father gave him the copy of the *Fable*, and hence tends to support the suggestion that has been advanced above that the peculiar time at which the poet came in contact with the book explains somewhat his misunderstanding of its doctrines.

In the second place, Mrs. Orr's statement, together with Browning's own letter to Fox, suggests reasons for the poet's great interest in Mandeville. The one mentions the "bright humour and sound practical sense in which the book abounds." The other refers to Mandeville's tendency to make a "case." It is significant to find Browning here interested, perhaps for the first time, in a thing that enthralled him the rest of his life. It is altogether likely that Mandeville accentuated in Browning or even induced in him the ruling passion of special pleading and "case" making. The trait is so deeply embedded in Browning's nature that it must have come from his own native mental activity; nevertheless Mandeville, the master of paradox, certainly supplied an impetus to Browning's tendency, and if he did not give him any material, at least suggested a striking method. This influence becomes the more significant when we recall that Browning spent the better part of his genius in making cases for such people as the lady in *The Glove*, Mr. Sludge, Prince Hohenstiel-Schwangau, Bishop Blougram, Pompilia, Caponsacchi, the hero of *Fifine at the Fair*, Ivan Ivanovitch, and a hundred others.[20]

Thus while Browning missed a comprehension of Mandeville's philosophy, he was nevertheless influenced by his style and method. He was impressed by the strong-minded boldness of the man, and described him in the *Parleying* as ready

19 Orr, *Life*, p. 53.

20 For a further discussion of Browning's use of paradox see Phelps, *Browning How to Know Him*, Ch. VI.

"to whisk out of his path any object that risked encounter."
A brusqueness in treating orthodox opinion is also noticed in
a reference to Mandeville's pooh-poohing Addison's "tye-
wig preachment." It was natural that the philosopher should
have made a very happy impression upon the young Browning, because of his humor, his practical sense, and his great
mastery of the art of paradox. So in summing up the influences of his youth Browning rightly included Mandeville in
the *Parleyings*, in spite of the fact that he had failed to comprehend Mandeville's philosophy.

Apparently Browning, in preparing to write his *Parleying With Bernard de Mandeville*, did not make a careful
study of the *Fable*. He seems to have refreshed his memory
chiefly by a glance at the Preface and at the *Vindication*,
which he remembered as the key to a "proper" interpretation of Mandeville. The few direct references that occur in
the *Parleying* all point to the *Vindication* and Preface; and
the whole tone of the poem suggests that Browning was rely-
ing chiefly on his early interpretation of Mandeville, rather
than on a consultation of the book itself. He frankly admits
that his knowledge of Mandeville is somewhat rusty:

> . . . so far I understood
> Thy teaching long ago.[21]

Because of his original misunderstanding of the philosophy of the *Fable of the Bees*, which was not corrected by any
careful study later on, Browning was led into the grotesque
situation of identifying himself with the foe of spirituality,
"the English Catiline," and the scoffer at all things that
Browning himself revered. The situation has its own irony.
Had Browning realized the true purport of Mandeville's
thought few men in England would have been more out-
raged. So astute a critic of philosophy as Samuel Taylor
Coleridge had written in Southey's copy of the *Fable:*

Can anyone read Mandeville's fable of the Bees, and not see

[21] *With Bernard de Mandeville*, ll. 38-39.

that it is a keen satire on the inconsistencies of Christianity, and so intended?[22]

And a critic of philosophical systems more nearly contemporary with Browning concluded that Mandeville

. . . leaves nothing but a bare, hideous chaos, entirely godless in the sense that it neither bears internal traces of Divine harmony, nor of the interference of Divine powers from without. Denying the reality of virtue, he sees no reason for providing any new form of belief round which the nobler impulses may gather. In short, he exhibits the result of taking the old theology and simply leaving out God. The result is naturally appalling. We have chaos without even a hint that some reconstructive process is necessary to supply the place of the old order. Without a God and without a hell and heaven, said theologians, there can be no virtue. Well, replies Mandeville in substance, we know nothing of God, and nothing of a future life; and I accept your conclusion that virtue is a humbug; . . . men of sense may laugh at it among themselves, though of course men of sense will not laugh in public. To say this, though not quite in plain words, and to say it with a grin, does not imply a very noble character.[23]

Surely no greater antithesis than this could be stated in answer to Browning's assurance that Mandeville had a "sound moral intention." The common consensus of nineteenth-century opinion—as indeed of all critical opinion upon Mandeville from Hutchinson, Berkeley, and Law, on down—was that he was "the sagacious sycophant of the baser instincts."

In short, Browning had absolutely nothing in common with Mandeville but a lively and ingenious mind that delighted in paradox. He believed that Mandeville had, in common with himself, a sound moral intention; but this similarity did not exist. In the same way Mandeville's belief in the doctrine of original sin was apparent to Browning

22 The Fable of the Bees, ed. Kaye, II, 453.
23 Leslie Stephen, Freethinking and Plainspeaking, New York, 1877, pp. 277-278.

alone.[24] Mandeville's system was really founded on self-love. With the analytical attitude of a modern scientist he had examined the origins of virtue:

. . . the nearer we search into human nature, the more we shall be convinced, that the moral virtues are the political offspring which flattery begot upon pride.[25]

Browning, who had his idea of the corruption of man's heart from the Scriptures, had attacked just such a position as Mandeville's in *Bishop Blougram's Apology:*

Philosophers deduce you chastity
Or shame, from just the fact that at the first
Whoso embraced a woman in the field,
Threw club down and forewent his brains beside,
So, stood a ready victim in the reach
Of any brother savage, club in hand;
Hence saw the use of going out of sight
In wood or cave to prosecute his loves:
I read this in a French book t'other day.
Does law so analyzed coerce you much?[26]

Thus the last similarity that Browning assumed existed between his philosophy and Mandeville's disappears; leaving no similarity whatsoever so far as philosophy is concerned. No two people could be more antithetical in purpose. There remain only the similarity in ingenuity of mind and the common delight in paradox which have already been discussed.

Thus there are decided elements of humor in Browning's attributing to Mandeville an optimistic and idealistic philosophy which the Dutch physician would have scorned. Browning, indeed, has a much closer kinship to Shaftesbury, Mandeville's arch-opponent, than to Mandeville himself.[27]

But it is still more humorous that Browning should have

24 See the passage from Mrs. Orr, quoted above, p. 9.
25 *The Fable of the Bees,* 1795, p. 18.
26 *Bishop Blougram's Apology,* ll. 825-834.
27 J. M. Robertson, in *Pioneer Humanists,* London, 1907, p. 263, is of this opinion. He suggests that Browning's elastic doctrines come through Pope.

called upon Mandeville to confute the doctrines of Thomas Carlyle. For Carlyle and Browning were in the process of maturing at about the same time, and were inheritors of the same methods and problems of thought. Consequently they are much more complementary figures in philosophy than they are opponents. They both broke from the Deism of the eighteenth century. They were both witnesses of the presence of God in mankind; and both uttered their appeal to the spirit of mankind. It was because they met on a common ground and had behind them a common background, that the difference between them was so apparent. It is more apparent than real. Hence it is rather ridiculous that Browning should have called in Mandeville, who was atheist, utilitarian, and philosopher of the senses and passions of mankind, to help him confute a brother-believer in the spirit.

II

It would be obvious that Thomas Carlyle was the antagonist against whom the *Parleying With Bernard de Mandeville* was directed, even if we had no other evidence than that contained in the poem itself. Not only are the sentiments ascribed to him in the *Parleying* familiar as those of Carlyle; but there is a recognizable portrait of the doleful prophet of Chelsea. He is introduced in this fashion:

> But what means this
> —Objected by a mouth which yesterday
> Was magisterial in antithesis
> To half the truths we hold, or trust we may,
> Though tremblingly the while?[28]

"Magisterial" was a word that Browning had used to describe Carlyle as early as 1845.[29] Carlyle had died in 1881; hence the fitting reference to him who was "yesterday" magisterial in antithesis. The longest description of his opponent

[28] *With Bernard de Mandeville*, ll. 39-43.
[29] See *Letters of R. B. and E. B. B.*, I, 27.

Browning gives in a passage which follows closely upon the former:

> Bernard de Mandeville, confute for me
> This parlous friend who captured or set free
> Thunderbolts at his pleasure, yet would draw
> Back, panic-stricken by some puny straw
> Thy gold-rimmed amber-headed cane had whisked
> Out of his pathway if the object risked
> Encounter, . . . grant this friend—
> (Whose groan I hear, with guffaw at the end
> Disposing of mock-melancholy)—grant
> His bilious mood one potion, ministrant
> Of homely wisdom, healthy wit![30]

The character is unmistakable. The "bilious mood," the "groan" and the "guffaw" are well-known characteristics of Carlyle. The "panic-stricken" quality of the philosopher is not so well known. Browning must have had in mind what Mazzini, whom he had introduced to Carlyle, had said in his essay upon the works of the Scotsman:

. . . from his lips, at times so daring, we seem to hear every instant the cry of the Breton mariner—"My God, protect me! My bark is so small and thy ocean so vast."[31]

The other quality here mentioned, the derision of mock-melancholy, is again a familiar characteristic of Carlyle. One has only to remember his chapter upon *The Sorrows of Teufelsdröckh*, or any one of a dozen other passages upon Byron, to realize how familiar it is:

. . . in the sickliest of recorded ages, when British Literature lay all puking and sprawling in Werterism, Byronism, and other Sentimentalism tearful or spasmodic (fruit of internal *wind*), Nature was kind enough to send us two healthy Men . . .[32]

[30] *With Bernard de Mandeville*, ll. 62-74.
[31] Reprinted in Mazzini, *Essays, The Writings of Thomas Carlyle*, Camelot Series, London, 1887, p. 128.
[32] Carlyle, *Sir Walter Scott*, in *The Works of Thomas Carlyle*, Centenary Edition, London, 1889-1923, *Critical and Miscellaneous Essays*, IV, 39-40.

And in a further passage Browning calls on Mandeville to answer Carlyle:

> Sage, once more repeat
> Instruction! 'Tis a sore to soothe not chafe.
> Ah, Fabulist, what luck, could I contrive
> To coax from thee another "Grumbling Hive"!
> My friend himself wrote fables short and sweet . . . [33]

Browning must have here had in mind Carlyle's method of illustrating a point by his stories, as he did, for example, in *The Diamond Necklace, Shooting Niagara,*[34] or perhaps *Fractions.* Browning may even have been thinking of *Sartor Resartus,* which is of course a prolonged fable.

Then too in the course of the argument Browning uses an illustration of Goethe's estate at Weimar. This of course was chosen distinctly for Carlyle's benefit, for his idolatry of Goethe needs no comment. In fact, Browning says plainly that his reference is one that will especially appeal to his opponent:

> And note—sufficient for all purposes—
> The ground-plan—map you long have yearned for—yes,
> Made out in markings—more what artist can?—
> Goethe's Estate in Weimar,—just a plan![35]

These points are of course all bits of description that tend to identify Browning's antagonist as Carlyle; and they are thoroughly supported by the philosophy which Browning attributes to the "parlous friend" whom he addresses.

But to put the matter beyond all dispute, Mrs. Orr, a close personal friend of Browning's, included in the third edition of her *Handbook to the Works of Robert Browning* (1887) a brief study of the *Parleyings,* in which she called Browning's opponent Carlyle throughout her discussion of the

---

[33] *With Bernard de Mandeville,* ll. 90-94.

[34] Browning disliked this essay intensely, and characterized it as "a grin through a horse-collar." See Moncure Daniel Conway, *Autobiography, Memories and Experiences,* New York and Boston, 1904, I, 412.

[35] *With Bernard de Mandeville,* ll. 173-176.

Parleying With Bernard de Mandeville. This is conclusive
when we remember that in the preface to the fifth edition,
dated January 7, 1890, Mrs. Orr stated that Browning had
read and corrected her *Handbook.* The book, too, had
Browning's own endorsement.[36] The matter is thus put beyond dispute.

Browning is attempting in the *Parleying* to answer the
gloomy philosophical views of Carlyle on the problems of
good and evil, and God's relation to the universe. But the
poem is more than mere answer to Carlyle; it amounts almost
to an attack upon him. Browning clung to his own philosophical beliefs with more and more tenacity and temper as
he grew older, and this fact partly explains the tone of the
Parleying. It is not altogether impersonal, and at times it becomes a little bitter and sneering. This is astonishing in the
light of the warm friendship that existed, and the mutual admiration that was so often expressed, between the two men.
Since the history of their relations has never been adequately
treated,[37] it will be necessary here to point out a few significant stages in the development of their friendship.

Their acquaintance began as early as 1839, for in that
year we find them both dining at Macready's with Harriet
Martineau and the Bullers.[38] The next year they met again
at Leigh Hunt's house.[39] On one occasion in 1840 they met
as Carlyle was leaving the lecture-hall, and Browning was
invited to visit Cheyne Row. From that time relations between the two became very cordial. Carlyle was Browning's
senior by seventeen years, and the young poet was flattered
by his interest, and very proud of the acquaintance. One of
the highest boasts that he could make to Elizabeth Barrett

[36] See Griffin and Minchin, p. 271, note 1.
[37] The best treatment, although an incomplete one, is to be found in
Alexander Carlyle's *The Correspondence between Carlyle and Browning,* in
the *Cornhill Magazine,* New Series, XXXVIII, 642-669.
[38] See Griffin and Minchin, p. 136.
[39] See *The Correspondence between Carlyle and Browning,* in *Cornhill
Magazine,* New Series, XXXVIII, 643.

was: "I know Carlyle and love him."[40] He described him as "dear, noble Carlyle"; and his letters to the poetess were full of what Carlyle had said or done. She in her turn characterized Carlyle as "the great teacher of the age, Carlyle, who is also yours and mine." The two men had been seeing a good deal of each other. Carlyle had gone to Hatcham[41] to meet Browning's family, and had delighted the poet's mother with his Scotch accent. The philosopher and the poet rode together fairly frequently in the next few years, and walked often. Browning wrote that "at night he would walk as far as Vauxhall Bridge on my way home"; and again, "We talked for three or four hours—he asked me to come again soon, and I will." They had, apparently, some memorable conversations, and it may well have been some of these which Browning reproduced in the *Parleying*. Carlyle, who foresaw Browning's greatness even in the early years,[42] was to recall their talks after twenty years:

I remember Browning as a fine young man, living in the neighbourhood of Croydon. I liked him better than any young man about here. He had simple speech and manners and ideas of his own. A good talk I recall with him, when I walked with him to the top of a hill, which had a fine prospect.[43]

The two men had many opportunities of exchanging views on many subjects during these years of walks and talks.

Thereafter, with Browning's departure for Italy upon his marriage, the meetings between them were infrequent and there was little correspondence. The tone of their relations remained warm and cordial. Browning's veneration for Carlyle must have deepened as he read the letter which offered

[40] The quoted bits that follow are taken, except when otherwise indicated, from the *Letters of R. B. and E. B. B.*, I, 16, 25, 27, 30, 151, 193, 448; II, 90, 98, 236, 276, 285.
[41] See Griffin and Minchin, p. 49.
[42] See *Letters of R. B. and E. B. B.*, II, 90.
[43] Moncure Daniel Conway, *Autobiography, Memories and Experiences*, New York and Boston, 1904, II, 22.

congratulations on his marriage and responded gratefully to his invitation to visit his wife and himself in Italy:

No marriage has taken place within my circle, these many years, in which I could so heartily rejoice. You I had known, and judged of; her, too, conclusively enough, if less directly; and certainly if ever there was a union indicated by the finger of Heaven itself, and so sanctioned and prescribed by the Eternal Laws under which poor transitory Sons of Adam live, it seemed to me, from all I could hear or know of it, to be this![44]

And there was great warmth in Browning's letter to Carlyle in 1850:

You know very well how happy and proud (for want of a better word) your friendship has made me—how happy and proud. It will always seem, as it does now, enough to have lived for.[45]

When the Brownings were back in London for a brief visit in 1850, they called on the Carlyles at Chelsea. On their return to Italy Carlyle accompanied them as far as Paris, allowing Browning to take care of all the details of the journey.[46]

Carlyle continued to think well of Browning's work. Speaking to Gavan Duffy he said that

. . . Browning had a powerful intellect, and among the men engaged in England in Literature just now was one of the few from whom it was possible to expect something.[47]

Carlyle liked very much, too, Browning's *Essay on Shelley* (1852), which he called "a solid, well-wrought, massive, manful bit of discourse,"[48] and urged him on to other work:

Seriously, dear Browning, you must at last gird up your loins

[44] This letter, written from Chelsea, June 23, 1847, is quoted in *The Correspondence between Carlyle and Browning*, in *Cornhill Magazine*, New Series, XXXVIII, 648.

[45] *Idem*, p. 650.

[46] See Orr, *Life*, pp. 165-167.

[47] Gavan Duffy, *Conversations with Carlyle*, New York, 1892, pp. 56-57.

[48] *The Correspondence between Carlyle and Browning*, in the *Cornhill Magazine*, XXXVIII, 659.

again; and give us a right stroke of work:—I do not wish to hurry you; far the contrary: but I remind you what is expected; and say with what joy I for one will see it arrive.[49]

Browning wrote in answer that he hoped "to write my best directly to you some day."[50] Then the correspondence lapsed until 1855, when Carlyle put Browning to work hunting references for him.[51] At the beginning of the next year Carlyle wrote to Browning in praise of *Men and Women:*

Nay, in a private way, I admit to myself that here apparently is *the finest* poetic genius, finest possibility of such, we have got vouchsafed us in this generation, and that it will be a terrible pity if we spill it in the process of elaboration.[52]

We hear little more of correspondence between these two. After Browning's return to England upon his wife's death, there was little need of letters. The friends seem to have been ever cordial, though there is little record of their meeting in the next thirteen years.

We get a glimpse of them again in 1875, when after the publication of *Aristophanes' Apology*, Carlyle asked Browning why he did not tell it all in plain straightforward statement. "As if," Browning exclaimed in describing his visit, "this did not make all the difference between a poet's treatment of a subject and a historian's or a rhetorician's!"[53] Carlyle did appreciate, however, the transcripts from Euripides in the poem; and he said to Browning soon after, "Ye won't mind me, though it's the last advice I may give ye; but ye ought to translate the whole of the Greek tragedians—that's your vocation."[54] But the poet did mind him, and in 1877 appeared his translation of *The Agamemnon of Aeschylus*,

[49] *The Correspondence between Carlyle and Browning*, in *Cornhill Magazine*, New Series, XXXVIII, 660.
[50] *Idem*, p. 657.
[51] See *idem*, pp. 661–664.
[52] *Idem*, p. 660.
[53] Quoted from Domett's unpublished diary in Griffin and Minchin, p. 256.
[54] Griffin and Minchin, p. 256.

the preface to which closed with a dedication of the piece to
Carlyle:

No, neither "uncommanded" nor "unrewarded": since it was
commanded of me by my venerated friend Thomas Carlyle, and
rewarded will it indeed become, if I am permitted to dignify it
by the prefatory insertion of his dear and noble name.

This happy relationship, warm though hardly intimate,
seems to have continued until Carlyle's death in February of
1881. Browning had evidently seen him in the months before
his death, for he told Domett that Carlyle was "anxious to
die."[55] A fortnight or so before the end came, Browning had
called at his house, but finding him lying on the sofa in a
comatose state, would not have him disturbed.[56]

After Carlyle's death Browning seems to have been
greatly disturbed by Froude's revelations concerning Carlyle. To quote from the account supplied by Domett:

Froude's subsequent "disclosures" awoke Browning's strong re-
sentment. He refused to believe that Carlyle was other than the
most tender-hearted of men. He was fond of telling how when
once he was walking with him they were passed by a butcher-
boy "savagely leathering his horse," and how Carlyle exclaimed
with passion, "Ah! if I could only get at that brute!"[57]

Yet it is possible that the disclosures did affect Browning. In
spite of his refusal to believe them, it would be strange indeed if they had not caused him to examine carefully his
own conception of Carlyle. Before Froude actually published the private papers of Carlyle and Jane Welsh Carlyle,
but after he had made known the "disclosures," Browning
found it necessary to deny a report that something had happened to his friendship with Carlyle. In 1881 he wrote:

I am astounded at the notion, as to how it could possibly arise,
that there was ever the slightest "falling out" between Carlyle

55 See Griffin and Minchin, p. 269.
56 See *idem*, pp. 268-269.
57 Quoted by Griffin and Minchin, p. 269.

and myself. Nothing of the kind ever happened during our long acquaintance.[58]

And in 1885 there is little sign of any change of mind on Browning's part. When C. E. Norton was contemplating a volume that would clear Carlyle's memory of much of the odium that had been attached to it since Froude's disclosures, Browning sent to him the letters Carlyle had written him, with the following comment:

The first of the letters was written, as you see, 44 years ago; and the goodness and sympathy which began so long ago continued unabated to the end of the writer's life. I repaid them with just as enduring an affectionate gratitude. It was not I who ventured to make the acquaintance nor ask the correspondence of Carlyle: his love was altogether a free gift, and how much it has enriched my life, I shall hardly attempt to say— certainly not at this moment, when I write in all the haste of approaching departure from home . . .[59]

But some five months later, on December 29, 1885, Browning still refused to write an account of the friendship:

I cannot undertake to write any account of our beloved friend at present. I feel just as you do respecting the misunderstanders, but am hardly able to say my whole mind aright just now, from abundance rather than lack of matter.[60]

In all probability the disclosures of Froude had penetrated deeper than Browning would admit. Clearly, from this letter, he was unable to tell just exactly what his opinion was; there were too many things that had to be fitted into his old conception of Carlyle.

Browning would never admit positively that his opinion had changed, but there are suggestions that it had. Mrs. Orr, who certainly was in a position to know, indicates that it had

[58] *Letters from R. B. to Various Correspondents,* 1st Series, I, 87.
[59] *New Letters of T. Carlyle,* ed. A. Carlyle, London, 1904, I, 235.
[60] *Ibid.*

not, and yet betrays rather significantly that Browning was somewhat shaken by the disclosures:

For none of these can his feelings have been more constant or more disinterested than that which bound him to Carlyle. He visited him at Chelsea in the last weary days of his long life, as often as their distance from each other and his own engagements allowed. Even the man's posthumous self-disclosures scarcely availed to destroy the affectionate reverence which he had always felt for him. He never ceased to defend him against the charge of unkindness to his wife, or to believe that in the matter of their domestic unhappiness she was the more responsible of the two.[61]

But Mrs. Orr goes on to supply a hint that goes far toward explaining any change of attitude that Browning may have had. Once Browning's faith in Carlyle was put to the test—refuse as he might to believe the accusations of cruelty —his own relations with him must have undergone very careful scrutiny. The results of that examination, and no other evidence, could have caused a change in Browning's attitude. The clue to his less friendly feelings toward Carlyle is supplied by Mrs. Orr:

Yet Carlyle had never rendered him that service, easy as it appears, which one man of letters most justly values from another: that of proclaiming the admiration which he privately expressed for his works. The fact was incomprehensible to Mr. Browning—it was so foreign to his own nature; and he commented on it with a touch, though merely a touch, of bitterness, when repeating to a friend some almost extravagant eulogium which in earlier days he had received from him tête-à-tête. "If only," he said, "those words had been ever repeated in public, what good they might have done me!"[62]

Here is the clue to the fault Browning found in Carlyle; it betrays the fact that Carlyle's attitude to or treatment of Browning was not all that the latter might have desired.

61 Orr, *Life,* p. 346.
62 *Idem,* pp. 346-347.

If we look back over the long acquaintance, we find that
things were not always as agreeable between them as they
appeared on the surface. As early as **1846** Browning had
quarrelled with Carlyle's condemnation of Italy.[63] A few
years later, according to Mrs. Browning, the poet found
fault with another of Carlyle's utterances:

> Robert curses & swears over Carlyle's Frederick, which is a
> relief to my own mind too. Never was there a more immoral
> book in the brutal sense.[64]

Mrs. Browning, it is interesting to note, had had some fears
before meeting Carlyle that she might not like him "in his
personality."[65] As for Mrs. Carlyle, she made no attempt to
conceal her aversion for the Brownings, and thought Browning "nothing . . . but a fluff of feathers."[66] Other entries in
her record indicate that her liking for him diminished rather
than increased.[67] Mrs. Orr's account of the journey to Paris
which Carlyle made in the Brownings' company suggests, inasmuch as her information came through Browning, that the
poet did not particularly enjoy having the entire responsibility for the details of the trip left to him.[68] The two men
differed, too, on the question of the Civil War in America,
Browning being an ardent anti-slavery man. He characterized Carlyle's *Shooting Niagara* as "a grin through a horse-
collar."[69] Nor should it be forgotten in this connection that
Carlyle criticized Browning's method of presentation in
Aristophanes' Apology.[70]

The truth is, I believe, that the relation between them was
continued exactly as it began; that is, with Carlyle as the pa-

[63] See *Letters of R. B. and E. B. B.*, II, 276.
[64] *Letters to Isa Blagden*, p. 14.
[65] Orr, *Life*, p. 165.
[66] *New Letters and Memorials of Jane Welsh Carlyle*, ed. A. Carlyle and
Sir J. Crichton-Browne, London, 1903, II, 39.
[67] See *idem*, pp. 45, 108-109.
[68] See Orr, *Life*, pp. 166-167.
[69] Conway, *Autobiography* . . ., I, 412.
[70] See above, p. 20.

tron of a very promising young man. As we have seen,
Browning was pleased and flattered by this relation in the
beginning. The difficulty was that as Browning's powers matured and as he began to gain prominence and recognition,
Carlyle continued to treat him with the same manner of
friendly condescension. This might well have irked Browning; and as his own fame grew, while Carlyle had somewhat
passed the height of his influence, it may have grown more
and more irritating. Carlyle had been sarcastic at Browning's expense a good many times;[71] and his magisterial manner may have become equally annoying. It is extremely
likely that during the last years of Carlyle's life much of the
reverence that Browning had once felt for him evaporated.
Thus while there was no open break between the two, there
was very probably an increasing feeling of annoyance and
forbearance on Browning's part. After Froude's disclosures,
when the poet was unable to say his "whole mind aright"
concerning Carlyle, he came eventually to the admission that
Carlyle had been, in his relations with him, rather less than
generous. Consequently there is in the *Parleying*, in spite of
the fact that Browning addresses Carlyle as "friend," a tone
rather ironical than reverential.

But the crux of the *Parleying* is after all the difference in
the beliefs of the two men. There was a striking antithesis in
their attitudes toward certain philosophical problems, an antithesis which they both noticed. The *Parleying* bears witness to it, for Browning; and for Carlyle, there is this statement concerning the poet:

But there's a great contrast between him and me. He seems very
content with life, and takes much satisfaction in the world. It's
a very strange and curious spectacle to behold a man in these
days so confidently cheerful.[72]

---

[71] See Griffin and Minchin, pp. 136, 256; and *Correspondence between
Carlyle and Browning,* in *Cornhill Magazine,* New Series, XXXVIII, 666-
667.

[72] Quoted by Henry Jones, *Browning as a Philosophical and Religious
Teacher,* Glasgow, 1902, p. 45. He mentions no source, so that it may well
be verbal from Carlyle.

Yet the contrast was not so great as either of them imagined. They were products of the same age, and were confronted with the same problems. The Deists had made a system of checks and balances of God, Man, and Earth. Wordsworth and Shelley had broken the Deistic conception and had found God in Nature. Carlyle and Browning carried the revolt further and found God in man. But once in the presence of the spirit in man, Carlyle looked about him and saw the old faith lifeless. Chaos reigned, and night sat umpire. To Browning there was a new heaven, and a new earth, and the old had passed away. For Browning was younger and naturally matured a little later. While Carlyle's limits in speculation were fairly well set in 1833, in *Sartor Resartus*, after which he went on elaborating but scarcely answering the grim questions he asked of the universe, Browning was just beginning to work out his problems in *Pauline*, which was published in the same year. He went on adapting his ideas, gradually subordinating knowledge to the doctrine of universal love. He seized intuitively upon evolution and turned it and scientific discovery into a new faith. But to Carlyle—as to Matthew Arnold who came still later when the first promise of science had proved false dawn—the old faith was dead and the new as yet unborn.

There is thus about Carlyle's utterances a tone of despair and pessimism. He did not see how anyone in that age could be "confidently cheerful," or take "satisfaction in the world." There is a story of his leading Emerson through the streets of London at midnight, asking him with grim humor every few steps if he believed in the devil now.[78] This is essentially typical of his attitude. The reality of the evil in the world was an ever-present factor in his thought. He could not deny it or ignore it. As he began in *Sartor Resartus* to inquire grimly into the relation of God to man, and of good to evil in their war in human action, so he continued to face

[78] Henry Jones, *Browning as a Philosophical and Religious Teacher*, p. 74.

the problem of evil. He found something of spirituality in man, in the conscience that prompted him to do right; but that discovery deepened his gloom rather than offered him any ray of hope. His whole pessimism arose from the fact that while God laid the heavy burden of duty on man, He offered no help, gave no sign of being interested or sympathetic. Thus the "Infinite Nature of Duty" hung over man; yet he got little happiness in doing his duty, and none at all if he did not:

What Act of Legislature was there that *thou* shouldst be Happy? A little while ago thou hadst no right to *be* at all. What if thou wert born and predestined to be Unhappy?[74]

God was an alien task-master who laid heavy duties on mankind's shoulders without offering any comfort, help, or sympathy. This slave-driving God only said sternly, "Bear!" The nature of duty was infinite, for evil had penetrated man to the heart. Morality offered little happiness, for it was but blind obedience to a foreign task-master; religion gave little comfort, for it was an awe of the unknowable with whom man can claim no kinship.[75] Nevertheless it was man's duty to do what he could against this omnipresent evil:

Thus, Evil, what we call Evil, must ever exist while man exists: Evil, in the widest sense we can give it, is precisely the dark, disordered material out of which man's Freewill has to create an edifice of order and Good.[76]

This was, according to Carlyle, man's sole destiny. He saw man in the presence of evil, subject to one law that he must obey above all others: he must *do*. Carlyle, despairing of the

[74] *The Everlasting Yea,* in *The Works of Thomas Carlyle,* Centenary Edition, London, 1889-1923, *Sartor Resartus,* p. 153.

[75] For this discussion of Carlyle's philosophy I am somewhat indebted to Henry Jones, whose *Browning as a Philosophical and Religious Teacher* is by all odds the best work on Browning's philosophy, and makes a comprehensive sweep of the thought of the age.

[76] *Characteristics,* in *The Works of Thomas Carlyle,* Centenary Edition, London, 1889-1923, *Critical and Miscellaneous Essays,* III, 28.

intervention of God in behalf of the good, and sometimes even the presence of God at all, uttered the cry that sums up his whole view:

Here on Earth we are Soldiers, fighting in a foreign land; that understand not the plan of the campaign, and have no need to understand it; seeing well what is at our hands to be done.[77]

So in the *Parleying* Browning represents him in his despairing attitude:

> "No sign"—groaned he—
> "No stirring of God's finger to denote
> He wills that right should have supremacy
> On earth, not wrong! . . ."[78]

This desire for God to give us some inkling that there is a plan in this chaos of life, is of the essence of Carlyle's attitude.

Yet it is equally a part of his philosophy that man, with his finite mind, cannot possibly comprehend God and His system, if there is one:

For the rest, let that vain struggle to read the mystery of the Infinite cease to harass us. It is a mystery which, through all ages, we shall only read here a line of, there another line of . . .[79]

And again:

We, the whole species of Mankind, and our whole existence and history, are but a floating speck in the illimitable ocean of the All . . . borne this way and that by its deep-swelling tides, and grand ocean currents;—of which what faintest chance is there that we should ever exhaust the significance, ascertain the go-

---

[77] *Characteristics*, in *The Works of Thomas Carlyle, Critical and Miscellaneous Essays*, III, 43.

[78] *With Bernard de Mandeville*, ll. 43-46.

[79] *Characteristics*, in *The Works of Thomas Carlyle, Critical and Miscellaneous Essays*, III, 43.

ings and comings? A region of Doubt, therefore, hovers forever in the background . . .[80]

Carlyle saw in the history of religions a series of attempts to explain the nature of the universe and to assign to man his place in it. From primitive paganism to mediaeval Christianity he saw a series of ideals conceived by man, realized, and outgrown. Yet he saw that those ideals had constantly grown more and more spiritual in their nature. But he saw no new faith now arising to take the place of the last. It was thus, from his point of view, an entirely natural remark that he made to Browning; but from Browning's it must have been a rather startling utterance:

On one occasion Mr. Carlyle made a singular remark. He was walking with Mr. Browning, either in Paris or the neighboring country, when they passed an image of the Crucifixion; and glancing towards the figure of Christ, he said, with his deliberate Scotch utterance, "Ah, poor fellow, *your* part is played out!"[81]

But even if the new faith has not yet arisen, Carlyle finds something of a solution of his problems. He believes in the spiritual element in man; and, in spite of the oppressive forces of evil, he manages to cling to his belief in God. He does this by admitting that man's little mind can never comprehend the nature of the illimitable, and that it is useless for him to try. The nature of God, and His attitude toward man, can never be comprehended in human terms.

Thus, discouraged as he was by his own view of things, Carlyle accepted the situation as he saw it, and even admitted that the situation was the best that could be hoped:

. . . could you ever establish a Theory of the Universe that were entire, unimprovable, and which needed only to be got by heart; man then were spiritually defunct, the Species we now

[80] *Characteristics,* in *The Works of Thomas Carlyle, Critical and Miscellaneous Essays,* III, 25-26.

[81] Orr, *Life,* p. 167.

name Man had ceased to exist. But the gods, kinder to us than we are to ourselves, have forbidden such suicidal acts.[82]

Thus Carlyle, while pessimistic, was nevertheless resigned. Understanding not the plan of the campaign, he felt that the principal thing was to fight; with so urgent a need for action, there was no need to understand.

With the same heritage of ideas, and the same problems to meet, Browning evolved a different sort of philosophy. As we have seen, he came just enough later than Carlyle to feel that there was a new hope for the world; and there is optimism at the basis of his whole belief. Whereas Carlyle started with the axiom that evil was essentially real, Browning started with the axiom that God was all-loving and all-powerful. But with the hypothesis that

> God's in his heaven—
> All's right with the world!

Browning had to meet the problem of evil and its reality. This brought him at once to a philosophical difficulty. For with his optimistic attitude, Browning refused to give up the belief that man, the creation of God, was really great too. Man had a dignity of his own, arising from the power of free will which he exerted in the moral struggle. Browning held with great tenacity to the idea of a universal benevolent order, and at the same time to the idea of man as a morally free person within that order. Yet—and this is the flaw in his argument—if God were all-loving He would wish to destroy evil, and if He were all-powerful He could do so. The idea of such a God is inconsistent with the existence of evil. Yet if man is to have free will, there must be evil for him to discriminate against and to fight against. Browning refused to degrade either God or man. God was power, wisdom, and love

[82] *Characteristics*, in *The Works of Thomas Carlyle, Critical and Miscellaneous Essays*, III, 38. The *Characteristics* is probably Carlyle's most metaphysical work; hence the large number of quotations from it in this discussion of metaphysical problems.

without limit. Man was king in the moral world, and that
world in which he was placed to strive was not perfect.

Browning solves the problem of reconciling an all-loving
God and the presence of evil in the world by casting doubt
upon facts that threaten his hypothesis of universal love.
Evil is not really evil; it is only apparent. God has placed it
in the world so that man may develop his moral nature. God
is thus like a father who while building a house has given his
son a few worthless boards to saw in order to make the boy
think he is helping. Or, as Jones put it, the world becomes
only "a kind of moral gymnasium, crowded with phantoms
wherein by exercise man makes moral muscle."[83] It is peril-
ously like playing a trick upon humanity in order to make
it progress, for the evil that spurs man on is nothing but
illusion.

Browning escapes from *this* difficulty by saying that man
ultimately cannot know that the evil is illusory. A certainty
of knowledge concerning the existence or non-existence of
evil is incompatible with moral life:

A full disclosure? Such would outrage law.[84]

If man knew absolutely that all things would ultimately turn
to good, or that evil was evil unchangeable forevermore,
there would be little point in striving. Man can exercise his
free will only on condition of being in absolute uncertainty;
his proper state is ignorance. Thus when Browning's hypothesis of universal love is threatened by the miseries and
evils of life he answers that man can have no knowledge of
whether the evil is real or not, and that man must believe
blindly in the goodness of God. Ignorance is in this ingenious way turned to a moral use by Browning.

In his philosophy of optimism, Browning not only asserts
that all is right with the world, but insists that things are

---

[83] Henry Jones, *Browning as a Philosophical and Religious Teacher*, p.
234.

[84] *With Bernard de Mandeville*, 1. 20.

getting better. Progress in human affairs is a necessary result of the existence of a kind, wise, and powerful God. As
we have seen, evil is necessary in order that man may progress. Human life is progress toward moral goodness
through opposition:

> . . . man must pass from old to new,
> From vain to real, from mistake to fact,
> From what once seemed good, to what now proves best.[85]

Earth is man's probation-place, in which he is to strive forever onward. This is the meaning of such poems as *Childe
Roland* and "*How they brought the Good News from Ghent
to Aix*"—poems which describe struggle toward no stated
end, struggle for the sake of the struggle and the ultimate
achievement.

Browning seized intuitively upon the facts of Evolution,
and saw progress through all nature up to man.[86] But in
man he saw a different kind of progress. In man evolution
continues its march into the realms of the mind and the
spirit. Man forever becomes better and wiser. So, with the
necessity for eternal moral progress in his mind, Browning
in the *Parleying With Gerard de Lairesse* asks:

> What were life
> Did soul stand still therein, forego her strife
> Through the ambiguous Present to the goal
> Of some all-reconciling Future?[87]

The development of the individual soul, as one may see from
Paracelsus, Sordello, Caponsacchi, and a hundred others of
Browning's heroes, becomes a matter of paramount importance. Man advances morally by fighting his way inch by
inch:

[85] *A Death in the Desert,* ll. 545-547.
[86] Browning treats the subject of evolution at some length in *The Parleying With Francis Furini,* and a discussion of his views on the subject will
be found in that chapter, pp. 193-200.
[87] *With Gerard de Lairesse,* ll. 367-370.

No, when the fight begins within himself,
A man's worth something. God stoops o'er his head,
Satan looks up between his feet—both tug—
He's left, himself, i' the middle: the soul wakes
And grows. Prolong that battle through his life!
Never leave growing till the life to come![88]

In this way the hypothesis of moral life as progressive is essential to Browning's optimistic philosophy; and he sees all things as symbols of man's moral progress toward the unattainable perfection of God.

Another aspect of the poet's optimistic philosophy is the necessity of showing that all things *are* right with the world. As we have seen, he believes in an all-loving God who could not allow real evil to exist. It therefore becomes necessary for Browning to prove that good exists in all things:

Beneath the veriest ash, there hides a spark of soul
Which, quickened by love's breath, may yet pervade the whole
O' the gray, and, free again, be fire—of worth the same,
Howe'er produced, for, great or little, flame is flame.[89]

God is at work mysteriously for good in even the most apparently wicked cases. The axiomatic faith that Browning had seized upon in *Pippa Passes*, that

> God's in his heaven—
> All's right with the world!

he spent the rest of his life defending. He saw evil as mere stuff for transmuting. Thus we find him searching the direst evils of the earth in order to show that within them lies the germ of good. This is the governing motive of his art, the motive which made him dramatize the conflicts and antagonisms of human life. He was not fully aware of the necessity for finding absolute good in his early days. He had seized

[88] *Bishop Blougram's Apology*, ll. 693-698.
[89] *Fifine at the Fair*, ll. 674-677. In l. 676 I have omitted a question mark, an omission which in no way falsifies the meaning, since it is merely part of a long rhetorical question.

upon the theme intuitively in *Pippa Passes*, had developed it
in *Men and Women* especially, at great length, and in *The
Ring and the Book* had made a herculean effort to show good
in the process of evolving from evil. But as time went on he
turned from dramatic examples and demonstrations of his
theory to philosophical disquisitions on the subject, until in
La Saisiaz, Ferishtah's Fancies, and the *Parleyings* themselves, he appears as a philosopher expounding his views.
For Browning, at first not definitely aware of the implications of his position, or of the difficulties in which it involved
him, found it increasingly harder to maintain that position,
and became more and more analytical as he defended it.

His optimistic philosophy, as we have seen, included an
all-loving and all-powerful God, and likewise free will and
moral progress for mankind. Under the consequent necessity
of admitting or disclaiming the reality of evil, Browning
made evil illusion, but insisted that man must not *know*
whether it was illusion or not. That is, ignorance became a
necessary part of his theory of an all-loving God. Then, too,
as he went on showing how good evolves from all things, and
how "the last is ever better than the first," he had more and
more to deny the evidence which his intellect brought him.
Thus Browning preserved his optimism by casting asper-
sions on the validity of man's knowing faculty; and as he
proclaimed with increasing vehemence his faith that God was
love,—the faith he had learned as a child from his mother,
and had temporarily rejected in his youth—he insisted on
the necessity of man's ignorance. His faith is thus ultimately
blind, and he is an intellectual agnostic:

> Knowledge means
> Ever-renewed assurance by defeat
> That victory is somehow still to reach . . .[90]

Knowledge, he insists in all the poems from *La Saisiaz* on,
is finite and earthly—a thing dependent on the peculiar

[90] *Ferishtah's Fancies, A Pillar at Sebzevar,* ll. 22-24.

make-up of our senses, and altogether relative to the individual.[91]

But if it is impossible to know anything intellectually, there are yet ways of comprehending the meanings of things. It is Browning's belief that God reveals Himself in man through the power of love. Even the most miserable wretch has some goodness in him, something of God; and it is through that germ of goodness, that power of love, that he reaches up to God. Thus it is through the heart that man is to comprehend the God who is love. God is like the sun, says Browning; and man has in his heart a tiny spark of light from God, that makes him a miniature sun. Thus while Browning takes away man's contact with God through knowledge, he restores it through love and faith. It is interesting that in all his poems, from *Paracelsus* on, Browning has been concerned with the relative values of love and knowledge; but from *Paracelsus*, where love was rated as equal to knowledge, love went on to usurp a more and more important place. Now at the last it has driven out knowledge altogether. This is illustrated in the context of the passage from *Ferishtah's Fancies* quoted above:

"Friend," quoth Ferishtah, "all I seem to know
Is—I know nothing save that love I can
Boundlessly, endlessly. My curls were crowned
In youth with knowledge,—off, alas, crown slipped
Next moment, pushed by better knowledge still
Which nowise proved more constant: gain, to-day,
Was toppling loss to-morrow, lay at last
—Knowledge, the golden?—lacquered ignorance!
As gain—mistrust it! Not as means to gain:
Lacquer we learn by: cast in fining-pot,
We learn,—when what seemed ore assayed proves dross,—
. . . The prize is in the process: knowledge means
Ever-renewed assurance by defeat

91 This curious aspect of Browning's philosophy is best illustrated in the *Parleying With Francis Furini*. See below, pp. 187-193. See also on Avison, pp. 269-270.

That victory is somehow still to reach,
But love is victory, the prize itself;
Love—trust to![92]

And the same theme is repeated in the *Parleying With Bernard de Mandeville*. There again knowledge is debased in order that Browning's optimistic philosophy may prevail.

III

The Parleying With Bernard de Mandeville affords Browning his opportunity of summing up, once and for all, his optimistic philosophy. His other poems have touched upon his beliefs, have even expounded them at great length, but the *Parleyings* are actually Browning's own last word on the subject. He throws off all disguise and speaks in his own person. His philosophical views are treated, of course, throughout the volume. Yet Browning's philosophical system, as a system, finds here in the *Parleying With Bernard de Mandeville* its fullest and most explicit expression.

As the poem opens Browning is sitting in his chair at midnight. He calls the spirit of Mandeville to him:

> Ay, this same midnight, by this chair of mine,
> Come and review thy counsels: art thou still
> Stanch to their teaching?—not as fools opine
> Its purport might be, but as subtler skill
> Could, through turbidity, the loaded line
> Of logic casting, sound deep, deeper, till
> It touched a quietude and reached a shrine
> And recognized harmoniously combine
> Evil with good, and hailed truth's triumph—thine,
> Sage dead long since, Bernard de Mandeville![93]

This is a truly poetic invocation, and it is ungrateful to criticize it. Yet, as we have seen, Browning had so completely misunderstood the teachings of Mandeville that

---

[92] *Ferishtah's Fancies, A Pillar at Sebzevar*, ll. 8-26.
[93] *With Bernard de Mandeville*, ll. 1-10.

perhaps the most valid idea in the passage is the thought
that Mandeville is misunderstood by many. Unfortunately
Browning must be included among the number.

What he desires of Mandeville is not more knowledge. It
is part of Browning's belief that we must do the best we can
with what knowledge we have, learn

> Man's proper play with truth in part, before
> Entrusted with the whole.[94]

He desires Mandeville to give him smiling witness that he
actually is doing his best with doubtful doctrine. So Mandeville is to face him silently, while he thinks and speaks:

A full disclosure? Such would outrage law.
Law deals the same with soul and body: Seek
Full truth my soul may, when some babe, I saw
A new-born weakling, starts up strong—not weak—
Man every whit, absolved from earning awe,
Pride, rapture, if the soul attains to wreak
Its will on flesh, at last can thrust, lift, draw,
As mind bids muscle—mind which long has striven,
Painfully urging body's impotence
To effort whereby—once law's barrier riven,
Life's rule abolished—body might dispense
With infancy's probation, straight be given
—Not by foiled darings, fond attempts back-driven,
Fine faults of growth, brave sins which saint when shriven—
To stand full-statured in magnificence.[95]

This passage is especially intricate,[96] but the meaning be-

[94] *With Bernard de Mandeville*, ll. 15-16. There is a very illuminating
discussion of this trait of Browning's character in Orr, *Life*, pp. 352-354.

[95] *With Bernard de Mandeville*, ll. 20-34.

[96] J. Bertram Oldham suggested that this passage was obscure, and
Furnivall undertook to make a grammatical analysis of it; see *Browning
Society Papers*, London, II, 342, 325*-326*. The analysis, however, leaves
the passage more mystifying than ever. Yet Browning's letter to Furnivall,
published in *Letters from R. B. to Various Correspondents*, 1st Series, II,
88, explains his meaning well enough: "Neither body nor mind is born to
attain perfect strength or perfect health at its first stage of existence re-

comes sufficiently clear in the next few lines. Browning is denying the efficacy of knowledge and affirming the necessity of growth through failure and moral struggle:

No: as with body so deals law with soul
That's stung to strength through weakness, strives for good
Through evil,—earth its race-ground, heaven its goal,
Presumably . . .[97]

This is Browning's familiar teaching concerning the purpose of evil in the world; but when he identifies this precept with Mandeville's ideas,

> . . . so far I understood
> Thy teaching long ago . . .[98]

the result is ludicrous. In spite of the incongruity the eighteenth-century philosopher is swallowed completely by Browning and we hear little more of him. For now Browning's musings are interrupted by an objection from another philosopher, who is to take most of his attention:

> But what means this
> —Objected by a mouth which yesterday
> Was magisterial in antithesis
> To half the truths we hold, or trust we may,
> Though tremblingly the while?[99]

Carlyle has appeared to expound his gloomy belief that here on earth we are merely soldiers fighting in a foreign land, in a campaign that we do not understand, with no sign from God that we shall conquer, or that there is a plan for the battle:

spectively, in each case, by the want of and desire for the thing as yet out of reach, they get raised towards it, and are educated by the process—as would not happen were the body strong all at once—or the soul at once perfect in apprehension."

[97] *With Bernard de Mandeville,* ll. 35-38.
[98] *Idem,* ll. 38-39.
[99] *Idem,* ll. 39-43.

> "No sign"—groaned he—
> "No stirring of God's finger to denote
> He wills that right should have supremacy
> On earth, not wrong! How helpful could we quote
> But one poor instance when he interposed
> Promptly and surely and beyond mistake
> Between oppression and its victim, closed
> Accounts with sin for once, and bade us wake
> From our long dream that justice bears no sword,
> Or else forgets whereto its sharpness serves!"[100]

If there were only some sign, we could mock at the things that tend to weaken our faith; we should be spared the increasing and sapping fear that perhaps the strife between good and evil will never cease. Suppose that there is no peace after the life on earth, but that the struggle still goes on, without any intervention of justice?

Bernard de Mandeville is called upon to confute the beliefs of this man who was at times so daring, and at times so fearful:

> Bernard de Mandeville, confute for me
> This parlous friend who captured or set free
> Thunderbolts at his pleasure, yet would draw
> Back, panic-stricken by some puny straw
> Thy gold-rimmed amber-headed cane had whisked
> Out of his pathway if the object risked
> Encounter, 'scaped thy kick from buckled shoe!
> As when folk heard thee in old days pooh-pooh
> Addison's tye-wig preachment, grant this friend—
> (Whose groan I hear, with guffaw at the end
> Disposing of mock-melancholy)—grant
> His bilious mood one potion, ministrant
> Of homely wisdom, healthy wit![101]

"My fine fellow Mandeville" is here described as the typical

100 *With Bernard de Mandeville*, ll. 43-52.
101 *Idem*, ll. 62-74.

dandy of Queen Anne's age;[102] and it is interesting to observe how in a few lines Browning has pictured the boldness of the man, and his brusqueness in treating orthodox opinion. It is he who is to scatter the morbid fears of Carlyle. For hear, says Browning, this continued cry of the doleful prophet of Chelsea:

> "With power and will, let preference appear
> By intervention ever and aye, help good
> When evil's mastery is understood
> In some plain outrage . . ."[103]

Without such a sign of the preference of God for the good, despair comes to the adherents of right. We know all too well how evil grows, like a many-headed monster. What a help it would be if wrong could be destroyed as soon as it appeared! It is this cry that Mandeville is to answer:

> Sage, once more repeat
> Instruction! 'Tis a sore to soothe not chafe.
> Ah, Fabulist, what luck, could I contrive
> To coax from thee another "Grumbling Hive"![104]

For it is another fabulist that Mandeville is to instruct. Browning suggests that he tell Carlyle a fable; and then puts into the mouth of Mandeville a parable of a Gardener

[102] Mandeville speaks of himself, quoting a contemporary opponent, as "well-dressed"; see *Fable of the Bees,* 1795, p. 276. It is almost the only suggestion we have concerning his appearance, yet Browning always thought of him as a "fine fellow"; see Orr, *Life,* p. 53. The story of Mandeville and Addison the poet may have heard from his father, who possessed a fund of unusual information about the lives of writers and artists; or he may have read it in Hawkins or Johnson.

[103] *With Bernard de Mandeville,* ll. 75-78.

[104] *With Bernard de Mandeville,* ll. 90-93. Browning knew the title of Mandeville's original pamphlet (1705) from the preface in his copy, for every edition after 1714 included the explanation: "The following Fable, in which what I have said is set forth at large, was printed above eight years ago*, in a six penny pamphlet, called, The Grumbling Hive, or Knaves turn'd Honest; and being soon after pirated, cried about the streets in a halfpenny sheet."

* "This was wrote in 1714."

and a field of tares and wheat—a theme sufficiently foreign
to the nature of that iconoclast, who would compare the body
politic to a bowl of punch,[105] liken religion to small beer,[106]
or in more serious mood would tell the fable of the lion and
the merchant.[107] Browning in all innocence gives him a bibli-
cal parable to speak, for Carlyle's benefit:

> Ask him—"Suppose the Gardener of Man's ground
> Plants for a purpose, side by side with good,
> Evil—(and that he does so—look around!
> What does the field show?) . . ."[108]

and suppose that this evil, planted purposely, should be destroyed as soon as it begins to show signs of life. That might
strike the simple as wise husbandry, but such swift sure ex-
tirpation scarcely suits wiser observers. Seed is planted that
it may thrive; if it is hindered in the process, the lesson of
the sower is lost—and that lesson may be

> . . . that every growth of good
> Sprang consequent on evil's neighborhood?[109]

So said Mandeville's shrewdness, according to Browning;
and Browning agrees with him. But they disagreed who held
that mere unintelligence sowed both good and evil. But once
you admit that understanding planted the seeds, why should
that understanding interfere with its own plan? Then
Browning insists that Carlyle should concede a use to evil—
a concession which Carlyle would have made, to be sure, since
he saw how man's free will was given him in order that he
might work against evil.[110] The difference between the views
of the two nineteenth-century philosophers is that Browning
would have an active, intelligent, and loving God making

105 See *Fable of the Bees,* 1795, pp. 55-56.
106 See *idem,* pp. 141-143.
107 See *idem,* pp. 101-105. Voltaire admired and versified this fable.
108 *With Bernard de Mandeville,* ll. 95-98.
109 *Idem,* ll. 112-113. Compare the passage from Mandeville quoted above,
p. 8.
110 See the passage quoted above, p. 27.

good come of evil every moment. Browning sees a greater
use for evil than Carlyle does. Hence the poet would not have
evil destroyed: to do so would be to defeat God's plan of
struggle and progress for mankind. It is thus that he states
his position:

> Let the sage
> Concede a use to evil, though there starts
> Full many a burgeon thence, to disengage
> With thumb and finger lest it spoil the yield
> Too much of good's main tribute! But our main
> Tough-tendoned mandrake-monster—purge the field
> Of him for once and all? It follows plain
> Who set him there to grow beholds repealed
> His primal law: his ordinance proves vain:
> And what beseems a king who cannot reign,
> But to drop sceptre valid arm should wield?[111]

In this way Browning turns the existence of evil to proof
that God is omnipotent and omniscient.

But Carlyle answers, re-interpreting Browning's own
fable:

> "Still there's a parable"—retorts my friend—
> "Shows agriculture with a difference!
> What of the crop and weeds which solely blend
> Because, once planted, none may pluck them thence?
> The Gardener contrived thus? Vain pretence!
> An enemy it was who unawares
> Ruined the wheat by interspersing tares.
> Where's our desiderated forethought? Where's
> Knowledge, where power and will in evidence?
> 'T is Man's-play merely! Craft foils rectitude,
> Malignity defeats beneficence.
> And grant, at very last of all, the feud
> 'Twixt good and evil ends, strange thoughts intrude
> Though good be garnered safely and good's foe
> Bundled for burning. Thoughts steal: 'even so—

111 *With Bernard de Mandeville*, ll. 121-131.

Why grant tares leave to thus o'ertop, o'ertower
Their field-mate, boast the stalk and flaunt the flower,
Triumph one sunny minute?' Knowledge, power
And will thus worked?"[112]

The difficulty, Browning makes Carlyle go on to say, is with man's mind. Man tries to "cram inside his finite mind God's infinitude," and all his difficulties arise from that. He tries to comprehend the incomprehensible, and to crowd spiritual things into a system made according to his human ideas. It works for a time—then suddenly there comes a stumble, and he discovers that the

". . . wings in rudiment,
Such as he boasts, which full-grown, free-distent
Would lift him skyward, fail of flight while pent
Within humanity's restricted space.
Abjure each fond attempt to represent
The formless, the illimitable! Trace
No outline, try no hint of human face
Or form or hand!"[113]

Here is Carlyle's belief in the spiritual element in man. Here too is his insistence on the fact that spiritual things are not to be comprehended in human terms; and that man's yearnings toward the spiritual fail because of the human restrictions imposed upon him.

This sounds very much like Browning's own denial of man's ability to have any ultimate knowledge of things. Yet Carlyle did not for a moment deny the evidence that his intellect brought him. In fact, his pessimism was the result of his refusal to shut his eyes to the evidence of the existence of evil. But he had not the belief which consoled Browning, the belief that God could be comprehended through the heart of man; and Browning, during the rest of the *Parleying*, sets forth to Carlyle this belief. He prepares the way by an an-

[112] *With Bernard de Mandeville*, ll. 132-150.
[113] *Idem*, ll. 163-170.

swer to Carlyle's objection that the universe cannot be comprehended in human terms. That, Browning would say, is
the only way we have of comprehending it. There are signs
and symbols, which we must interpret with "mind's eye."
This phrase to Browning ever means, not the intellect, but
the informing power of the emotional imagination. He offers
to Carlyle a symbol which should appeal to him:

> Friend, here's a tracing meant
> To help a guess at truth you never knew.
> Bend but those eyes now, using mind's eye too,
> And note—sufficient for all purposes—
> The ground-plan—map you long have yearned for—yes,
> Made out in markings—more what artist can?—
> Goethe's Estate in Weimar,—just a plan!
> A. is the House, and B. the Garden-gate,
> And C. the Grass-plot—you've the whole estate
> Letter by letter, down to Y. the Pond,
> And Z. the Pig-sty. Do you look beyond
> The algebraic signs, and captious say
> "Is A. the House? But where's the roof to A.,
> Where's Door, where's Window? Needs must House have such!"
> Ay, that were folly. Why so very much
> More foolish than our mortal purblind way
> Of seeking in the symbol no mere point
> To guide our gaze through what were else inane,
> But things—their solid selves?[114]

Orion's dots form a constellation, and only the simple suppose that they are meant to be taken literally as a picture of
a man with flesh and joints. Look through the sign, Browning urges, to the thing signified.

And now Carlyle is permitted to speak once more. What
he has to say is reminiscent of his question to Browning, why

[114] *With Bernard de Mandeville,* ll. 170-188. For the appropriateness of
the choice of a symbol relating to Goethe, see David Alec Wilson, *Carlyle
to the French Revolution,* London, 1924, the Goethe entries; and *Correspondence between Goethe and Carlyle,* ed. C. E. Norton, London, 1887,
passim; and Carlyle's essays on Goethe.

ML

he did not tell the whole story of *Aristophanes' Apology* in plain, straightforward statement.[115] Why symbolize? There are words which describe our notions of abstract attributes; why use human ones?

> "What need of symbolizing? Fitlier men
> Would take on tongue mere facts—few, faint and far,
> Still facts not fancies: quite enough they are,
> That Power, that Knowledge, and that Will,—add then
> Immensity, Eternity: these jar
> Nowise with our permitted thought and speech.
> Why human attributes?"[116]

And Browning responds:

> A myth may teach:
> Only, who better would expound it thus
> Must be Euripides not Æschylus.[117]

The remainder of the poem is given up to the myth by which Browning reveals his philosophical views. It begins with a picture of nature, which is to be the background for Browning's own version of the Prometheus story:

> Boundingly up through Night's wall dense and dark,
> Embattled crags and clouds, outbroke the Sun
> Above the conscious earth, and one by one
> Her heights and depths absorbed to the last spark
> His fluid glory, from the far fine ridge
> Of mountain-granite which, transformed to gold,
> Laughed first the thanks back, to the vale's dusk fold

115 See above, p. 20.

116 *With Bernard de Mandeville*, ll. 198-204.

117 *With Bernard de Mandeville*, ll. 204-206. Porter and Clarke suggest in their notes to this passage in the Florentine edition of Browning, that the choice of Euripides over Aeschylus is due to the fact that the latter confined himself to orthodox interpretations of Greek myths, while Euripides often indulged in original interpretations of them. This is undoubtedly true; yet I believe the deeper reason for the choice may be more personal. Browning had dedicated his translation of Aeschylus' *Agamemnon* to Carlyle. This time he chooses the warm and human Euripides instead of Aeschylus.

On fold of vapor-swathing, like a bridge
Shattered beneath some giant's stamp. Night wist
Her work done and betook herself in mist
To marsh and hollow there to bide her time
Blindly in acquiescence. Everywhere
Did earth acknowledge Sun's embrace sublime
Thrilling her to the heart of things: since there
No ore ran liquid, no spar branched anew,
No arrowy crystal gleamed, but straightway grew
Glad through the inrush—glad nor more nor less
Than, 'neath his gaze, forest and wilderness,
Hill, dale, land, sea, the whole vast stretch and spread,
The universal world of creatures bred
By Sun's munificence, alike gave praise—
All creatures but one only: gaze for gaze,
Joyless and thankless, who—all scowling can—
Protests against the innumerous praises? Man,
Sullen and silent.[118]

While all the rest of nature acknowledges the power and
bounty of the sun, man alone is aggrieved. He, like the other
things in nature, is dependent upon the sun, but he shows
little gratitude for that:

Man speaks now: "What avails Sun's earth-felt thrill
To me? Sun penetrates the ore, the plant—
They feel and grow: perchance with subtler skill
He interfuses fly, worm, brute, until
Each favored object pays life's ministrant
By pressing, in obedience to his will,
Up to completion of the task prescribed,
So stands and stays a type. Myself imbibed
Such influence also, stood and stand complete—
The perfect Man,—head, body, hands and feet,
True to the pattern: but does that suffice?"[119]

[118] *With Bernard de Mandeville,* ll. 207-231. For the type of landscape
described in this passage see the discussion of Browning's use of landscape,
below, pp. 221-225.
[119] *With Bernard de Mandeville,* ll. 235-245.

Nature and physical growth will do for the beast, but man has evolved a mind and a soul that demand more than mere existence. He has outgrown his natural environment.

> How of my superadded mind which needs
> —Not to be, simply, but to do, and pleads
> For—more than knowledge that by some device
> Sun quickens matter: mind is nobly fain
> To realize the marvel . . .[120]

An intellectual comprehension of the influence of the sun is not enough; man must comprehend emotionally his relation to the scheme of things. It is not enough to be the greatest of God's creatures—would not be enough to be able to conquer each of the animals. For man, all-developed, is still incomplete:

> Let the oak increase
> His corrugated strength on strength, the palm
> Lift joint by joint her fan-fruit, ball and balm,—
> Let the coiled serpent bask in bloated peace,—
> The eagle, like some skyey derelict,
> Drift in the blue, suspended, glorying,—
> The lion lord it by the desert-spring,—
> What know or care they of the power which pricked
> Nothingness to perfection? I, instead,
> When all-developed still am found a thing
> All-incomplete: for what though flesh had force
> Transcending theirs—hands able to unring
> The tightened snake's coil, eyes that could outcourse
> The eagle's soaring, voice whereat the king
> Of carnage couched discrowned? Mind seeks to see,
> Touch, understand, by mind inside of me,
> The outside mind—whose quickening I attain
> To recognize—I only.[121]

Man is distinguished from the rest of creation by the mind— which to Browning means not the intellect, but the emotions

---

[120] *With Bernard de Mandeville,* ll. 246-250.
[121] *Idem,* ll. 254-271.

or the imagination[122]—and it is through this faculty that he attains contact with God. And then Browning, still speaking ostensibly for man, begins to expound his favorite theme. He does not want intellectual comprehension; he wants to experience through his emotions that he has a kinship with God:

> . . . were Sun's use understood,
> I might demonstrate him supplying food,
> Warmth, life, no less the while? To grant one spark
> Myself may deal with—make it thaw my blood
> And prompt my steps, were truer to the mark
> Of mind's requirement than a half-surmise
> That somehow secretly is operant
> A power all matter feels, mind only tries
> To comprehend! Once more—no idle vaunt
> 'Man comprehends the Sun's self!' Mysteries
> At source why probe into? Enough: display,
> Make demonstrable, how, by night as day,
> Earth's centre and sky's outspan, all's informed
> Equally by Sun's efflux!—source from whence
> If just one spark I drew, full evidence
> Were mine of fire ineffably enthroned—
> Sun's self made palpable to Man."[123]

This was the complaint of man until Prometheus helped him. Browning changes the story to suit his purpose, interpreting Prometheus' gift as the power to serve man by showing him how to find the sun in little, and in little to comprehend it:

> Thus moaned
> Man till Prometheus helped him,—as we learn,—
> Offered an artifice whereby he drew
> Sun's rays into a focus,—plain and true,
> The very Sun in little: made fire burn

122 See Orr, *Handbook*, p. 342.
123 *With Bernard de Mandeville*, ll. 284-300.

And henceforth do Man service—glass-conglobed
Though to a pin-point circle—all the same
Comprising the Sun's self, but Sun disrobed
Of that else-unconceived essential flame
Borne by no naked sight. Shall mind's eye strive
Achingly to companion as it may
The supersubtle effluence, and contrive
To follow beam and beam upon their way
Hand-breadth by hand-breadth, till sense faint—confessed
Frustrate, eluded by unknown unguessed
Infinitude of action? Idle quest!
Rather ask aid from optics. Sense, descry
The spectrum—mind, infer immensity![124]

Thus does Browning establish a connection between man and
God, by means of the emotional and moral consciousness.
Just as the little image of the sun that we make with a mag-
nifying glass is indeed the sun in little, with all its properties
of burning, roundness, and light, just so the heart of man is
a little picture of the great, good, and wise God out beyond
our senses and our intellectual comprehension, ruling this
world. It is his final answer to Carlyle's pessimism. Carlyle
had wanted a sign of God's preference for good; he had seen
no way by which man could know anything of the universe;
he had complained of the use of symbols, and he wanted the
triumph of evil explained. By means of his myth Browning
depicts his own optimistic philosophy: he finds hopefulness
in man himself. As man is against evil, so is God, for man is
the image of God, in little; and thus God can be comprehended somewhat, in human terms. He answers Carlyle in-
directly by setting up his own beliefs. And so the *Parleying*
ends:

Little? In little, light, warmth, life are blessed—
Which, in the large, who sees to bless? Not I
More than yourself: so, good my friend, keep still
Trustful with—me? with thee, sage Mandeville![125]

124 *With Bernard de Mandeville*, ll. 300-317.
125 *Idem*, ll. 318-321.

CHAPTER II

THE PARLEYING WITH
DANIEL BARTOLI

I

*T*HE *Parleying With Daniel Bartoli* is unique among the *Parleyings* because it is the only one among the seven that is not "mere gray argument." It is a swift and unstressed narrative, coupled with a psychological study of the three main persons involved, told in Browning's best manner; that is, in the humorously-serious manner of *Red Cotton Night-Cap Country*. In perfection of form and in depth of psychology it rivals such triumphs as *A Forgiveness* or *The Glove*, the latter of which it closely resembles. Yet in spite of the absence of metaphysics, the *Parleying* manages to be one of the clearest expressions of the mature opinions of the poet upon a fundamental characteristic of his art. It is of little consequence that Bartoli, like several of the other "people of importance," should drop out of the poem at a very early stage.

We can date more precisely Browning's first acquaintance with the works of Daniel Bartoli, the Jesuit historian of the seventeenth century, than we can date his acquaintance with the works of any other man with whom he parleyed. It was in the year 1830 that Angelo Cerutti, an Italian refugee in England, who was instructor in Italian to the poet and his sister, prepared for his pupils an edition of Bartoli's *Dei Simboli Trasportati al Morale*, which he considered one of the three best of Bartoli's works.[1] The names of "Robert Browning, Esquire," at that time eighteen years of age, and of his sister, appear in the list of subscribers for this reprint.

For the next fifteen years Browning seems to have had the

[1] Griffin and Minchin, p. 20.

Simboli always by him. It has been customary since Mrs. Orr's *Handbook* appeared to speak of the *Simboli* as Browning's favorite reading in these years.[2] Griffin and Minchin go so far as to say:

> For years the *Simboli* formed his favourite reading, and partly on account of its contents, partly on account of the purity of its style, he took it with him to Italy in 1838; and thus it happened that upon the cover of this octavo volume he wrote in pencil during the voyage his *Good News from Ghent* and *Home Thoughts from the Sea*.[3]

I doubt, however, that the *Simboli* became a favorite of Browning's. Whenever he mentions Bartoli, even in the *Parleying* itself, his references are other than approving. The truth is that Browning admired Bartoli's learning and ingenuity but objected to the use to which the Jesuit father turned those qualities.[4] The *Simboli* was the constant companion of Browning between the years 1830 and 1845 for precisely the same reason that Cerutti's Italian Grammar was. In these years Browning was either preparing himself for a visit to Italy or for a life there, and he was familiarizing himself with the language of that country. A letter to Elizabeth Barrett concerning the Grammar is indicative of his habit:

> . . . yesterday morning as I turned to look for a book, an old fancy seized me to try the 'sortes' and dip into the first page of the first I chanced upon, for my fortune; I said 'what will be the event of my love for Her'—in so many words—and my book turned out to be— 'Cerutti's Italian Grammar!'—propitious source of information . . . the best to be hoped.[5]

As Browning was studying Italian, it was most natural that

---

2 Orr, *Handbook*, p. 346.

3 Griffin and Minchin, p. 20.

4 See the descriptive note which Browning attached to the first edition of the *Parleyings*, p. 53, quoted below, p. 54. See also *Letters of R. B. and E. B. B.*, I, 535-536.

5 *Letters of R. B. and E. B. B.*, I, 464.

he should carry his old text-book with him on his first trip to
Italy. Aboard the Norham Castle on the evening of Friday
April 27, he was reading the *Simboli* and wrote upon its
cover *Home Thoughts from the Sea.* The book was again in
his hand a few days later when he wrote *"How They Brought
the Good News from Ghent to Aix."*[6] One can hardly say
that the book kept him enthralled. Yet Browning probably
resorted again to Bartoli when he went upon his second trip
to Italy in 1844. Certainly, when he was preparing to take
Elizabeth Barrett to Italy he read the *Simboli* again. In a
letter to her on March 6, 1846, we get the only specific reference that Browning makes to Bartoli and his *Simboli* before
the *Parleying* in 1887. It is at once significant and characteristic:

As for 'what people say'—ah—Here lies a book, Bartoli's
'Simboli' and this morning I dipped into his Chapter XIX. His
'Symbol' is 'Socrate fatto ritrar su' Boccali' and the theme of
his dissertating, 'L' indegnità del mettere in disprezzo i più
degni filosofi dell' antichità.' He sets out by enlarging on the
horror of it—then describes the character of Socrates, then
tells the story of the representation of the 'Clouds,' and thus
gets to his 'symbol'—'le pazzie fatte spacciare a Socrate in
quella commedia . . . il misero in tanto scherno e derisione del
pubblico, che perfino i vasai dipingevano il suo ritratto sopra
gli orci, i fiaschi, i boccali, e ogni vasellamento da più vile servi-
gio. Così quel sommo filosofo . . . fu condotto a far di se par
le case d'Atene una continue commedia, con solamente vederlo
comparir così scontraffatto e'ridicolo, come i vasai sel forma-
vano d'invenzione'—

There you have what a very clever man can say in choice
Tuscan on a passage in Aelian which he takes care not to quote
nor allude to, but which is the sole authority for the fact.
Aelian, speaking of Socrates' magnanimity, says that on the
first representation, a good many foreigners being present who
were at a loss to know 'who could be this Socrates'—the sage

[6] See Griffin and Minchin, pp. 127-128. This copy of the *Simboli* is now
in the library of Balliol College, Oxford.

himself stood up that he might be pointed out to them by the auditory at large . . . 'which' says Aelian—'was no difficulty for them, to whom his features were most familiar,—*the very potters being in the habit of decorating their vessels with his likeness*'—no doubt out of a pleasant and affectionate admiration. Yet see how 'people' can turn this out of its sense,—'say' their say on the simplest, plainest word or deed, and change it to its opposite! 'God's great gift of speech abused' indeed![7]

Browning very evidently read Bartoli for the "choice Tuscan" to be found in his works; but the more significant thing for us is the nature of Browning's criticism of Bartoli, and his rejection of the interpretation of the Jesuit historian. Browning did not care for the "Don's" trick of turning the miracles and wonders of nature, or the ordinary events of history, to some moral end. To him historical fact had a righteousness of its own. This criticism by Browning in 1846 is important because it is the attitude which he held toward Bartoli to the end of his life. In the *Parleying* Browning attempts to sum up briefly the general nature of Bartoli by giving a typical example of the historian's manner. But when he has told the story of Saint Scholastica muzzling the lion,

> "Now, Saint Scholastica, what time she fared
> In Paynimrie, behold, a lion glared
> Right in her path! Her waist she promptly strips
> Of girdle, binds his teeth within his lips,
> And, leashed all lamblike, to the Soldan's court
> Leads him,"[8]

he turns impatiently away:

> Ay, many a legend of the sort
> Do you praiseworthily authenticate:
> Spare me the rest.[9]

[7] *Letters of R. B. and E. B. B.,* I, 535-536.
[8] See *With Daniel Bartoli,* ll. 245-250.
[9] *Idem,* ll. 250-252.

In recounting miraculous legends and in pointing morals,
Bartoli seems to Browning to be misusing the gift of speech.
This criticism of the Jesuit historian had been first suggested
to Browning by Angelo Cerutti in his preface to the *Simboli*
in 1830. The poet took over Cerutti's characterization of
Bartoli wholeheartedly, so much so that when he came to
parley with Bartoli, he used Cerutti's words for almost his
whole description:

A learned and ingenious writer. "Fu Gesuita e Storico della
Compagnia; onde scrisse lunghissime storie, le quali sarebbero
lette se non fossero ripiene traboccanti di tutte le superstizioni
. . . Egli vi ha ficcati dentro tanti miracoloni, che diviene una
noia insopportabile a chiunque voglia leggere quelle storie: e
anche a me, non mi bastò l' animo di proseguire molto avanti."
—Angelo Cerutti.[10]

In the *Parleying* Browning seems not to have consulted the
Simboli at all. He takes his whole conception of Bartoli from
Cerutti's preface, and from his own memory. At the very beginning of the poem the Jesuit father is called in, only to be
dismissed until the poem is almost two-thirds done:

Don, the divinest women that have walked
Our world were scarce those saints of whom we talked.
My saint, for instance—worship if you will!
'T is pity poets need historians' skill:
What legendary's worth a chronicle?[11]

Preferring the facts of history to all the miracles of legend,
Browning in the *Parleying* uses Bartoli as a spring-board
from which he leaps into more congenial matters. The difference between the natures of the two men, Bartoli and Browning, is the genesis of the *Parleying*. Bartoli's love of the

---

[10] Browning attached this note to p. 53 of the first edition of the *Parleyings,* in order to give his readers some idea of the nature of Bartoli. It
was necessary to do this for the sake of his plan. It is taken from the preface of *De' Simboli Trasportati al Morale* dal P. Danielo Bartoli . . . edizione coretta e emendata da Angelo Cerutti. Londra, 1830.

[11] *With Daniel Bartoli,* ll. 1-5.

WITH DANIEL BARTOLI 55

miraculous and the incredible seems always to have had the
effect upon Browning of forcing him by contrast to glorify
some secular hero and some human deed. Thus the *Parleying*
concerns itself chiefly with the delineation of the kind of
woman that Browning thinks is worthy of sainthood, in contrast to Bartoli's kind of saint. Perhaps this also accounts
for the fact that *"How They Brought the Good News"* and
Home Thoughts from the Sea were written upon the fly-
leaves of Browning's copy of the *Simboli*, for the one is in
glorification of a secular hero, and the other is in praise of
Nelson and authentic history.

If we turn now to the works of Bartoli in order to form
some conception of the influence which that writer had upon
Browning we find ourselves facing a difficult problem.
Browning was apparently not acquainted with Bartoli's
greatest work, the *History of the Jesuits in Japan, China
and Asia.*[12] In his library there seems to have been only the
Simboli.[13] That work, comprising three large books with fifteen chapters to each book, about a thousand pages in all, is
a compilation of all the wonders of nature and of man which
Bartoli could cull from out-of-the-way sources of Greek
and Roman history. Stories concerning the source of the
Nile, the inundations of that river, the shadow of Bucepha-
lus, or the deeds of valor of Alexander, Hercules, or Hanni-
bal, fill the book. Several chapters are concerned with the
history of the theatrical productions in the Athenian theatre.
More space is given up to the man-made wonders of the
earth—the towers at Cizico or the urn of Severus. Bartoli
manages to turn all of these subjects into texts from which

[12] The full title is *Dell' Istoria della Compagnia di Gesù. L' Asia, del
Giappone, della Cina,* Firenze, 1829-1832, 12 vols.

[13] Of this work there were two copies when the library of Browning was
dispersed in 1913. One was the edition prepared by Cerutti which Browning
had had since 1830, and upon the cover of which he wrote the poems. The
other was evidently bought in 1886 when Browning was collecting material
for the *Parleyings*. See Sotheby, *Catalogue*, item no. 368. The second copy
is in the Wellesley College library.

he preaches some moral sentence. As we have seen, it was this
trait of Bartoli's which had caused Browning to express his
impatience to Elizabeth Barrett, " 'God's great gift of
speech abused' indeed!"

Nevertheless, while Browning may have rejected the
moral, he must have picked up an enormous amount of information from the *Simboli* concerning the history of Greece
and Rome. For example, Bartoli's chapter which Browning
quoted to Elizabeth Barrett, *Socrate fatto Ritrar su' Boccali* . . .,[14] is a mine of information concerning the Greek
theatre. The same may be said for other chapters in Bartoli's
book *La Tragedia e la Commedia* . . .,[15] *La Spelonca delle
Tragedie d'Euripide,*[16] and to some extent for the chapter
entitled *Il Teatro di Pompeo.*[17] Scattered throughout, too,
are passages of much interest upon the same subject.[18] The
Simboli must certainly have served as an introduction for
Browning to the great period of the Athenian drama. Indeed, when in 1871 he came to write *Balaustion's Adventure,*
and more particularly in 1874 when *Aristophanes' Apology*
was being written, Browning had reason to be grateful to
the *Simboli. Aristophanes' Apology,* written in nine weeks
at Mers, a little sea village on the outskirts of Tréport, is remarkable for the extensive knowledge it displays of the
plays of Aristophanes and what the scholiasts have said
about the plays. So much is this so that many thought that
it was "probably written after one of Mr. Browning's Oxford Symposia with Jowett."[19] But after the plays themselves with their scholiastic comments, Browning is more indebted to Bartoli than anyone else. Bartoli, indeed, crowds

[14] *Simboli,* II, xv. My references are from the edition published at Venice in 1831. As the pagination is entirely illogical, I refer to book and chapter, adding the page reference where necessary.
[15] *Idem,* III, i.
[16] *Simboli,* III, vii.
[17] *Idem,* II, iv.
[18] See especially Bartoli's remarks upon the *Agamemnon; idem,* III, xi,
pp. 86-87.
[19] *Letters from R. B. to Various Correspondents,* 1st Series, I, 34.

his volume with gossip and story of Athenian life, from
which Browning has freely drawn. The figure of Euripides
as he appears in the English poet's description is particularly like Bartoli's description of him.[20]

One of the chapters named above, *Il Teatro di Pompeo*
. . ., may have supplied Browning with detail for his poem,
The Bishop Orders his Tomb, which was being written in
1844 when Bartoli was much in Browning's mind. The rich
materials of which the theatre was built are all to be found
in Browning's poem.[21] The *Simboli* may also have first suggested to Browning the possibility of a poem upon Sordello.[22] Browning may have heard there too of Zeuxis, the
Greek painter who was so skilful that he could make men believe his scenes were real.[23] Bartoli, I think, filled Browning's
mind with such diverse facts as these. His great service to
Browning lay in the fact that he was a rich storehouse of detailed information.

Of particular interest to us here are the many miraculous
conquests, or at least extraordinary conquests, of lions that

[20] See *Aristophanes' Apology*, ll. 252-320; and *Balaustion's Adventure*, ll.
289-304.
[21] See *Simboli*, III, iv, especially pp. 44-55.
[22] See *idem*, I, xi, p. 12;
"Ricordami della gentilissima descrizione che Virgilio fece con la penna di
Dante, a Sordello, del luogo dov' egli abitava sotterra: non beato come i
Campi Elisi, nè misero come l'inferno, un terzo non so che men di questo, e
di quegli: come a dire allegro senza allegrezza, e doloroso senza dolore.
Così dunque parla Virgilio:

> Loco è là giù, non tristo di martiri,
> Ma di tenebre solo, ove i lamenti
> Non sonan come guai, ma son sospiri.
> Quivi sto io co'parvoli innocenti.
>
> *Purg. cap. 7.*

Oh quanto è più il poter dire d'un animo in un corpo infermo, e perciò
Tristo di martiri, che il suo lamentarsi non suona come guai, ma son sospiri!
Il dolore ha il suo proprio decoro; e può dare un bellissimo veder di sè il
mostrarsi addolorato: operando la virtù in un uomo ciò che l'arte potè nel
metallo d'una memorabil figura, che mi par ben degna d'esporsi ad essere
considerata."
[23] See below, p. 208.

occur in the *Simboli*.[24] Bartoli is continually using the old story of Hercules overcoming the Nemean lion to point his moral. It is perhaps because of the constant appearance of this beast that Browning in the *Parleying* chose the legend of Saint Scholastica muzzling a lion, as expressing an incident characteristic of the *Simboli*. Of greater interest, however, is another conquest of lions from the *Simboli* which Browning seems to have had in mind when in 1845 he was writing *The Glove*. Bartoli writes characteristically, with unconscious humor:

> Ricordivi dell' avvenuto a quel giovine Africano che abbattutosi a trovar nel diserto un lioncino nel covo senza la madre, nel rapì; e portatolo alla sua abitazione in Cartagine, sel venne a gran cura allevando e domandolo fino a renderlo non solamente di feroce mansueto, ma di libero servo, *Usque adeo, ut sarcinis impositis, aselli modo per urbem ageret* (*Max. Tyr. Serm. 32*). Ma quanto prima ne videro l'indegnità que' savii del Senato Cartaginese, ne parve loro sì male, che si adunarono sopra ciò a consiglio: e fomatane causa e giudicio rimisero per sentenza illeone in libertà, e'l suo domatore dannarono nella testa; perrochè reo (dissero) d'una violenza da tiranno usata con la natura; la quale avendo fatto e costituito il leone re degli animali, e datagli anima nobile e signorile, spiriti generosi e magnanimi, corpo voce e portamento e forze convenienti a tal personaggio: costui l' aveva non solo ingiuriosamente avvilito, ma fatto d'un leone un mostro, trasformandolo in un giumento da soma.[25]

In describing his lion in *The Glove*, Browning must have had this passage in mind. Particularly does this seem to be the case when Browning is subtly discounting the achievement of De Lorge in leaping into the lion's pit to retrieve the lady's glove.[26] Not only is Bluebeard, the lion, homesick and "leagues in the desert already," but Browning is careful to

---

[24] See *Simboli*, I, vi, p. 131; vii, p. 143; II, ii, pp. 213-214; III, iv, pp. 40 and 57; viii, p. 216; ix, p. 12; xii, p. 139; xiii, p. 159.

[25] *Simboli*, I, vi, pp. 131-132.

[26] For this light on Browning's treatment of the achievement of De Lorge I am indebted to William Lyon Phelps's excellent account of *The Glove* in *Robert Browning, How to Know Him*, pp. 250-255.

show that the men who captured lions in the desert risked
their lives every day. The lady speaks:

> When I looked on your lion, it brought
> All the dangers at once to my thought,
> Encountered by all sorts of men,
> Before he was lodged in his den,—
> From the poor slave whose club or bare hands
> Dug the trap, set the snare on the sands
> With no King and no Court to applaud,
> By no shame, should he shrink, overawed,
> Yet to capture the creature made shift,
> That his rude boys might laugh at the gift . . .[27]

In this manner Bartoli supplied the poet with a considerable number of details for his poems, particularly for those
written about 1845, when Browning was reading the *Simboli*
steadily. For the next thirty years Bartoli seems to have
been forgotten. He plays his part briefly, as we have seen, in
Aristophanes' Apology in 1874, and finally reappears to be
acknowledged when Browning in 1887 is summoning up
those "men whose works connected themselves with the intellectual sympathies and the imaginative pleasures of his very
earliest youth."

Yet in the *Parleying* itself Browning attempts to characterize the Jesuit historian in a sentence or two, and then dis-
misses him summarily. Bartoli comes in for the briefest of
notices, once as the *Parleying* begins, and again when it is
about three-quarters done. He lends his name to the piece
and stands as a contrast to the things of secular modern history which Browning wishes to praise:

> Don, the divinest women that have walked
> Our world were scarce those saints of whom we talked.
> My saint, for instance—worship if you will!
> 'T is pity poets need historians' skill:
> What legendary's worth a chronicle?[28]

27 *The Glove*, ll. 133-142.
28 *With Daniel Bartoli*, ll. 1-5.

Browning differs at the outset from Bartoli. From this point forward he ignores the Jesuit father altogether until he has cited a practical instance of what he, Browning, considers worthy of saintship in a story which has not the remotest connection with Bartoli. At the end of his tale he returns to Bartoli to strike him off in a phrase in what he conceives is the historian's own manner:

> "Now, Saint Scholastica, what time she fared
> In Paynimrie, behold, a lion glared
> Right in her path! Her waist she promptly strips
> Of girdle, binds his teeth within his lips,
> And, leashed all lamblike, to the Soldan's court
> Leads him." Ay, many a legend of the sort
> Do you praiseworthily authenticate:
> Spare me the rest.[29]

In this attempt to characterize Bartoli there is the poet's old objection to the miraculous and the legendary. But there are two main difficulties with the characterization. Browning speaks of the "divinest women . . . those saints of whom we talked." Now neither the *Simboli* nor any other work by Bartoli is devoted to a discussion of saintly women. The *Simboli* hardly dealt with the Christian world at all. The second difficulty is with the incident by which Browning attempted to typify Bartoli. The saint he chose for that purpose was Saint Scholastica, and the miracle was the conquest of the lion when she was in Paynimrie. That the incident has all the air of a direct quotation is due to Browning's art. But this particular saint—I can say it after long and careful search —does not appear in Bartoli's works. Further, nowhere in hagiology is this particular miracle ascribed to the sister of Saint Benedict, who is the only saint canonized under the name of Scholastica. It does not appear, moreover, that Saint Scholastica was ever in "Paynimrie." Bartoli was not so much interested in the legends of the early Christian saints

---

[29] *With Daniel Bartoli*, ll. 245-252.

WITH DANIEL BARTOLI 61

as in the history of the later Jesuit orders. It may be said
finally that Saint Benedict himself is rarely mentioned in the
works of Bartoli. The name and the miracle of Saint Scholastica are fabricated for the occasion.

It is likely that Browning has confused Daniello Bartoli,
the Jesuit historian, with Adolfo Bartoli, historian of Italian
Literature. In Adolfo Bartoli's *Storia della Litteratura
Italiana,* Firenze, 1881, the critic discusses in the fourth volume *La Nuova Lirica Toscana.* In dealing with Dante and
Petrarch, Adolfo Bartoli notices the rise of new types of
women in Italian Literature in the persons of Beatrice and
Laura. The fifth and tenth chapters of the fourth volume he
entitles *La Donna Angelicata* and *Organismo Della Vita
Nuova E la Donna Pietosa.* Browning may have grafted
these ideas into his conception of Daniello Bartoli, author of
the *Simboli.*

Nevertheless, the incident which Browning gives is fairly
representative of Daniello Bartoli's love of miracle and legend. It is a concrete example of the kind of history he delights in telling. The reasons why the poet fabricated the
legend of Saint Scholastica are not far to seek. The word
"scholastic" describes rather neatly the pedantic learning of
Don Bartoli. The word means, too, a certain rank in the
Jesuit orders.[30] In a sense it is descriptive of the historian as
well as of his works. Browning's love of obscure and forgotten
people as well as his obvious delight in the sound of the word
may have directed his choice of Saint Scholastica. The
deeper reason, however, I believe to be this. The story which
makes up the greater part of the *Parleying* is of a woman,
and of a woman who deserves saintship according to Browning because she is admirable in her dealings in the world of
actuality, not of legend. Saint Scholastica and her miracle
serve to make the contrast effective and thus emphasize

[30] See *New English Dictionary.* The fifth definition under the word *scholastic* reads: "A member of the third grade in the organization of the Society of Jesus."

Browning's own views. The name, Saint Scholastica, was dictated by the exigencies of the *Parleying*. It made little difference to Browning whether or not the saint or her miracle had any verity whatever.

For the greater part of his *Parleying* and the swift and beautiful tale told therein Browning owes "thanks to no legend but a chronicle." Bartoli dismissed, the poet begins at once the dramatic story of the druggist's daughter who refused to become a duchess because it would have been detrimental to the welfare of the duke, her affianced husband; tells of her subsequent marriage to a youth who saw her true worth, and of the later careers of these two men whose lives she has touched. The story is significant. Browning's choice of such a story is dictated by his desire to exemplify one of the greatest characteristics of his own poetic art. Not only is it indicative of the ever-increasing tendency in his poetry to find subjects from actual history and in actual people, but it is a perfect example of his characteristic method of work. All of his life he was looking for the deeper psychological truth which lay behind the ordinary act. The world sees only externals, and makes hasty judgments. It is the business of the poet, says Browning, to delve and find the true motive. Thus in his poem, *The Glove*, Browning makes Peter Ronsard follow the lady as she goes out amid hooting and laughter:

> Clement Marot stayed; I followed after,
> And asked, as a grace what it all meant?
> If she wished not the rash deed's recallment?
> "For I"—so I spoke—"am a poet:
> Human nature,—behoves that I know it!"[31]

When he discovers the facts, the poet usually reverses for us the judgment of the world. This trait in Browning's nature continually leads him to "make a case" for his characters. It leads him into a justification of Pompilia and Caponsacchi,

[31] *The Glove*, ll. 118-122.

and at another time of Elvire's husband in *Fifine at the Fair*. These are but typical incidents among scores that might be named, for this trait of psychological delving into motives is Browning's forte and unique gift to English poetry. So Browning naturally chooses in contrast to Bartoli's saint's legend a story from actual history upon which he can exercise his peculiar talent of revealing the subtle psychological motives of his characters. Bartoli, as we have seen, seems always to have stimulated Browning to the expression of his own ideas, usually opposed to those of Bartoli.

The story, which Browning relates in the *Parleying With Bartoli*, Mrs. Orr tells us, is "a well-known episode in the lives of Charles IV., Duke of Lorraine, and the Marquis de Lassay."[32] But neither Mrs. Orr nor any other commentator has given us a further clue to Browning's precise source, and the story occurs in many memoirs of the reign of Louis XIV.[33] Mrs. Orr's information may well have come from the mouth of Browning himself, as she mentions no source whatever. The *Memoires* of the Marquis de Lassay[34] are so obviously the exact account upon which Browning depended for his story that no one reading them can doubt it. Browning was probably led to the *Memoires* for his story by a work he had long known, the *Biographie Universelle*,[35] which Griffin suggests he read in its entire thirty volumes when he was a boy. The *Biographie* gives the story in very abbreviated form, and gives also the lives of the main personages before and after the event, and supplies the one detail which de Lassay's *Memoires* did not suggest for the story, the fact that by occupation Marianne Pajot's father was a drug-

[32] Orr, *Handbook*, p. 346.

[33] Usually in very brief form. A good example may be seen in *Memoires de Saint Simon*, Paris, 1873, I, 292-293.

[34] This work goes often under the title *Recueil de Differentes Choses*, Par M. de Lassay. It is from Vol. I of the edition published in four volumes at Lausanne in 1756, that I shall quote.

[35] *Biographie Universelle*, Paris, 1819, 50 Vols., XXV, 60; and XXIII, 412-414. For some idea of the extent of the influence of this work upon the poet, see Griffin and Minchin, p. 25.

gist.[36] The fact that Browning seems to have used the *Memoires* upon only this one occasion would lead one to believe that the poet followed the suggestion of the *Biographie* to read the story at greater length in the *Memoires*. The *Premier Partie* of the *Memoires* is the book of Marianne, and is a "Recit de ce qui se passa dans le moment que M. le Duc de Lorraine alloit epouser Mlle. Marianne (*Marie-Anne Pajot*)." Since the story as de Lassay gives it has not been previously suggested as a source for Browning's narrative, and since it affords at once both a striking parallel and a perfect opportunity to see the poet's method of work, I quote the account from the *Memoires* almost in full:

Quelques années après la Paix des Pyrenées, le Duc de Lorraine vint en France, où il fit un Traité avec le Roi, par lequel il lui cédoit ses Etats à des conditions écrites en plusieurs endroits, trop longues pour être mises ici, & de plus, inutiles à ce que j'ai dessein de dire. Après avoir fait ce Traité, il s'en repentit, & ne voulut plus qu'il eût d'exécution.

Pendant tout ce tems-là il voyoit au Luxembourg, chez *Madame*, que étoit sa soeur, & chez *Mademoiselle*, une Fille, que sa beauté, ses graces & son esprit avoient mis dans le monde d'un air bien différent de celui qu'elle y devoit avòir par sa naissance; elle s'appelloit *Marianne*, & n'étoit que Femme-de-chambre de *Mademoiselle:* ses qualités aimables & ses manieres nobles qui avoient plu à tout le monde toucherent le Duc *de Lorraine* qui en devint passionément amoureux: il s'apperçut bien-tôt que ce n'étoit pas une conquête aisée, & il l'estima assez pour la vouloir faire Duchesse de *Lorraine*, il lui dit donc qu'il vouloit l'épouser.

On peut aisément imaginer l'effet que fit une telle proposition sur une jeune personne dont l'ame étoit noble & élevée; elle regarda un honneur si surprenant avec modestie, mais elle n'en fut point éblouie au point de s'en croire indigne. M. *de Lorraine* parla à ses parens de ses intentions, & la chose alla si loin qu'il y eut un Contrat de Mariage fait dans toutes les formes; que les Bans furent publiés, & le jour pris pour faire le mariage.

[36] See *Biographie Universelle*, XXV, 60.

Comme tout cela ne se fit pas avec un grandmistere, *Madame*, Soeur de M. *de Lorraine*, en étant avertie fit tout ce qu'elle put auprès de lui, pour l'empêcher de faire un Mariage si inégal; mais voyant que tout ce qu'elle lui pouvoit dire étoit inutile, elle eut recours au Roi & à la Reine Mere, & les supplia d'empêcher ce Mariage.

D'un autre côté, M. *le Tellier* instruit de ce qui se passoit, & qui avoit fait avec M. *de Lorraine* le Traité par lequel il donnoit ses Etats, vint trouver le Roi, & lui dit qu'il se présentoit l'occasion du monde la plus favorable pour engager M. *de Lorraine* à finir une affaire aussi avantageuse à la France qu'étoit le Traité en question; qu'il falloit aller trouver Mademoiselle *Marianne*, & lui dire que, si elle vouloit obliger M. de *Lorraine* à exécuter ce Traité, le Roi nonseulement n'empêcheroit point son Mariage, mais qu'il la reconnoîtroit Duchesse *de Lorraine;* & que si elle ne lui obéissoit pas, il accorderoit à *Madame* la grace qu'elle lui demandoit avec tant d'instance, qui étoit de la faire mettre dans un Couvent. La proposition ayant été agréée (*sic*) par le Roi, M. *le Tellier* lui dit qu'il n'y avoit pas un moment à perdre, parce que le Mariage se devoit faire la nuit même; qu'il eût donc la bonté de lui donner un Officier & trente de ses Gardes, & qu'il iroit sur le champ chercher Mademoiselle *Marianne* pour lui parler ce qui fut exécuté. Il la trouva à table avec M. *de Lorraine* & sa Famille qui étoit assemblée chez un de ses Oncles, où se faisoit le Festin de nôces, en attendant minuit, pour s' aller marier.

Je crois que la surprise fut grande de voir arriver M. *le Tellier* qui demanda à parler en particulier à la Marièe. Il remplit son ordre en homme qui avoit fort envie de réussir, il lui fit envisager tout ce qu'elle avoit à craindre & à espérer, & il lui dit enfin qu'il ne tenoit qu'à elle d'être reconnue le lendemain Duchesse *de Lorraine* par le Roi; qu'elle n'avoit qu'à faire signer à M. de Lorraine un Papier qu'il avoit apporté avec lui, & qu'il lui montra, & qu'elle seroit reçue au Louvre avec tous les Honneurs dûs à un si grand rang; mais que si elle refusoit de faire ce que Sa Majesté souhaitoit, qu'il y avoit a la porte un de ses Carosses, trente Gardes du Corps & un Enseigne qui avoit ordre de la mener au Couvent de la Ville-l'Evêque, ce que Madame demandoit avec beaucoup d'empressement.

L'alternative étoit grande, & il y avoit lieu d'être tentée. *Marianne* ne balança pas un moment, & elle répondit à M. *le Tellier* qu'elle aimoit beaucoup mieux demeurer *Marianne*, que d'être Duchesse *de Lorraine*, aux conditions qu'on lui proposoit; & que si elle avoit quelque pouvoir sur l'esprit de M. *de Lorraine*, elle ne s'en serviroit jamais pour lui faire faire (*sic*) une chose si contraire à son honneur & à ses intérêts; qu'elle se reprochoit déja assez le Mariage que l'amitié qu'il avoit pour elle lui faisoit faire. M. *le Tellier* touché d'un procédé si noble, lui dit, qu' on donneroit, si elle vouloit, vingtquatre heures pour y songer. Elle lui répondit que son parti étoit pris, & qu'elle n'avoit que faire d'y penser davantage, & puis elle rentra dans la Chambre où étoit la Compagnie pour prendre congé de M. *de Lorraine*, qui ayant appris de quoi il étoit question se mit dans des transports de colere effroyables; après l'avoir calmè autant qu'elle pût, elle donna la main à M. *le Tellier*, laissant la Chambre toute remplie de pleurs, & monta dans le Carosse du Roi sans verser une seule larme.

Quelques jours après elle renvoya à M. *de Lorraine* par une de ses Tantes, pour un million de pierreries qu'il lui avoit données, lui disant qu'il ne lui convenoit pas de les garder, n'ayant pas l'honneur d'être sa Femme: Elle demeura à la Ville-l'Evêque, où il y avoit ordre de ne la point laisser voir à M. *de Lorraine* tout le temps qu'il resta en France, ce qui fut quatre ou cinq mois, étant gardée par une Compagnie aux Gardes, dans la crainte qu'on avoit qu'il ne l'enlevât, ayant même fait quelque tentatives pour cela, & elle n'en sortit que lorsqu'il fut retourné en *Lorraine*, d'où il demanda, (sçachant qu'elle étoit en liberté) que si elle vouloit le venir trouver dans ses Etats avec sa Mere, ou quelqu'une de ses Tantes, il acheveroit un Mariage qu'il souhaitoit toujours passionnément. La crainte qu'elle eût de lui, si elle étoit une fois en lieu où il fut le maître, fit qu'elle lui répondit qu'elle ne pouvoit point se résoudre à aller en *Lorraine*, sans être auparavant sa femme.

Il lui écrevit pendant un tems assez long beaucoup d'autres Letters, par lesquelles il lui disoit qu'il viendroit l'épouser en France s'il n'avoit pas peur d'y être arrêté, étant brouillé avec le Roi: mais effrayée par beaucoup d'examples de légéreté qu'il avoit déja donnés en de pareilles occasions, elle ne put jamais se rassurer; & elle lui repondit toujours sur le même ton.

J'ai écrit une action aussi belle & aussi singuliere que celle-là pour mon Fils & pour ses enfans, afin qu'ils en conservent la mémoire & qu'ils tâchent à imiter une mere si vertueuse; j'ose même leur dire qu'une Fille qui avoit tant de noblesse dans l'ame est peut-être préférable à une Demoiselle dont les Peres sont parvenus par des voies basses & honteuses, aux honneurs qui ont illustré leur Maison.

M. *le Tellier* qui étoit demeuré fort des Amis de *Mlle Marianne* depuis leur conversation, l'a contée bien des fois en sa vie, & il parloit toujours d'elle avec admiration: l'Abbesse de la Ville-l'Eveque & les Religieuses ne lui donnoient pas moins de louanges.

Bien des années aprés, s'etant trouvée en un commerce assez familier avec le Roi, il lui demanda un jour si elle lui avoit pardonné de l'avoir empêchée d'être Duchesse *de Lorraine;* elle lui répondit qu'ayant contribué depuis, a lui faire épouser un homme de condition* qu'elle aimoit & dont elle croyoit être áimee, elle lui avoit pardon né aisément d'avoir rompu son mariage avec un Souverain, qui l'auroit rendue moins heureuse qu'elle n'étoit.[37]

* M. le Marquis *de Lassay,* auteur de ce Recueil. Il avoit épousé en premieres noces *Marie-Marthe Sibour.* Cette Dame étant morte au mois de Janvier 1675, il se remaria à Marie-Anne Pajot, ce mariage fut tenu secret pendant quelques tems; mais le Marquis *de Montataire* pere de M. de Lassay, paroissant en disposition de se remarier, son fils qui appréhendoit que dans une seconde alliance M. de *Montataire,* ne prit des engagements contraires à ses intérêts, si son mariage restoit plus longtems caché, le sollicita vivement de ne plus differer à y donner un consentement authentique, c'est ce que l'on va voir dans les Lettres suivantes.

In this account every ramification of fact in Browning's story in the *Parleying,* save the one mentioned above,[38] is provided for. But the psychology of the personages, the conversation, and the dramatization of the poem are Browning's very own. Browning has of course heightened the significance of some parts of the story and modified that of others, and these changes are full of meaning for the student

[37] De Lassay, *Recueil* . . ., I, 5-19.
[38] See above, p. 63.

of his art. Yet in all matters of fact Browning has followed
de Lassay in his smallest detail. We can best see this by a
study of the poem.

II

THE *Parleying* begins with Browning's denial that the divinest women of the earth have been the canonized saints of
whom Bartoli speaks. Browning would speak in behalf of a
secular saint, a creature not of legend but of actual history.
And so in the first five lines of the *Parleying* Browning dis-
misses Bartoli, and plunges at once into the business of depicting *his* kind of saint:

> Come, now! A great lord once upon a time
> Visited—oh a king, of kings the prime,
> To sign a treaty such as never was:
> For the king's minister had brought to pass
> That this same duke—so style him—must engage
> Two of his dukedoms as an heritage
> After his death to this exorbitant
> Craver of kingship.[39]

The story is launched, and the personages who first appear,
though no names are mentioned throughout the *Parleying*,
are the Duke of Lorraine, Louis XIV, and his minister, le
Tellier. There was nothing for the duke to do but agree to
the cession of his lands after his death. But unfortunately
for the king, the duke visited his sister before signing the
treaty, and there met Marianne Pajot:

> Now, as it happened, at his sister's house
> —Duchess herself—indeed the very spouse
> Of the king's uncle,[40]—while the deed of gift
> Whereby our duke should cut his rights adrift
> Was drawing, getting ripe to sign and seal—
> What does the frozen heart but uncongeal

39 *With Daniel Bartoli*, ll. 6-13.
40 That is, she was Duchess of Orleans.

And, shaming his transcendent kin and kith,
Whom do the duke's eyes make acquaintance with?
A girl.[41] "What, sister, may this wonder be?"
"Nobody! Good as beautiful is she,
With gifts that match her goodness, no faint flaw
I' the white: she were the pearl you think you saw,
But that she is—what corresponds to white?
Some other stone, the true pearl's opposite,
As cheap as pearls are costly. She's—now, guess
Her parentage! Once—twice—thrice? Foiled, confess!
Drugs, duke, her father deals in—faugh, the scents!—
Manna and senna—such medicaments
For payment he compounds you. Stay—stay—stay!
I'll have no rude speech wrong her! Whither away,
The hot-head? Ah, the scapegrace! She deserves
Respect—compassion, rather! Right it serves
My folly, trusting secrets to a fool!
Already at it, is he? She keeps cool—
Helped by her fan's spread. Well, our state atones
For thus much license, and words break no bones!"
(Hearts, though, sometimes.)[42]

It is highly instructive to observe how the poet has put warmth, life, and reality into the cold figures of the chronicle, at the same time following closely the facts therein. But we continue the narrative, which next describes the duke's resolution after he has talked with Marianne:

Next morn 't was "Reason, rate,
Rave, sister, on till doomsday! Sure as fate,
I wed that woman—what a woman is
Now that I know, who never knew till this!"
So swore the duke. "I wed her: once again—
Rave, rate, and reason—spend your breath in vain!"[43]

[41] Marianne Pajot, "une femme-de-chambre de Mlle. de Conti." See *Biographie Universelle*, XXIII, 412.
[42] *With Daniel Bartoli*, ll. 16-42.
[43] *Idem*, ll. 42-47.

And so the business proceeded:

> At once was made a contract[44] firm and fast,
> Published the banns were, only marriage, last,
> Required completion when the Church's rite
> Should bless and bid depart, make happy quite
> The coupled man and wife for evermore:
> Which rite was soon to follow. Just before—
> All things at all but end—the folk o' the bride
> Flocked to a summons. Pomp the duke defied:
> "Of ceremony—so much as empowers,
> Naught that exceeds, suits best a tie like ours—"
> He smiled—"all else were mere futility.
> We vow, God hears us: God and you and I—
> Let the world keep at distance! This is why
> We choose the simplest forms that serve to bind
> Lover and lover of the human kind . . ."[45]

Garrulousness is a part of the duke's nature. He says at great length that he chooses the simple way "of God's man and woman." It is a love match. All his life the duke has been told that it was his privilege to have mistresses at his discretion if he so desired, though of course one legal wife; now he asks,

> ". . . Prove I so inept
> A scholar, thus instructed? Dearest, be
> Wife and all mistresses in one to me,
> Now, henceforth, and forever!" So smiled he.[46]

The duke's long speeches upon his love are due to Browning's invention, though he has authority from the situation in the chronicle. They are significant for an interpretation of the duke's character and Browning's meaning.[47] But

44 Upon this contract the *Recueil*, p. 7, has a note: "On voit ce Contrat de Mariage imprimé dans plusieurs Receuils. Il fut passé le 18 Avril 1662."
45 *With Daniel Bartoli*, ll. 48-62.
46 *Idem*, ll. 74-77.
47 See below, pp. 82-83.

meanwhile the story proceeds; the king hears of the marriage:

> Good: but the minister, the crafty one,
> Got ear of what was doing—all but done—
> Not sooner, though, than the king's very self,
> Warned by the sister on how sheer a shelf
> Royalty's ship was like to split.[48]

The Grand Monarch is prompt:

> "I bar
> The abomination! Mix with muck my star?
> Shall earth behold prodigiously enorbed
> An upstart marsh-born meteor sun-absorbed?
> Nuptial me no such nuptials!" "Past dispute,
> Majesty speaks with wisdom absolute,"
> Admired the minister: "yet, all the same
> I would we may not—while we play his game,
> The ducal meteor's—also lose our own,
> The solar monarch's: we relieve your throne
> Of an ungracious presence, like enough:
> Balked of his project he departs in huff,
> And so cuts short—dare I remind the king?—
> Our not so unsuccessful bargaining.
> The contract for eventual heritage
> Happens to *pari passu* reach the stage
> Attained by just this other contract,—each
> Unfixed by signature though fast in speech.
> Off goes the duke in dudgeon—off withal
> Go with him his two dukedoms past recall.
> You save a fool from tasting folly's fruit,
> Obtain small thanks thereby, and lose to boot
> Sagacity's reward. The jest is grim:
> The man will mulct you—for amercing him?
> Nay, for . . . permit a poor similitude!
> A witless wight in some fantastic mood

[48] *With Daniel Bartoli*, ll. 78-82. Compare this passage with the *Recueil*, pp. 8-9, quoted above, p. 65.

Would drown himself: you plunge into the wave,
Pluck forth the undeserving: he, you save,
Pulls you clean under also for your pains.
Sire, little need that I should tax my brains
To help your inspiration!" "Let him sink!
Always contriving"—hints the royal wink—
"To keep ourselves dry while we claim his clothes."[49]

I quote at length in order to show how Browning has made
real by his understanding of psychology a scene which is
certainly suggested in the *Recueil*, but is little more than
suggested.[50] Browning has developed rather than changed
the material of his source. The story goes forward rapidly:

Next day, the appointed day for plighting troths
At eve,—so little time to lose, you see,
Before the Church should weld indissolubly
Bond into bond, wed these who, side by side,
Sit each by other, bold groom, blushing bride,—
At the preliminary banquet, graced
By all the lady's kinsfolk come in haste
To share her triumph,—lo, a thunderclap!
"Who importunes now?" "Such is my mishap—
In the king's name! No need that any stir
Except this lady!" bids the minister:[51]
"With her I claim a word apart, no more:
For who gainsays—a guard is at the door.
Hold, duke! submit you, lady, as I bow
To him whose mouthpiece speaks his pleasure now!
It well may happen I no whit arrest
Your marriage: be it so,—we hope the best!
By your leave, gentles! Lady, pray you, hence!
Duke, with my soul and body's deference!"[52]

49 *With Daniel Bartoli*, ll. 82-114.
50 See *Recueil*, pp. 9-10, quoted above, p. 65.
51 In these details Browning is following closely *Recueil*, pp. 10-11,
quoted above, p. 65.
52 *With Daniel Bartoli*, ll. 115-133.

In the next moment, while pandemonium reigns inside, the
lady and the minister talk quietly alone:

Doors shut, mouth opens and persuasion flows
Copiously forth. "What flesh shall dare oppose
The king's command? The matter in debate
—How plain it is! Yourself shall arbitrate,
Determine. Since the duke affects to rate
His prize in you beyond all goods of earth,
Accounts as naught old gains of rank and birth,
Ancestral obligation, recent fame,
(We know his feats)—nay, ventures to disclaim
Our will and pleasure almost—by report—
Waives in your favor dukeliness, in short,—
We—('t is the king speaks)—who might forwith stay
Such suicidal purpose, brush away
A bad example shame would else record,—
Lean to indulgence rather. At his word
We take the duke: allow him to complete
The cession of his dukedoms, leave our feet
Their footstool when his own head, safe in vault,
Sleeps sound. Nay, would the duke repair his fault
Handsomely, and our forfeited esteem
Recover,—what if wisely he redeem
The past,—in earnest of good faith, at once
Give us such jurisdiction for the nonce
As may suffice—prevent occasion slip—
And constitute our actual ownership?
Concede this—straightway be the marriage blessed
By warrant of this paper! Things at rest,
This paper duly signed, down drops the bar,
To-morrow you become—from what you are,
The druggist's daughter—not the duke's mere spouse,
But the king's own adopted: heart and house
Open to you—the idol of a court
'Which heaven might copy'—sing our poet-sort.
In this emergency, on you depends
The issue: plead what bliss the king intends!
Should the duke frown, should arguments and prayers,
Nay, tears if need be, prove in vain,—who cares?

> We leave the duke to his obduracy,
> Companionless,—you, madam, follow me
> Without, where divers of the body-guard
> Wait signal to enforce the king's award
> Of strict seclusion: over you at least
> Vibratingly the scepter threats increased
> Precipitation! How avert its crash?"[53]

Thus does the minister put the problem to the lady, the poor druggist's daughter. If we compare this long passage with the short, simple, and almost brutal alternatives which are presented to her in the *Recueil*,[54] we see at once that Browning is at no pains to minimize the lady's temptation. She stands between threat and promise, and her problem, put simply, is this: Will she use her influence with the duke in behalf of the king, her reward being that she should become duchess and favorite with the king? The consequence of not complying is imprisonment. But as she sees the question it becomes: Will she for her own gain betray the interests and the honor of the man she is to marry? It is a momentous choice; but, says the chronicle, "Marianne ne balança pas un moment . . ."[55] Browning's lady is no less decisive:

> "Re-enter, sir! A hand that's calm, not rash,
> Averts it!" quietly the lady said.
> "Yourself shall witness."
>   At the table's head
> Where, mid the hushed guests, still the duke sat glued
> In blank bewilderment, his spouse pursued
> Her speech to end—syllabled quietude.
>
> "Duke, I, your duchess of a day, could take
> The hand you proffered me for love's sole sake,
> Conscious my love matched yours; as you, myself
> Would waive, when need were, all but love—from pelf

To potency. What fortune brings about
Haply in some far future, finds me out,
Faces me on a sudden here and now.
The better! Read—if beating heart allow—
Read this, and bid me rend to rags the shame!
I and your conscience—hear and grant our claim!
Never dare alienate God's gift you hold
Simply in trust for him! Choose muck for gold?
Could you so stumble in your choice, cajoled
By what I count my least of worthiness
—The youth, the beauty,—you renounce them—yes,
With all that's most too: love as well you lose,
Slain by what slays in you the honor! Choose!
Dear—yet my husband—dare I love you yet?"[56]

Her fate has been decided. She, of course, must go under
guard with the minister, for never for a moment does she
consider betraying the interests and honor of the duke. She
is pleading that he save his own honor. If he tears the paper,
she will be taken away, but she will love him forever. She is
fighting to hold her faith in him. If he does not tear the paper, he will lose her person and heart at once. It is needless to
say that the subtle psychological depth of the problem is due
to Browning rather than to the *Recueil*. This is of considerable importance in our ultimate interpretation of the poem.
But the question has been put squarely to the duke and we
await his answer:

How the duke's wrath o'erboiled,—words, words and yet
More words,—I spare you such fool's fever-fret.
They were not of one sort at all, one size,
As souls go—he and she. 'T is said, the eyes
Of all the lookers-on let tears fall fast.
The minister was mollified at last:
"Take a day,—two days even, ere through pride
You perish,—two days' counsel—then decide!"[57]

[56] *With Daniel Bartoli*, ll. 178-201.
[57] *Idem*, ll. 202-209. One finds all these details in the *Recueil*, p. 13,
quoted above, p. 66.

But Marianne wishes no reprieve, and an immediate choice is
forced upon the duke:

> —"If I shall save his honor and my soul?
> Husband,—this one last time,—you tear the scroll?
> Farewell, duke![58] Sir, I follow in your train!"
>
> So she went forth: they never met again,
> The duke and she. The world paid compliment
> (Is it worth noting?) when, next day, she sent
> Certain gifts back—"jewelry fit to deck
> Whom you call wife." I know not round what neck
> They took to sparkling, in good time—weeks thence.[59]

The first part of the story is ended, but there is a sequel:

> Of all which was the pleasant consequence,
> So much and no more—that a fervid youth,[60]
> Big-hearted boy,—but ten years old, in truth,—
> Laid this to heart and loved, as boyhood can,
> The unduchessed lady: boy and lad grew man:
> He loved as man perchance may: did meanwhile
> Good soldier-service, managed to beguile
> The years, no few, until he found a chance:
> Then, as a trumpet-summons to advance,
> Outbroke the love that stood at arms so long,

[58] The Florentine edition is incorrectly punctuated here, with a question
mark. I have corrected it to agree with the first edition.

[59] *With Daniel Bartoli,* ll. 210-218. Browning has authority for this belief concerning the duke's fickleness in the *Recueil,* p. 15, note:
". . . ce Prince avoit déja épousé la Duchesse Nicole, fille de Henri II.
Duc de Lorraine, puis sous prétexte que ce Mariage étoit nul, il se maria à
la Princesse Cantecroix, du vivant de la quelle il prétendoit épouser Marie-
Anne Pajot, depuis il voulut épouser Mademoiselle de S. Remi, ensuite il
devint passionnément amoureux de Mademoiselle de Ludres . . ." etc. See
Recueil, p. 15, where after the affair of Marianne it is said, "il acheveroit un
Mariage qu'il souhaitoit toujours passionnément . . ."

[60] This is, of course, de Lassay himself. The facts which Browning uses
here are from the *Recueil,* and in more concise form may be found in the
Biographie Universelle, XXIII, 412 ff. Browning adds de Lassay's long
love for Marianne to the character, because it strengthens his hero and his
own moral as well. See below, pp. 82, 85.

Brooked no withstanding longer. They were wed.
Whereon from camp and court alike he fled,
Renounced the sun-king, dropped off into night,
Evermore lost, a ruined satellite:
And, oh, the exquisite deliciousness
That lapped him in obscurity![61] You guess
Such joy is fugitive: she died full soon.[62]
He did his best to die—as sun, so moon
Left him, turned dusk to darkness absolute.
Failing of death—why, saintship seemed to suit:
Yes, your sort, Don! He trembled on the verge
Of monkhood: trick of cowl and taste of scourge
He tried:[63] then, kicked not at the pricks perverse,

[61] Browning makes de Lassay's obscurity and renunciation of the world much more complete than it really was. De Lassay married Marianne in 1673 and she died in 1678. De Lassay fought the campaign of Flanders in 1675. See the *Biographie Universelle,* as above. Browning, in all likelihood, got his idea of the self-exile from a letter which de Lassay wrote after the death of Marianne:
"A quinze ans, je l'ai connue; & à quinze ans j'ai commenceé à l'aimer; depuis, cette passion a toujours réglé ma vie, & il n'y a rien que je ne lu aye sacrifié; je la perds, cette chere Femme; je n'ai été dans le monde que pour elle; je n'en veux plus sans elle; on peut juger quelle est mon amitié, par le sacrifice que lui avois fait, & par celui que je lui vais faire . . ." *Recueil,* p. 54.
[62] One reads on p. 50 of the *Recueil:*
"Après la prise de Cambrai & autres places; la paix fut conclue par le Traité de Nimigue en 1678. Marie-Anne Pajot, Marquise de Lassay, mourut quelque tems après." The marriage lasted five years.
[63] The following excerpts from the letters of de Lassay quoted from *Recueil,* pp. 51 ff., will show his poignant grief upon the death of Marianne. Browning condenses skilfully, yet follows closely:
Ceci a été écrit dans le tems que je venois de perdre cette *Marianne,* que j'avois assez aimer pour quitter tout, dans l'espérance de passer ma vie avec elle.
Dieu à rompu la seule chaîne qui m'attachoit au monde; je n'ai plus rien à y faire qu'a mourir; je regarde la mort comme un moment heureux; on n'en souffre les horreurs qu'une fois en sa vie; & je les viens de sentir, avec cette différence, que d'ordinaire on a l'esprit si abattu dans ces derniers momens, qu'on n'en a qu'un sentiment imparfait; & moi j'en sens toute l'amertume, & je l'avale à longs traits. Que je me trouve jeune! la longueur de ma vie me paroît insupportable quand je la compare a la longueur des jours que j'ai passés depuis la perte effroyable que j'ai faite; je suis de-meuré seul sur la terre; que c'est un triste séjour! si je n'etois pas sujet à la mort, mon état ne se pourroit supporter; ma seule consolation est que je ferai le même chemin qu'a fait ma chere *Marianne,* & qu'il ne lui est rien arrivé qui ne m'arrive; elle est partie la premiere, & j'espere que je la

> But took again, for better or for worse,
> The old way in the world, and, much the same
> Man o' the outside, fairly played life's game.[64]

Here is grief expressed too poignantly to be entirely impersonal. It transcends both de Lassay and the situation in the
story. And we shall see before we have done that this is as
much a description of Browning himself as it is of de Lassay,
even though the poet is following the chronicle closely[65] in
the fact of the tale.

Then suddenly Browning reminds us of the contrast between his kind of saint and that other kind of Bartoli's; that
is, of Saint Scholastica muzzling the lion. He turns impatiently from such superficial saintliness:

> This much of no debate
> Admits: my lady flourished in grand days
> When to be duchess was to dance the hays
> Up, down, across the heaven amid its host:
> While to be hailed the sun's own self almost—
> So close the kinship—was—was—
> Saint, for this,
> Be yours the feet I stoop to—kneel and kiss!
> So human? Then the mouth too, if you will!
> Thanks to no legend but a chronicle.[66]

The poem should have ended here. But Browning is not quite
content, and must pursue his thoughts a little further. He
must turn back to the forsaken duke to wonder at greater
length what became of him. For this turn in his story, too,
as we have seen, the *Receuil* supplied suggestion.[67] So
Browning follows him into his subsequent career:

suivrai bien-tôt; quand on a connu le plaisir d'aimer & d'être aimé par une
personne qui ne vivoit que pour vous, & pour qui seule on vivoit, on ne veut
plus de la vie a d'autres conditions . . . Je n'oserois demander la mort à
Dieu, mais je l'appelle par mes desires . . .

    64 *With Daniel Bartoli*, ll. 219-244. After the death of Marianne, de Las-
say went into Hungary to fight against the Turks. See *Recueil*, pp. 64 ff.
    65 See above, p. 77, note 63.
    66 *With Daniel Bartoli*, ll. 252-260.
    67 See above, p. 76, note 59, or *Recueil*, p. 15 and note.

One leans to like the duke, too: up we'll patch
Some sort of saintship for him—not to match
Hers—but man's best and woman's worst amount
So nearly to the same thing, that we count
In man a miracle of faithfulness
If, while unfaithful somewhat, he lay stress
On the main fact that love, when love indeed,
Is wholly solely love from first to last—
Truth—all the rest a lie. Too likely, fast
Enough that necklace went to grace the throat
—Let's say of such a dancer as makes doat
The senses when the soul is satisfied—
Trogalia, say the Greeks—a sweetmeat tried
Approvingly by sated tongue and teeth,
Once body's proper meal consigned beneath
Such unconsidered munching.
                  Fancy's flight
Makes me a listener when, some sleepless night,
The duke reviewed his memories, and aghast
Found that the Present intercepts the Past
With such effect as when a cloud enwraps
The moon and, moon-suffused, plays moon perhaps
To who walks under, till comes, late or soon,
A stumble: up he looks, and lo, the moon
Calm, clear, convincingly herself once more!
How could he 'scape the cloud that thrust between
Him and effulgence? Speak, fool—duke, I mean![68]

And as the duke speaks there rises before us the Present
which has intercepted the Past. It is one of the strangest ap-
paritions in literature. The poem which follows, set off as it
is by its distinct verse-form and its repellent but fascinating
imagery, is at once a plea for the duke upon the grounds of
general human frailty, and an insistence upon his better nature. For Browning believed that this man who had once
truly loved could not be altogether bad. The latent quality

[68] *With Daniel Bartoli,* ll. 261-286.

of the man will flame some day. But now the apparition
comes, and the duke addresses it:

> "Who bade you come, brisk-marching bold she-shape,
>   A terror with those black-balled worlds of eyes,
> That black hair bristling solid-built from nape
>   To crown it coils about? O dread surmise!
> Take, tread on, trample under past escape
>   Your capture, spoil and trophy! Do—devise
> Insults for one who, fallen once, ne'er shall rise!

> "Mock on, triumphant o'er the prostrate shame!
>   Laugh 'Here lies he among the false to Love—
> Love's loyal liegeman once: the very same
>   Who, scorning his weak fellows, towered above
> Inconstancy: yet why his faith defame?
>   Our eagle's victor was at least no dove,
> No dwarfish knight picked up our giant's glove—

> " 'When, putting prowess to the proof, faith urged
>   Her champion to the challenge: had it chanced
> That merely virtue, wisdom, beauty—merged
>   All in one woman—merely these advanced
> Their claim to conquest,—hardly had he purged
>   His mind of memories, dearnesses enhanced
> Rather than harmed by death, nor, disentranced,

> " 'Promptly had he abjured the old pretence
>   To prove his kind's superior—first to last
> Display erect on his heart's eminence
>   An altar to the never-dying Past,
> For such feat faith might boast fit play of fence
>   And easily disarm the iconoclast
> Called virtue, wisdom, beauty: impudence

> " 'Fought in their stead, and how could faith but fall?
>   There came a bold she-shape brisk-marching, bent
> No inch of her imperious stature, tall
>   As some war-engine from whose top was sent
> One shattering volley out of eye's black ball,
>   And prone lay faith's defender!' Mockery spent?
> Malice discharged in full? In that event,

"My queenly impudence, I cover close,
  I wrap me round with love of your black hair,
Black eyes, black every wicked inch of those
  Limbs' war-tower tallness: so much truth lives there
'Neath the dead heap of lies. And yet—who knows?
  What if such things are? No less, such things were.
Then was the man your match whom now you dare

"Treat as existent still. A second truth:
  They held—this heap of lies you rightly scorn—
A man who had approved himself in youth
  More than a match for—you? for sea-foam-born
Venus herself: you conquer him forsooth?
  'T is me his ghost: he died since left and lorn,
As needs must Samson when his hair is shorn.

"Some day, and soon, be sure himself will rise,
  Called into life by her who long ago
Left his soul whiling time in flesh-disguise.
  Ghosts tired of waiting can play tricks, you know!
Tread, trample me—such sport we ghosts devise,
  Waiting the morn-star's re-appearance—though
You think we vanish scared by the cock's crow."[69]

III

To even the casual reader the likeness of the story told in
this *Parleying* to Browning's poem, *The Glove*, written and
published in 1845, is patent. The stories, stripped of ever so
little of their superficial dress, are essentially the same. The
most striking similarity is the presence of the youthful lover.
The young man of *The Glove* observed the whole action at
the lion's pit, and followed the disgraced lady to marry her.
De Lassay pursues a similar course in the *Parleying*. Both
lovers are considerably younger than the ladies involved.
Each remains quietly in the background until his moment
arrives, each being willing to "first earn" the prize he seeks.

[69] *With Daniel Bartoli*, ll. 287-342.

They are both superior in social position to the ladies they wed.[70] But above all, they are both endowed with that first of virtues, the ability to discern a soul's true worth where the superficial glance discovers only superficial values. Both lovers know the true motives of their ladies without explanation. Since these things are so, it is significant that the youthful lover in the story of *The Glove* is Browning's own addition to, and comment upon, Leigh Hunt's story.

The lady of *The Glove* is in her motives also Browning's creation. Leigh Hunt's poem on the same subject had ended with King Francis's strictures upon ladies who needlessly risked their lovers' lives, after De Lorge had rescued the glove from the lion's pit and had flung it in the lady's face.[71] Browning adds the whole of the lady's case, defends her right to test De Lorge's wordy love, approves her satisfaction with the result, and rewards her with a youthful lover who understands her. The lady of *The Glove* is Marianne Pajot in another guise. Marianne too listened to the fine speeches of a boundless passion, tested the real worth of that love and found it wanting. That the test is slightly different is hardly significant, since Browning inherited the situation in *The Glove* from Leigh Hunt. The important thing is that Browning took the part of the two women involved in similar problems, justified the women in the same psychological manner, and rewarded them similarly.

Then, too, the third figure of the drama, the duke who loves Marianne, has his parallel in De Lorge in *The Glove*. Both are verbose in love. Both fail in understanding. The subsequent life of De Lorge, which is Browning's invention, is very like the subsequent life of the duke. De Lorge married another beauty of the court, who was not only faithless, but who mocked him and mistreated him. She made him fetch

---

70 This was true because the lady of *The Glove* was disgraced and driven from court after the affair at the lion's pit.

71 Leigh Hunt's *The Glove and the Lion* appeared in the *New Monthly Magazine* in 1836. Browning was particularly interested in this periodical.

her gloves from where she had left them—in the king's chamber. The similarity of his career to the duke's is at once patent.

Not only are the main figures and situations in the two poems strikingly alike, but minor figures and incidents bear out the similarity. It seems that Peter Ronsard, the poet, who in Browning's version of *The Glove* tells the story with a sympathetic understanding of the lady's motives, was suggested by one trait of the minister le Tellier's nature; for, says de Lassay,

M. *le Tellier* qui étoit demeuré fort des Amis de Mlle. *Marianne* depuis leur conversation, l'a contée bien des fois en sa vie, & il parloit toujours d'elle avec admiration . . .[72]

It behoves a prime minister as well as a poet to know human nature.

Other small likenesses may be noticed. The lion in the legend of Saint Scholastica may be reminiscent of the lion in *The Glove*.[73] Also when the duke is musing on his recollections there occurs the line, "No dwarfish knight picked up our giant's glove." There is a further suggestive likeness in the mock-serious style in which the two stories are told.

The likenesses are so startling and so numerous that one is forced to the conclusion that the *Recueil* served as a source not only for the *Parleying* but for the changes which Browning made in the story of *The Glove* as well. This would place Browning's acquaintance with de Lassay's *Memoires* at least as early as 1845.[74] At that time, it will be remembered, the poet was courting Elizabeth Barrett, and incidentally preparing himself for Italy by reading Bartoli's *Simboli*. Con-

[72] *Recueil*, p. 17.

[73] This further connection is significant. I have already suggested that the lion of *The Glove* may have its source in Bartoli; see above, pp. 58-59.

[74] This is not at all unlikely considering that Browning came to the *Recueil* through the *Biographie Universelle*. Practically every poem Browning wrote between 1835 and 1845 owes something to the *Biographie Universelle*. See Griffin and Minchin, p. 25. He seems actually to have consulted this work on every occasion.

sequently when he thought of parleying with Bartoli, the whole memory of the *Recueil* and the part it played in the making of *The Glove* came inevitably to his mind.

But both Bartoli, whom he read in preparation for his life in Italy, and *The Glove* could hardly have failed to remind him of his courtship of Elizabeth Barrett in the years between 1845 and 1847. For *The Glove* was written not only under the influence of the *Recueil*, but under the influence of Browning's new love for Elizabeth Barrett. He realized fully for the first time that love gives power to the lover to see the soul of his beloved as no one else can. This is the great virtue of the youthful lovers in *The Glove* and in the story of the *Parleying;* and this again is the gift for which Elizabeth Barrett was most grateful to the poet. She was perpetually thanking him for his understanding of her—in her letters,[75] in her poems, and it must have been so in her conversations as well. He understands her as she is, accepts her, desires her:

> Because thou hast the power and own'st the grace
> To look through and behind this mask of me
> (Against which years have beat thus blanchingly
> With their reins), and behold my soul's true face,
> The dim and weary witness of life's race,—
> Because thou hast the faith and love to see,
> Through that same soul's distracting lethargy,
> The patient angel waiting for a place
> In the new Heavens,—because nor sin nor woe,
> Nor God's infliction, nor death's neighborhood,
> Nor all which others viewing, turn to go,
> Nor all which makes me tired of all, self-viewed,—
> Nothing repels thee, . . . Dearest, teach me so
> To pour out gratitude, as thou dost, good![76]

[75] See *Letters of R. B. and E. B. B.*, I, 183, 211, 223, 248, and in fact almost every letter she wrote to him in the summer and fall of 1845. *The Glove* was published in *Dramatic Romances and Lyrics* (*Bells and Pomegranates*, No. VII), in November, 1845.

[76] *Sonnets from the Portuguese*, XXXIX.

Thus the almost miraculous understanding of the lady by the youthful lover in *The Glove* and in de Lassay's story has its parallel in Browning's own inmost experience.

In other important respects the story parallels his own experience. Elizabeth Barrett was an invalid, withdrawn from the world, who felt that her life was too sad and hopeless to burden him with. "I had done *living*, I thought, when you came and sought me out!"[77] is her continual cry. Her situation is like that of the outcast lady of *The Glove*. And like the outcast lady she is several years older than her lover. Browning is, of course, the waiting lover, and it is significant to find Elizabeth Barrett describing him thus:

> But thou are not such
> A lover, my Belovèd: thou canst wait
> Through sorrow . . .[78]

In short, the details which Browning put into *The Glove* in 1845 are those which were inevitably, and I think consciously, suggested to his mind by his own situation.

The fact that Elizabeth Barrett had been especially pleased by *The Glove* was another association in Browning's mind. She had thanked him especially for his chivalrous treatment of the lady:

And for your 'Glove,' all women should be grateful,—and Ronsard, honoured, in this fresh shower of music on his old grave . . . though the chivalry of the interpretation, as well as much beside, is so plainly yours, . . . could only be yours perhaps. And even *you* are forced to let in a third person . . . close to the doorway . . . before you can do any good. What a noble lion you give us too, with the 'flash on his forehead,' and 'leagues in the desert already' as we look on him. And then, with what a 'curious felicity' you turn the subject 'glove' to another use and strike De Lorge's blow back on him with it, in the last paragraph of your story! And the versification! And the lady's speech—(to return!) so calm, and proud—yet a little bitter![79]

77 *Letters of R. B. and E. B. B.*, I, 211.
78 *Sonnets from the Portuguese*, XL.
79 *Letters of R. B. and E. B. B.*, I, 261.

Thus we see that *The Glove* is connected not only with the *Recueil*, but is inextricably bound up with the period of Browning's courtship, and his reading of Bartoli.

But if *The Glove* is closely connected with Browning's own experience—and it is hard to see how one can escape that conclusion—much more so, and much more consciously so, is the *Parleying With Daniel Bartoli*. One cannot dissociate Marianne Pajot—"My saint, for instance—worship if you will"—from Elizabeth Barrett Browning any more than one can dissociate Pompilia or Balaustion from her. Marianne, one remembers "jamais pour lui faire une chose si contraire à son honneur & à ses intérêts . . ."; [80] she would not harm the man she loved. Browning could not have written Marianne's long speech renouncing the duke without remembering the cry of Elizabeth Barrett when he pressed her to marry him:

> . . . if I were different in some respects and free in others by the providence of God, I would accept the great trust of your happiness, gladly, proudly and gratefully; and give away my own life and soul to that end. I *would* do it . . . *not, I do* . . . observe! it is a truth without a consequence; only meaning that I am not all stone—only proving that I am not likely to consent to help you in wrong against yourself . . . [81]

We see the same thing in her sonnets:

> O Belovèd, it is plain
> I am not of thy worth nor for thy place!
> And yet, because I love thee, I obtain
> From that same love this vindicating grace,
> To live on still in love, and yet in vain,—
> To bless thee, yet renounce thee to thy face. [82]

---

[80] *Recueil*, p. 12.

[81] *Letters of R. B. and E. B. B.*, I, 202. See also pp. 206-223. One cannot read the *Sonnets from the Portuguese* without realizing that the point of view of Elizabeth Barrett toward Browning there is precisely that of Marianne Pajot toward the duke in the *Parleying*. Compare Sonnet XI:
> And therefore if to love can be desert,
> I am not all unworthy.
with ll. 184-186, 199, of the *Parleying*.

[82] *Sonnets from the Portuguese*, XI. See also VIII-X.

This is the ever-recurring cry in 1845. Like Marianne Pajot, Elizabeth Barrett refused to hurt her lover by marrying
him. It was his own wife whom the poet had in mind when he
wrote in praise of Marianne,

> Saint, for this,
> Be yours the feet I stoop to—-kneel and kiss!
> So human? Then the mouth too, if you will![83]

That Elizabeth Barrett is meant here cannot be doubted.
The *human* side of the poetess was Browning's discovery, the
side of the moon that the world never saw:

> This I say of me, but think of you, Love!
> This to you—yourself my moon of poets!
> Ah, but that's the world's side, there's the wonder,
> Thus they see you, praise you, think they know you!
> There, in turn I stand with them and praise you—
> Out of my own self, I dare to phrase it.
> But the best is when I glide from out them,
> Cross a step or two of dubious twilight,
> Come out on the other side, the novel
> Silent silver lights and darks undreamed of,
> Where I hush and bless myself with silence.[84]

The word "human" is ever his thought of her in contrast to
the intellectual poetess that the world knew. Notice that he
addresses her two selves in his famous invocation to her:

> O lyric Love, half angel and half bird,
> And all a wonder and a wild desire,—
> Boldest of hearts that ever braved the sun,
> Took sanctuary within the holier blue,
> And sang a kindred soul out to his face,—
> Yet human at the red-ripe of the heart . . .[85]

Hawthorne, visiting the Brownings, remarked that Mrs.
Browning was "sweetly disposed towards the human race,

[83] *With Daniel Bartoli*, ll. 257-260.
[84] *One Word More*, ll. 187-197.
[85] *The Ring and the Book*, I, 1383-1388.

though only remotely akin to it."[86] But to Browning she was ever *human*.[87]

As Marianne Pajot in the *Parleying* is representative of Elizabeth Barrett Browning, so is the youthful lover, de Lassay, a representation of Robert Browning. In common with the other lovers, he has that perfect insight which makes him see beauties unseen by the general. The seclusion of de Lassay and Marianne after their marriage, exaggerated as it is by the poet, finds its sure parallel in the flight of the Brownings from the English world to Italy. Browning is describing himself when he cries:

> And, oh, the exquisite deliciousness
> That lapped him in obscurity! You guess
> Such joy is fugitive: she died full soon.[88]

Is not this pure autobiography? And may not the same be said of de Lassay's grief, and his subsequent return to the world?[89] In the end they both

> . . . took again, for better or for worse,
> The old way in the world, and, much the same
> Man o' the outside, fairly played life's game.[90]

These are like the descriptions Browning gives of himself in his letters, once his passionate grief is past. From the coast of Brittany some months after Mrs. Browning's death, he wrote: "I am getting 'mended up' here and shall no doubt last my proper time, for all the past."[91] Perhaps he too had "tried to die." In the next year, acting under advice, he re-

---

[86] *French and Italian Note-Books*, Cambridge, 1883, p. 294.

[87] Browning may have got this characterization of his wife from her characterization of Euripides; see *Balaustion*, end of poem.

[88] *With Daniel Bartoli*, ll. 233-235.

[89] Compare Orr, *Life*, pp. 238 ff., and *Recueil*, pp. 51 ff., for the passionate outburst of grief in the two men.

[90] *With Daniel Bartoli*, ll. 242-244.

[91] Quoted from a letter to his friend Story, reprinted in Griffin and Minchin, pp. 224-225.

solved that no suitable invitation should go unaccepted, and thus entered the world again.[92]

It only remains now to treat the enigmatic figure of the duke. In the *Parleying* Browning puts together for him a makeshift sainthood, for he believed that his love for Marianne had been genuine. Perhaps this was an indirect tribute to the lady, showing that whoever touched her could not fail to be glorified. The duke, too, like the lover of Cynara, had been faithful in his fashion. In the face of vicissitudes he had held "to the main fact of love." It is this that gives him strength in later years to review his memories. He finds to his dismay that the present intercepts the past, as the cloud covers the moon. He has flitted on to other women—but he finds that she is the lasting reality, just as the watcher of the skies finds his moon clear of the cloud once more.

The poem at the end of the *Parleying* is addressed to the woman who has come between the man and his memory. For this other woman Browning had authority in his source. But the space which he gives to the duke, and the sympathy with which he treats him and the peculiarly personal nature of the language he uses, leads the reader to question whether this section of the poem may not also have its biographical significance. Is this the later Browning speaking? Has the present intercepted the past for him? Is the subsequent career of the duke, when Marianne has left him, a representation of Browning's career—with modifications, of course,—after Mrs. Browning's death? Can it be said of him that "Here lies he among the false to Love"? It is impossible to escape the suspicion that Browning himself speaks in the man who is waiting like a ghost to rise,

Called into life by her who long ago
Left his soul whiling time in flesh-disguise.[93]

Mrs. Browning had always been the "moon of poets" to

92 Griffin and Minchin, p. 227.
93 *With Daniel Bartoli*, ll. 337-338.

her husband since his famous apostrophe to her in *One Word More*. The reference to the moon in the *Epilogue* to *Ferishtah's Fancies* (dated December 1, 1883) is most certainly to her. There the moon finally breaks through the clouds to lend comfort to a dark life. In the poem that concludes the *Parleying With Daniel Bartoli* the figure is used again. Only in this latter case the clouds that obscure the moon are said quite plainly to represent another woman. The duke

> Found that the Present intercepts the Past
> With such effect as when a cloud enwraps
> The moon and, moon-suffused, plays moon perhaps
> To who walks under, till comes, late or soon,
> A stumble: up he looks, and lo, the moon
> Calm, clear, convincingly herself once more!
> How could he 'scape the cloud that thrust between
> Him and effulgence? Speak, fool—duke, I mean.[94]

Then the duke speaks of the "bold she-shape" who came and conquered him, and ends with the threat to reassert, some day, his former strength. Clearly this is Robert Browning's confession that he has been false, at least in thought, to the memory of Elizabeth Barrett. Intimate friends of Browning knew that in the year 1883 he had proposed to, and been refused by, a certain lady of title. Whether she is the "queenly impudence" who overcame him, cannot be definitely stated. The fact remains that in his later years at least one woman obscured the memory of his dead wife. The fact also remains that he regretted it bitterly. Perhaps the bitterest part of the irony and tragedy of this event in Browning's life lay in the fact that he had foreseen it. A reading of *Any Wife to Any Husband* (1855) leads one to suspect the poet of possessing prophetic powers, or at least of having taken with amazing accuracy the measure of his own nature. The passionate nature which had made his great love affair so wonderful, demanded finally some more substantial expression

[94] *Idem,* ll. 279-286.

than the years of loyalty to his wife's memory had given. It
is no discredit to him that he should have been eager for
human companionship in his old age. He is his own accuser
—perhaps because he realized that the great love affair of
his life had become to the public a legend of faithfulness, and
to himself the proof of the doctrine of elective affinities.

The young lover and the duke both give great biographical significance to the *Parleying With Daniel Bartoli.*
Browning could not have written the lines describing Marianne Pajot without seeing their application to his own life.
In a volume which is patently autobiographical it is incon-
ceivable that Elizabeth Barrett Browning should not take a
prominent place. Furthermore, Browning never wrote a volume after his wife's death without putting in it somewhere a
tribute to her. In December 1864, he wrote to his friend and
confidante, Isa Blagden,

> I hope to do much more yet; and that the flower of it will be
> put into Her hand somehow.[95]

He announced his definite purpose in the first work he
undertook after Elizabeth Barrett Browning had died:

> Never may I commence my song, my due
> To God who best taught song by gift of thee,
> Except with bent head and beseeching hand—. . .
> —Never conclude, but raising hand and head
> Thither where eyes, that cannot reach, yet yearn . . .[96]

So in the *Parleyings,* in which Browning avowedly unlocked
his heart, she must become the saint *he* worships, whose feet
he stoops to. The poet did not forsake his expressed purpose
of using his poetry to find, despite the distance and the dark,
some interchange of grace with his dead wife.

[95] *Letters to Isa Blagden,* p. 109.
[96] *The Ring and the Book,* I, 1395-1403.

CHAPTER III

THE PARLEYING WITH
CHRISTOPHER SMART

I

THE *Parleying* with the mad poet, Christopher Smart, 1722-1771, is the briefest and at the same time one of the most illuminating of the *Parleyings*. It is the only one to deal directly[1] with Browning's own chosen mode of expression, the art of poetry. Smart's *Song to David* was among the imaginative pleasures of his youth, and it had an influence upon his early poems. But the *Song to David* was far more than an imaginative pleasure; it was a stimulus to Browning's thoughts and ideas. The problem of how Smart, in the midst of his mediocre verse-writing, could have written one great poem, the *Song to David*—and that one when he was confined in a madhouse, as the legend went—continually puzzled Browning. The problem brings with it all sorts of questions about how the mind of the poet works, what his function is, and what the function of poetry should be. Thus Smart, not only through his influence on the work of Browning, but through this indirect influence on his ideas, serves as a constant by which we may measure Browning's growth both in the practice and in the theory of poetry. So in summing up the influences of his youth Browning rightly includes Christopher Smart. It is interesting to see him turning back in his old age to the mad poet, from whose personality his own was always widely different and from whose type of poetry he had long since departed; and it is still more interesting to hear him call upon Smart to bring a message to the poets of 1887.

[1] *The Parleying With Gerard de Lairesse,* though not concerned directly with poetry, deals with it at some length.

In all likelihood Browning's acquaintance with Christopher Smart dates from the year 1824. In July of that year Reuben Browning, his favorite uncle, gave him Smart's translation of the works of Horace—probably the poetical one.[2] The sad life-story of the poet, with its several striking incidents, Browning probably learned soon after; for his book-loving father knew "especially the lives of the poets and painters, concerning whom he ever had to communicate some interesting anecdote not generally known."[3] In the Browning library were some Smart manuscripts which the elder Browning probably showed to his son.[4] But Browning's knowledge of Smart was not confined to the translations and these bits of manuscript. Apparently he read widely in Smart's poetry, and as we learn also from the *Parleying*, he knew well the magnificent *Song to David*. Since it was this last-mentioned work that inspired him to parley with Christopher Smart, it will be necessary to give a brief account of the bibliography of the *Song* in order to trace Browning's knowledge of it. Since, moreover, the *Song* is so inextricably bound up in Browning's mind with the circumstances under which Smart wrote it, certain of those significant circumstances will be touched upon in passing.

Christopher Smart had been the Seatonian prize poet at Cambridge, had written much hack work,[5] and toward the

2 See Griffin and Minchin, p. 6. Smart translated Horace into prose in 1756 and into verse in 1767. There would have been little point in giving Browning a prose crib; yet on the other hand it should be pointed out that Browning thought of Smart as being already a translator of Horace in 1763. See *With Christopher Smart*, l. 181.

3 Introductory notes by Reuben Browning to a small volume of sketches by Robert Browning, senior. Quoted in Griffin and Minchin, p. 8.

4 See Sotheby, *Catalogue*, items no. 280 and 281. These manuscripts are a translation of Psalm cxxxi, and a poem *On Gratitude, To the Memory of Mr. Seaton*, autographed with Smart's full name. The fact that these items are undated points unquestionably to their having been the property of the poet's father rather than of the poet himself, and thus to their having been in the library during the poet's youth.

5 See Boswell, *Life of Johnson*, ed. Hill, II, 395, for the curious tradition that Smart sold his services to the bookseller, Gardner, for ninety-nine years.

end of a very unhappy life, in which he had been deeply religious and rarely sober, he had finally been driven mad by his cares and ill health. Madness had in fact been very near to him from birth, and had upon at least three occasions overwhelmed him. His nephew, Hunter, writing of him said:

Though the fortune as well as the constitution of Mr. Smart required the utmost care, he was equally negligent in the management of both, and his various and repeated embarrassments acting upon an imagination uncommonly fervid, produced temporary alienations of the mind; which at last were attended with paroxysms so violent and continued as to render confinement necessary.[6]

He was confined in Bedlam in 1751,[7] and in the year 1756 suffered a dangerous fit of illness, in which he was again out of his mind.[8] In 1763 he was again confined in a madhouse, where he was visited by Samuel Johnson and where he wrote the *Song to David*. When he was liberated there was still some doubt whether he had entirely recovered his sanity,[9] and in fact it is not certain that he was sane when he died in King's Bench Prison on May 21, 1771.

The form which his madness took was closely allied to, and perhaps only an accentuation of, the normal tendencies of his life. He was deeply religious, and Dr. Johnson's classic pronouncement upon his condition in 1763 makes much of this aspect of his mania:

'Madness frequently discovers itself merely by unnecessary deviation from the usual modes of the world. My poor friend Smart shewed the disturbance of his mind, by falling upon his knees, and saying his prayers in the street, or in any other un-

[6] *The Life of Christopher Smart,* prefixed to *The Poems, of the late Christopher Smart,* Reading, 1791, 2 vols., I, xx.

[7] On October 8, 1751, Thomas Gray wrote to Horace Walpole: "He is lousy, and he is mad: he sets out this week for Bedlam." See *The Works of Thomas Gray,* ed. Gosse, New York, 1895, II, 215.

[8] See his *Hymn to the Supreme Being, On Recovery from a dangerous Fit of Illness,* in *Poems,* 1791, I, 52-62.

[9] See *The Life of Christopher Smart,* as above, pp. xxiii-xxvi.

usual place. Now although, rationally speaking, it is greater madness not to pray at all, than to pray as Smart did, I am afraid there are so many who do not pray, that their understanding is not called in question."[10]

Another time Johnson spoke with Burney concerning Smart:

BURNEY. 'How does poor Smart do, Sir; is he likely to recover?'
JOHNSON. 'It seems as if his mind had ceased to struggle with the disease; for he grows fat upon it.'
BURNEY. 'Perhaps, Sir, that may be from want of exercise.'
JOHNSON. 'No, Sir; he has partly as much exercise as he used to have, for he digs in the garden. Indeed, before his confinement, he used for exercise to walk to the ale-house; but he was *carried* back again. I did not think he ought to be shut up. His infirmities were not noxious to society. He insisted on people praying with him; and I'd as lief pray with Kit Smart as any one else. Another charge was, that he did not love clean linen; and I have no passion for it."[11]

It was during Smart's confinement in 1763 that the *Song to David* was written. The tradition is that he indented at least a part of the *Song* on the wainscot with his key, in default of writing materials.[12] In the autumn of 1763, when Smart had just been released from the madhouse, the *Song* was published in a thin quarto pamphlet. In 1765, when he got out his volume, *A Translation of the Psalms of David*, the *Song to David* fittingly concluded the work. This volume is now very rare. But when Smart's poems were collected and published by his kinsman, Hunter, in 1791 under the title, *Poems, of the late Christopher Smart . . . consisting of his Prize Poems, Odes, Sonnets and Fables, Latin and English Translations*, the *Song* was not included. It was given only

---

[10] Boswell, *Life of Johnson*, ed. Hill, I, 459.
[11] *Idem*, pp. 459-460.
[12] A story not entirely disproved, but in bad repute of late. Blunden in his edition of *A Song to David*, London, 1924, states in the *Address* (p. 15), his belief that the story was started by an enemy paragrapher. But see *Notes and Queries*, 2d Series, III, 433.

the briefest mention in a footnote to the *Memoir* of Smart's
life prefixed to the first of the two volumes:

> Besides the works contained in this edition, our Author wrote
> a Poem called *a Song to David*, and a *new Version of the Psalms.*
> . . . These . . . were written after his confinement, and bear
> for the most part melancholy proofs of the recent estrange-
> ment of his mind.[13]

Neither Dr. Anderson nor Chalmers, in making their collections of the works of English poets for the readers of the
early nineteenth century, was able to procure a copy of the
Song, which shows how rare the volumes had become.[14]
That the *Song to David* should have been omitted from
the collected works of Smart is one of the most astonishing
judgments that can be conceived. For the *Song* is the one
poem in the English language in which the original glory
and splendor of the Psalms of David are caught. The secret
of its success lies in the fact that it is not an attempt at
translation or paraphrase, but an original poem written by
a man who was so thoroughly steeped in the spirit of the
Psalms that he achieved in his own poem their tone of exaltation. It is a splendid catalogue of the beauties of the world
which God has made:

> Glorious the sun in mid career;
> Glorious th' assembled fires appear;
>   Glorious the comet's train:
> Glorious the trumpet and alarm;
> Glorious th' almighty stretch'd-out arm;
>   Glorious th' enraptured main:
>
> Glorious the northern lights astream;
> Glorious the song, when God's the theme;
>   Glorious the thunder's roar:
> Glorious hosanna from the den;
> Glorious the catholic amen;
>   Glorious the martyr's gore:

[13] *The Life of Christopher Smart*, as above, I, xliii, note.
[14] See *Extracts Respecting Smart's Song to David*, prefixed to *A Song to David*, London, 1827, pp. 3-4.

> Glorious—more glorious is the crown
> Of Him, that brought salvation down
>   By meekness, call'd thy Son;
> Thou at stupendous truth believ'd,
> And now the matchless deed's achiev'd,
>   DETERMIN'D, DAR'D, and DONE.[15]

The *Song* is not only exalted in tone, but it is full of richness and color. For Smart's conception of the whole earth as the chapel of the Most High gives to his poem a rich, ornate, and colorful character. It is in essence a psalm of thanksgiving for the good things of earth. The following stanzas are characteristic:

> Of gems—their virtue and their price,
> Which hid in earth from man's device,
>   Their darts of lustre sheathe;
> The jasper of the master's stamp,
> The topaz blazing like a lamp
>   Among the mines beneath.
>
> .   .   .   .
>
> The wealthy crops of whit'ning rice
> 'Mongst thyine woods and groves of spice,
>   For ADORATION grow;
> And, marshall'd in the fenced land,
> The peaches and pomegranates stand,
>   Where wild carnations blow.
>
> .   .   .   .
>
> Rich almonds colour to the prime
> For ADORATION; tendrils climb,
>   And fruit-trees pledge their gems;
> And Ivis with her gorgeous vest,
> Builds for her eggs her cunning nest,
>   And bell-flowers bow their stems.[16]

This was the poem which Rossetti characterized as "the only

---

[15] *A Song to David,* stanzas lxxxiv-lxxxvi.
[16] *Idem,* stanzas xxvi, lx, and liii. See also stanzas xxx-xxxvii and lxxxi.

great accomplished poem of the eighteenth century,"[17] and
which Browning quite independently declared placed its
author for once with Milton on the one hand and Keats on
the other.[18] It is, indeed, poetry of exceptional greatness;
and it is totally out of and different from the manner and
style of the eighteenth century. It was probably this difference from the spirit of the age that made the eighteenth century neglect it and cast it out as the product of a deranged
mind, and that eventually made the nineteenth century—
especially the romanticists—receive it so whole-heartedly.
For if the *Song* was slighted in its own century, it certainly
came into its own in the next.

To Browning the poem, far from being something to be
overlooked in Smart, was the poet's one claim to greatness.
It is the only work of Smart's that he mentions in the *Parleying*, dismissing the others with the label of "safe mediocrity." He describes the relation of the *Song* to the rest of the
works by an elaborate simile, and attempts to give his
readers a little of the thrill he had when he discovered it:

> I was exploring some huge house, had gone
> Through room and room complacently, no dearth
> Anywhere of the signs of decent taste,
> Adequate culture: wealth had run to waste
> Nowise, nor penury was proved by stint:
> All showed the Golden Mean without a hint
> Of brave extravagance that breaks the rule.
> The master of the mansion was no fool
> Assuredly, no genius just as sure![19]

Exploring the mansion, he goes on and on with neither hope
nor fear of what may be coming next, until suddenly, push-

---

[17] See his letter to Hall Caine, published in *The Athenaeum*, February 19, 1887.

[18] See *Letters from R. B. to Various Correspondents,* 1st Series, II, 69. See also *With Christopher Smart,* ll. 95-96.

[19] *With Christopher Smart,* ll. 17-25.

ing a door open, he enters the Chapel. This represents, of course, the *Song to David:*

> It was the Chapel. That a star, from murk
> Which hid, should flashingly emerge at last,
> Were small surprise: but from broad day I passed
> Into a presence that turned shine to shade.
> There fronted me the Rafael Mother-Maid,
> Never to whom knelt votarist in shrine
> By Nature's bounty helped, by Art's divine
> More varied—beauty with magnificence—
> Than this: from floor to roof one evidence
> Of how far earth may rival heaven.[20]

There follows a magnificent description of the richness of the place. Then, when he goes forth from the Chapel, eager for new discoveries, he finds again the same dull commonplace:

> Big with anticipation—well-nigh fear—
> Of what next room and next for startled eyes
> Might have in store, surprise beyond surprise.
> Next room and next and next—what followed here?
> Why, nothing! not one object to arrest
> My passage—everywhere too manifest
> The previous decent null and void of best
> And worst, mere ordinary right and fit,
> Calm commonplace which neither missed, or hit
> Inch-high, inch-low, the placid mark proposed.[21]

Therefore Browning represents Smart at every opportunity as a poet who has once and once only attained the level of true greatness.

Admittedly the *Song to David* is Smart's greatest work. I would not for a moment detract from the wonder of the poem, but perhaps the love of paradox, or love of the mysterious, has made Browning state the case too strongly. He is

20 *With Christopher Smart,* ll. 36-45.
21 *Idem,* ll. 65-74.

undeniably fascinated by the fact that the *Song* leapt up
like a blaze "with black behind and blank before," and
puzzled by the question "why only once the fire-flame was."
He associates the poem, rightly enough, with Smart's confinement; but he perverts the facts concerning Smart's mental condition. As we have seen, Smart had early shown a
tendency toward madness even while he was still at Cambridge, and madness of the same definite sort overtook him
several times.[22] Yet Browning always represents him as being only once afflicted with mental disorder:

> The man was sound
> And sane at starting . . .

and after the one madness

> . . . the untransfigured man
> Resumed sobriety,—as he began,
> So did he end nor alter pace, not he![23]

The fact that Smart's greatest poem was coincident with his
madness somehow leads Browning to explain the poem as the
result of a divine revelation. The fact that the achievement
of the *Song* was never equalled, consequently leads him to
consider the madness that inspired it an isolated event. In
the same way his explanation of the *Song* as one of the
operations of heaven leads him not so much to overestimate
the greatness of that one poem, as to underestimate the value
of all the others.

As a matter of fact, *A Song to David* is very much of a
piece with the rest of Smart's works. Smart was a man of
talent before he wrote the *Song*, though not a genius; and it
is distinctly worthy of notice that the five Seatonian prize
poems that he executed upon the various attributes of the
Deity[24] clearly foreshadow both in manner and tone, as well

[22] See above, pp. 94-95.
[23] *With Christopher Smart*, ll. 76-77 and 84-86.
[24] While a fellow at Cambridge Smart five times won the Seatonian
Prize in poetry: 1750, *On the Eternity of the Supreme Being;* 1751, *On the*

as in subject, the magnificent *Song*. In the poems before Smart's confinement and in those after there may be seen the same poetic cataloguing of the strengths and beauties of the earth. Of course neither the Seatonian prize poems nor the *Psalms* and miscellaneous poems are poetically transfigured as is the *Song*. Nevertheless, they are composed of the same elements, and it is significant that thirty or more of Smart's poems are done in the same verse as the *Song*. Browning was lured too far by his paradox; yet Hugh Walker, ignorant, I think, of Browning's judgment, said of the *Song:*

> But of this I am sure, that it contains evidence of a reach of imagination beyond all comparison greater than Smart had ever displayed before; and further, that it gives evidence of an intellectual force superior to anything he had ever yet possessed.[25]

Both, I think, would have reconsidered their pronouncements had they made a careful study of Smart's works.[26] Blunden, the latest editor of the *Song*, sees it as a consummation,[27] as it most surely is, of all Smart's other poems. Just as his madness was an accentuation of his natural tendencies, so the *Song* was the culmination of his poetry. During his madness he attained, apparently, a state of religious exaltation that was capable of producing the poem; but all that had gone before was the natural preparation for it, as all that followed after was a natural consequence.

To return now to the history of Browning's acquaintance with the *Song*, it should first of all be pointed out that Browning's account of the place of the *Song* in the works of Smart seems to apply very aptly to his own experience with

Immensity of the Supreme Being; 1752, *On the Omniscience of the Supreme Being;* 1753, *On the Power of the Supreme Being;* 1755, *On the Goodness of the Supreme Being.* The *Hymn to the Supreme Being,* referred to above, also shows masterly design and high poetry.

25 In *Yale Review,* 2d Series, no. 4, October, 1914, pp. 86–87.

26 For the fact that Browning's was a judgment from memory and not from study, see below, p. 106.

27 *A Song to David,* ed. Blunden, London, 1924, *Address,* pp. 20–21.

the *Song* and the other poems. He first formed the opinion that Smart was characterized by a "safe mediocrity." In all probability this means that he knew Smart from his translation of Horace and, it is likely, from the manuscript poems in his father's library as well. It may mean that he had read some of the poems in the collected edition of 1791. Then suddenly he discovered the *Song*. Thereafter he read other things of Smart—perhaps reading in the collected edition for the first time, perhaps completing his acquaintance with it. But his high hopes of finding more wonders like the *Song* were never realized.

Browning first read the *Song* some time during or after the year 1827. Writing sixty years later to Furnivall, who was interested in knowing where he had got hold of the *Song*, Browning says:

I am surprised at an edition appearing so early as in 1819; that which I bought professed to be just out some years later.[28]

But when we turn to the bibliographer of Smart, G. J. Gray,[29] we find that he has listed no edition between 1819 and 1895. The problem of the edition that "professed to be just out" some years after 1819 has puzzled many, and has been ignored by many others, notably by Gosse and those who have accepted his statements as final.[30] Browning obviously meant an edition of the poem by itself, not a reprint in any collection or anthology. His memory was not here playing him false. There was a separate edition of *A Song to David* in 1827. In 1819 J. F. Dove had printed for Rodwell and Martin, New Bond Street, London, Smart's *Song*, with Advertisement, Extracts Respecting Smart's *Song to David*,

---

[28] *Letters from R. B. to Various Correspondents,* 1st Series, II, 69.

[29] *A Bibliography of the Writings of Christopher Smart . . .* in *Transactions of the Bibliographical Society,* London, 1900-1902, VI, 269 ff.

[30] See Gosse, *Gossip in a Library,* New York, 1891, p. 197. Gosse speaks of the editor of the 1819 edition as the "Rev. R. Harvey," but upon what grounds I am unable to say. The *Advertisement* states that the rarity of the work is the reason for its being here reprinted, but does not mention the editor's name.

the Argument, the text, and a few explanatory notes, the
whole comprising fifty-five pages. In 1827, John Rodwell
and B. J. Holdsworth, evidently successors to Rodwell and
Martin, had printed for themselves, this time by R. Clay, *A
Song to David*.[31] With the exception of the title-page and
the notes, which vary slightly from the earlier edition, it is
identical with the issue of 1819. A copy of this edition of
1827 was most certainly the book by which Browning first
came in contact with the *Song*. Since the Advertisement was
the same in the 1819 and 1827 editions, it was quite natural
that the latter "professed to be just out."

Furthermore, the pamphlets of 1819 and 1827 reprinted
critical extracts from Chalmers' *English Poets* and *The
Quarterly Review* which repeated the traditional story of the
writing of the *Song to David*. This is significant in view of
the fact that Browning, who must surely have known more
of Smart's life than that single tradition, made use only of
that, in the *Parleying*. Griffin and Minchin suggest that
Browning learned from his father "the sad life-story of the
eighteenth century poet,"[32] and indeed the incidents of
Smart's life are so striking that it is hardly possible that
they escaped that encyclopaedic book-lover. It is likely too
that Browning was acquainted with Dr. Johnson's remarks
upon Smart,[33] though he makes no use of them in the *Parleying*. But the point which was apparently impressed upon
Browning again and again was the tradition concerning
Smart's manner of writing the *Song*. The critical extract
from Chalmers, reprinted in the pamphlet of 1827, read:

. . . this piece was composed by him during his confinement,

[31] *A Song to David. By the late Christopher Smart, M. A. Fellow of
Pembroke Hall, Cambridge; and Translator of Horace . . .*, London, 1827.
This title-page differs from that dated 1819 in that the earlier one says
Prose Translator of Horace. The notes appended to the 1827 edition are a
very little fuller than those of the earlier edition, but the total pagination
is the same.

[32] See Griffin and Minchin, p. 8.

[33] Quoted above, pp. 94-95.

when he was debarred the use of pen, ink, and paper, and was obliged to indent his lines with the end of a key upon the wainscot. This poem was not admitted into the edition of his Works published in 1791, but the grandeur and originality of the thoughts will apologize for my introducing the only part of it I have been able to recover.[34]

This passage comes very near supplying all the information that Browning needed for his *Parleying*,[35] and we find him putting it into verse:

> ". . . This scribble on the wall was done—in lieu
> Of pen and paper—with—ha, ha!—your key
> Denting it on the wainscot! Do you see
> How wise our caution was? Thus much we stopped
> Of babble that had else grown print: and lopped
> From your trim bay-tree this unsightly bough—
> Smart's who translated Horace! . . ."[36]

The presence of the traditional story, which Browning thus versified in the *Parleying*, in the edition of the *Song* of 1827, makes it still more a certainty that this was the edition to which he referred in his letter to Furnivall.

The words, "professed to be just out," carry the implication that Browning bought his copy of the *Song* soon after the date of publication. At any rate, by 1835 he had become well enough acquainted with the rest of Smart's work to have formed his unique conception of the genius of that writer. Mrs. Orr states, in the *Handbook* which Browning himself read and corrected,[37] that the poet had Christopher Smart in mind when he wrote in *Paracelsus*,

[34] *Extracts Respecting Smart's Song to David*, prefixed to *A Song to David*, London, 1827, pp. 3-4.

[35] In this connection it is interesting to note that if Browning had read carefully the *Memoir* of Smart's life prefixed to the edition of 1791—the only collected edition—he would not have made the error of supposing that Smart went mad only once. Yet his knowledge of this edition may have dictated ll. 179-180 of the *Parleying*.

[36] *With Christopher Smart*, ll. 175-181.

[37] Orr, *Handbook*, p. 350.

> One man shall crawl
> Through life surrounded with all stirring things,
> Unmoved; and he goes mad: and from the wreck
> Of what he was, by his wild talk alone,
> You first collect how great a spirit he hid.[38]

This judgment upon Smart is, in little, the same judgment that Browning pronounced, with much the same wonder, in 1887.

Though the influence of Smart upon Browning was great, the history of Browning's further contacts with the works of Smart is briefly told. He found another reprint of the *Song* in Chambers' *Cyclopaedia,* published in 1844. The same letter to Furnivall which has been quoted states concerning a later reading of the poem,

I think it was the reprint in Chambers that I saw—not in Chalmers; indeed I am sure of it, although I discovered it there on an occasion that would excuse much mistiness in my memory.[39]

What this occasion was we can only guess, for Browning does not tell us exactly at what date he read Chambers. In the same letter to Furnivall, however, he states that it is "nearly fifty years" since he has read the *Song.*[40] Briefly, the facts seem to be that Browning first read the *Song* for himself in the reprint of 1827, remembered it vividly through the next seventeen years, and rediscovered it when it appeared in Chambers' *Cyclopaedia* in the fall of 1844. It is not without significance that in December of 1844—the year of publication—and in January of 1845 Browning was cultivating his acquaintance with Elizabeth Barrett.[41] Perhaps,

---

[38] *Paracelsus,* I, 770-774.

[39] *Letters from R. B. to Various Correspondents,* 1st Series, II, 68.

[40] See *ibid.* Browning begins his answer to Furnivall: "Don't trouble yourself about Smart on my account—unnecessarily, since, after nearly fifty years, I remember the whole pretty well."

[41] Browning speaks of seeing Elizabeth Barrett as his "Chapel Scene" and uses language to describe his approach to her which is similar to his description of his discovery of the Chapel in the *Parleying.* Compare *With Christopher Smart,* ll. 26-36, with *Letters of R. B. and E. B. B.,* I, 2, 6.

since the dates coincide so exactly, it was the advent of this
new and great experience which made Browning say that he
discovered the *Song* in the *Cyclopaedia* at a time "that
would excuse much mistiness in my memory." Moreover,
after the two began to correspond regularly in the latter
month, one of the recurring subjects of their letters was the
poem, *Saul*, upon which Browning was then working, and in
which the influence of Smart is very evident.[42] It is therefore
extremely likely that Browning's reading of the *Song* in
Chambers belongs to this period; particularly when we recall that soon afterward his residence in Italy began, and he
turned away from English to Italian subjects.

Apparently Browning read little of Smart thereafter. It
was not that he turned against Smart; it was rather that the
poet's work had become a part of his thought, so that recur-
rence to his poems was scarcely necessary. The letter to
Furnivall is final on this point. Although Browning had not
read Smart for nearly fifty years, he remembered him well,
and could still repeat some of his stanzas from memory:

> Don't trouble yourself about Smart on my account—un-
> necessarily, since, after nearly fifty years, I remember the
> whole pretty well. . . . Depend upon it, no goody-goody writer
> ever conceived or executed the stanzas I could repeat—as I did,
> with all the effect I supposed would follow—to people of au-
> thority enough: Tennyson, the present Bishop of London, and,
> last year to Wendell Holmes, who had asked me innocently at
> Oxford, "whether I knew the wonderful poem."[43]

This, it must be remembered, was in 1887.

It is small wonder then, in view of Browning's detailed acquaintance with the *Song*, that it exercised a great influence
upon him. The influence of the style of Smart was very great
during the early years, and the influence of the poet's personality was equally great, but much more permanent. Most

[42] See *Letters of R. B. and E. B. B.*, I, 60, 76, 179, 182, 191, 261, 277, 325.
For the influence of Smart upon *Saul*, see below, pp. 116-118.
[43] *Letters from R. B. to Various Correspondents*, 1st Series, II, 68-69.

of these influences, touching closely as they do upon Browning's theory and practice of poetry, properly belong in the following section of this discussion. Certain other significant ones, however, will be discussed here; but it should not be forgotten that these are by no means all, or even the greatest.

The thing about Smart that had particularly caught Browning's imagination was the fact that once and once only the eighteenth-century poet had reached the heights of genius, and that once was when he was confined to a madhouse. Abnormal psychology always profoundly interested Browning. It is not impossible that he got the idea for his title of *Madhouse Cells*, under which *Johannes Agricola* and *Porphyria's Lover* were first published in 1836,[44] from his keen interest in Smart's case. As we have seen,[45] that interest had already borne fruit in *Paracelsus*, the year before.

The idea of "oneness"—that is, that an event could happen once and only once in a lifetime—is a curious thought that any suggestion of Smart's name seems automatically to have brought to Browning. The idea by deep and subtle penetration pervaded his mind to such an extent that whenever he spoke of any poet he was likely to bring in the thought of uniqueness. Thus in *Memorabilia*, in 1855, in speaking of Shelley, he says,

> Ah, did you once see Shelley plain,
> And did he stop and speak to you . . . ?

The man was alive both before and after the event, just as Smart was alive both before and after writing *A Song to David*, but his life was a featureless moor save for the one eagle's feather. And further, observe the first line of *How it strikes a Contemporary:*

> I only knew one poet in my life . . .

---

44 In the *Monthly Repository,* Vol. X (N.S.), 43-46.
45 See above, pp. 104-105.

This same idea at once rises from and forms Browning's conception of Smart's genius. It was to find one other expression before the final and explicit one in the *Parleying*. In 1878 Browning wrote *The Two Poets of Croisic*. The first of these poets, it will be remembered, was René Gentilhomme, who wrote "rubbish unutterable" to compliment the Prince of Condé, the man expected by all to be the next king. One day as René sat rhyming

> . . . suddenly flashed lightning, searing sight
> Almost, so close to eyes; then, quick on flash,
> Followed the thunder, splitting earth downright . . .
>
> So, for the moment, all the universe
> Being abolished, all 'twixt God and him,—[46]

he saw clearly that the Prince would never be king. He versified his prophecy and gave it to the Prince. When within a year the prophecy was seen to be true, René was hailed as unequalled among poets, and made Royal Poet by King Louis. And René's genius?

> At the word, it winks,
> Rallies, relapses, dwindles, deathward sinks.[47]

He could claim nothing but mediocrity before his prophecy, and nothing worthy the name of poet afterward. But Browning is deeply interested in his case:

> Well, I care—intimately care to have
>   Experience how a human creature felt
> In after-life, who bore the burden grave
>   Of certainly believing God had dealt
> For once directly with him: did not rave
>   —A maniac, did not find his reason melt
> —An idiot, but went on, in peace or strife,
> The world's way, lived an ordinary life.[48]

---

[46] *The Two Poets of Croisic*, ll. 249-251, 281-282.
[47] *Idem*, ll. 391-392.
[48] *Idem*, ll. 465-472.

Browning could not have written these lines without thinking of Smart. For though the story of René Gentilhomme has some historical basis, it is difficult to think that Browning's version was not colored by his recollection of the mad poet, or that his choice of subject was not directed by his favorite theme—a theme which was to find its final expression nine years later in the *Parleying.*

For in the *Parleying With Christopher Smart* this idea of "oneness" is repeatedly touched upon. It is not only that the madness that produced the *Song* was a unique experience to Smart, as Browning sees it; but the idea recurs with variations. Browning plays upon the theme of the suddenness of the visitation, and the phrase changes from "once" to "all at once." Smart is like the man who designed the beautiful chapel in the commonplace house—a chapel which has the rare virtue of combining the old art and the new; and the phrase becomes "for once." The achievement not only stations Smart "for once on either hand with Milton and with Keats," but it empowers him to claim affinity with the "superhuman poet-pair" for "one moment" and "in one point only." The final variation, before Browning returns to his original theme, is that

> Such success
> Befell Smart only out of throngs between
> Milton and Keats that donned the singing-dress—
> Smart, solely of such songmen, pierced the screen
> 'Twixt thing and word . . .[49]

Then Browning goes back to his main point, the great question "why only once the fire-flame was." The "once" theme and its variations can be found, in Section VI of the *Parleying*, either openly expressed or definitely implied, ten times in fifty lines.

[49] *With Christopher Smart,* ll. 110-114. The brief quotations in this paragraph are all from Section VI.

II

Bᴜᴛ perhaps even more interesting to Browning than the uniqueness of Smart's experience was the great question of how it could be explained. Ultimately, of course, it is inexplicable, but each man's imagination is challenged to attempt to account for it. Browning's explanation is a part of his religious belief; he makes no lengthy analysis, but he hints at his solution repeatedly. Thus when, in his exploration of the house, he suddenly comes upon the Chapel, his exclamation is:

> So—thus it is thou deck'st,
> High heaven, our low earth's brick-and-mortar work?[50]

He describes the wonders of the Chapel as "Art's response to earth's despair."[51] In recounting Smart's history he suggests again the working of heaven:

> . . . all at once the ground
> Gave way beneath his step, a certain smoke
> Curled up and caught him, or perhaps down broke
> A fireball wrapping flesh and spirit both
> In conflagration. Then—as heaven were loth
> To linger—let earth understand too well
> How heaven at need can operate—off fell
> The flame-robe, and the untransfigured man
> Resumed sobriety . . .[52]

The thing is a miracle, the intervention of heaven. Explain it any way you like, says Browning, it is still a miracle:

> No matter if the marvel came to pass
> The way folk judged—if power too long suppressed
> Broke loose and maddened, as the vulgar guessed,
> Or simply brain-disorder (doctors said),
> A turmoil of the particles disturbed
> Brain's workaday performance in your head,
> Spurred spirit to wild action health had curbed . . .[53]

50 *With Christopher Smart*, ll. 34-35.
51 *Idem*, ll. 52-53.
52 *Idem*, ll. 77-85.
53 *Idem*, ll. 127-133.

However it happened, the fact remains that it did happen; and that fact, Browning implies continually, is a miracle. It is another sign of the working of God in man.

So Browning goes on to question just what *did* happen, and his answer brings us face to face with his idea of what the highest poetry is. Somehow the poet sees old sights so clearly that their essential meaning appears all new, and while that vision lasts he has the power so to seize upon the expressive word that he can impart to others his own vision. To quote Browning's own words,

> Was it that when, by rarest chance, there fell
> Disguise from Nature, so that Truth remained
> Naked, and whoso saw for once could tell
> Us others of her majesty and might
> In large, her lovelinesses infinite
> In little,—straight you used the power wherewith
> Sense, penetrating as through rind to pith
> Each object, thoroughly revealed might view
> And comprehend the old things thus made new,
> So that while eye saw, soul to tongue could trust
> Things which struck word out, and once more adjust
> Real vision to right language, till heaven's vault
> Pompous with sunset, storm-stirred sea's assault
> On the swilled rock-ridge, earth's embosomed brood
> Of tree and flower and weed, with all the life
> That flies or swims or crawls, in peace or strife,
> Above, below,—each had its note and name
> For Man to know by,—Man who, now—the same
> As erst in Eden, needs that all he sees
> Be named him ere he note by what degrees
> Of strength and beauty to its end Design
> Ever thus operates—(your thought and mine,
> No matter for the many dissident)—
> So did you sing your Song, so truth found vent
> In words for once with you?[54]

Beside the thought that Smart had enabled other people to

see old things anew by the magic of words that his vision had
given him, Browning in this passage touches upon the general function of poetry. In fact he here says of poetry what
he had earlier pointed out about painting, that man sees
clearly only those things that art has enabled him to see. Fra
Lippo Lippi had spoken for him concerning painting:

> For, don't you mark? we're made so that we love
> First when we see them painted, things we have passed
> Perhaps a hundred times nor cared to see . . . [55]

And so in poetry man needs to have things named for him,
described for him, before he really notes them; and when
they are thus named for him, he begins to see the wonders of
the design of the universe. This, Browning points out, is his
belief and Smart's: that such a catalogue of the lovely
things of the earth serves to show men the power of God.

As a matter of fact, Christopher Smart had no such carefully analyzed theory of poetry. His poems were simply the
outpourings of a religious spirit inspired by the Psalms and
by his own desire to praise God. The nearest he ever came to
expressing a theory of poetry was in the lines:

> I speak for all—for them that fly,
> And for the race that swim;
> For all that dwell in moist and dry,
> Beasts, reptiles, flow'rs and gems to vie
> When gratitude begins her hymn. [56]

This, it will be recognized, is not so much a theory of poetry
as it is a part of Smart's mood of adoration. Yet there is this
to be said about Smart's unanalyzed theory of poetry: to
adopt the style of Smart is to comprehend his theory.
Browning for a time was profoundly influenced by his style,

[55] *Fra Lippo Lippi*, ll. 300-302.

[56] See *The Presentation of Christ in the Temple*, in *Hymns and Spiritual
Songs for the Fasts and Festivals of the Church of England*, appended to
the edition of *The Psalms* translated by Smart and published in 1765;
quoted in Blunden's edition of the *Song*, pp. 73-74.

and consequently it is not strange for him to be identifying himself in this way with Smart.

Turning now to the influence of Smart upon Browning, we should see that there are in reality two sorts of influence to be kept in mind as we trace Browning's poetical development. One of these is the effect of the style of Smart on the style of Browning; the other is the effect upon Browning of thinking about the personality and poetry of Smart.

Browning, as we have seen, had become acquainted with the *Song to David* about 1827. The influence of Smart upon his idea of what poetry should be showed itself in his first volume, *Pauline*, published in 1833. In this poem, which is largely a catalogue of the things that Browning found lovely in the earth,[57] the lyrical and emotional elements outweigh altogether the intellectual. A great deal of *Pauline* is given up to description of nature for its own sake. In other words, Browning's idea of poetry as it is shown in his first poem is not at all moral or didactic. He is quite content to catch the beauty of the earth, the fleeting emotion, the hopeless sorrow, or the knightly tale. His celebrated definition,

> . . . a perfect bard was one
> Who shadowed forth the stages of all life . . .[58]

meant to him that he should shadow forth his every emotion, and every interaction between himself and nature. *Pauline*, in short, combined a strong interest in the workings of his own mind, with descriptions of natural beauty. It was the former quality that was singled out by the keen and searching criticism of John Stuart Mill:

With considerable poetic powers, the writer seems to me possessed with a more intense and morbid self-consciousness than I ever knew in any sane human being . . . he should not attempt

---

57 See below, pp. 223–225.

58 *Pauline*, ll. 883–884. This is generally taken to mean the stages of the life of man. Browning's meaning, I am sure, is the subjective one.

to show how a person may be *recovered* from this morbid state,
—for *he* is hardly convalescent . . .[59]

This criticism had the immediate effect of making Browning
inspect very carefully his theory of poetry. He turned away
from this very subjective sort of poetry, and became objective and dramatic. After the change he insisted continually
that his opinions should not be read from the opinions of his
characters.

So beginning with his very next poem, *Paracelsus* (1835),
Browning himself ceases to speak directly. But his interest
still lies in psychology, and his purpose becomes the chroni-
cling of the stages of life in other people's bosoms.[60] Moreover, while he would have insisted that he was not to be identified with his characters, the choice of subject and manner
of treatment everywhere necessarily reveal the interests of
the poet himself. In *Paracelsus*, for example, Browning is
groping his way toward some solution of the problem of
what the business of a poet is. This search was undoubtedly
hastened by the criticism of Mill. But the problem had already been forced upon Browning by his interest in the character of Christopher Smart. As we have seen, Smart was
present in his mind at the writing of *Paracelsus*;[61] the mad
poet furnished much more than a passing reference for that
poem. He enters into the problem of the business and character of a poet. There appear in *Paracelsus* two contrasted
types of poets, Paracelsus and Aprile. Paracelsus is funda-
mentally interested in matters of the intellect, while Aprile
is the exponent of the idea of love. Love takes the form of
admiration for all earthly things; and Aprile himself takes
delight in the sheer beauty of spontaneous song. This, it
need scarcely be pointed out, is very close to being a description of Christopher Smart.

[59] Quoted from Griffin and Minchin, pp. 59-60. Though Mill's criticism
was not printed, Browning knew it shortly after it was written. *Letters of
R. B. and E. B. B.*, I, 29.
[60] See *Paracelsus*, II, 465-471.
[61] See above, pp. 104-105.

It should be remarked in passing that there is also in
Paracelsus a direct influence of Smart's poetic style. For
while Browning has turned to the objective method, there is
still a great richness of detail, especially in the songs, which
is suggestive of Smart. The gorgeous lyric beginning

> Heap cassia, sandal-buds and stripes
> Of labdanum, and aloe-balls,[62]

owes its being, for example, to the author of *A Song to
David*.

In *Sordello* (1837) Browning is still occupied with the
problem of what the nature of the true poet is, and the whole
of the poem is concerned somewhat with it. The two poets appear once more. There is Sordello, who is interested in man
and man's intellect and actions. Contrasted with him there is
Eglamor, who delights in singing of the glories of nature.
But when *Sordello* is compared with *Paracelsus* it will be
seen that the problem has changed slightly. Eglamor is nar-
rower in the scope of his abilities than Aprile; and Sordello
is a greater figure as a poet than Paracelsus. Browning has,
in brief, taken one of the qualities that he earlier gave to the
lyrical poet Aprile—the lyrical treatment of the emotions
and passions of man—away from Eglamor and has given it
to the intellectual poet Sordello. The choice between the two
is therefore less difficult than it was in the former case, and
Browning naturally decides in favor of Sordello. Yet even
here Browning could not give the lyrical delight in nature
over to utter defeat; and the ultimate decision is that Sordello prevails by assimilating Eglamor's type of poetry into
his own.

Yet the fact that Browning had proved to himself, mentally, that the intellectual type of poet was to be preferred,
does not indicate that he had yet become that sort of poet
entirely. As John Stuart Mill pointed out, Browning was
prone to suggest a cure when he had not yet succeeded in

[62] *Paracelsus*, IV, 190-191.

curing himself.[63] Consequently, while Browning has given
the decision to intellectual poetry, and is tending more and
more toward it in practice, he has by no means given up the
lyrical. Thus *Pippa Passes* (1841) denotes an advance in
Browning's lyrical abilities. The whole poem is a triumph of
lyrical expression. A mood similar to Smart's adoration here
underlies Browning's philosophy that all things in earth are
to be turned to good for the glory of God. Consequently the
songs of Pippa are in spirit very like those of Smart.

As we have seen, Browning reacquainted himself with the
Song to David in 1844 and 1845, and it is at this time that
the influence of Smart's style is seen most clearly in his work.
It is entirely possible, for example, that a stanza in the *Song*
helped Browning to some of the lines in his *Home Thoughts
from Abroad* (1845). Compare these lines with Browning's
poem:

> For ADORATION, beyond match,
> The scholar bulfinch aims to catch
>   The soft flute's iv'ry touch;
> And, careless on the hazle spray,
> The daring redbreast keeps at bay
>   The damsel's greedy clutch.[64]

It is, however, in *Saul*, published in the same year, that
Smart's hand is most clearly seen. The very suggestion for
the poem came in all probability from the works of Smart.
In the preface to his *Ode for Musick on Saint Cecilia's Day*,
Smart had written:

It would not be right to conclude, without taking notice of a
fine subject for an Ode on S. Cecilia's Day, which was suggested
to the Author by his friend the learned and ingenious Mr.
Comber, late of Jesus College in this University; that is David's
playing to King Saul when he was troubled with the evil Spirit.
He was much pleased with the hint at first, but at length was

---

[63] See above, pp. 113-114.
[64] *A Song to David*, stanza lxv. Browning loved to recite this stanza;
see Gosse, *Gossip in a Library*, p. 199.

deterred from improving it by the greatness of the subject, and
he thinks not without reason. The chusing too high subjects has
been the ruin of many a tolerable Genius.[65]

It is amusing to hear Smart, who had written many times
about the Supreme Being, suggest that anything is "too
high" a subject. His objection to it was probably owing to
the difficulties that a too complicated psychological problem
would entail. Browning, on the other hand, had no such objections to a tangled psychological problem, and accepted
the challenge. The *Song to David* itself repeats the suggestion of the subject:

> Blest was the tenderness he felt
> When to his graceful harp he knelt,
>   And did for audience call;
> When Satan with his hand he quell'd
> And in serene suspence he held,
>   The frantic throes of Saul.[66]

Again, in his prize poem, *On the Goodness of the Supreme
Being*, Smart addressed "Israel's sweet Psalmist" at great
length, ending thus:

> . . . for thy tuneful touch
> Drove trembling Satan from the heart of Saul,
> And quell'd the evil Angel.[67]

But the most convincing proof that Browning's *Saul*—at
least the part of it published in 1845—was the child of
Christopher Smart is the nature of the poetry. The first nine
sections of *Saul* are largely a catalogue of the good things
of the earth that the king of Israel should have been thankful for. This, of course, is in the true tradition of Smart.

In *Saul*, moreover, the problem that has been engrossing
Browning for many years comes to its climax. Here again
there is the problem of the two poets, and the problem of

[65] *The Poems, of the late Christopher Smart*, Reading, 1791, I, (40).
[66] *A Song to David*, stanza xxvii.
[67] *The Poems, of the late Christopher Smart*, I, (113).

what true poetry should do; except that the two poets do not
actually appear in person. The struggle between them is the
struggle between the two tendencies in Robert Browning
himself. He began *Saul* in one manner, found himself unable
to finish it, and so published it as a fragment in *Bells and
Pomegranates* in 1845.[68] That manner was, as has been said,
the manner of Christopher Smart; but it is indicative of
Browning's own natural tendencies that he could not be satisfied to complete the poem in the same manner. There was
more to be said on the subject than that type of poetry permitted him to say. So the poem was left as it was, and presently Browning went to Italy. The period of leisure that he
enjoyed there gave him an opportunity to develop his own
moral and religious opinions—a development which shows
itself fully for the first time in *Christmas-Eve and Easter-
Day* (1850). He had found himself, found his own characteristic manner, and was now ready to proclaim his message
to his century. The great change in Browning was his turn
to metaphysical and philosophical thinking. He was ever
ready after 1850 to come forward with instruction.

So when Browning went back to *Saul*, which he published
with ten new sections in 1855, in *Men and Women*, he had
not only new ideas and a new manner, but a different view of
what poetry should be. Thus the two parts of *Saul* are
clearly indicative of Browning's change in poetic theory.
The second part goes more deeply, intellectually and psychologically, into the characters of Saul and David. But the
great change is the introduction of the element of didacticism. Browning has found himself and his characteristic
manner, but it is no longer the manner of Smart. *Saul* is the
barometer which shows the change in Browning's point of
view.

In this connection it is interesting to observe that Browning, in the same year that he appended the didactic sections

[68] Reflections of Browning's dissatisfaction with the early sections of
Saul may be seen in *Letters of R. B. and E. B. B.*, I, 178-179, 261.

to *Saul*, registered an objection to didacticism in poetry. In *"Transcendentalism: A Poem in Twelve Books,"* he up-braided a fellow-poet for talking instead of singing:

> 'Tis you speak, that's your error. Song's our art:
> Whereas you please to speak these naked thoughts
> Instead of draping them in sights and sounds . . .[69]

And Browning prefers the magician John of Halberstadt, who can make roses break "over us, under, round us every side," to musty transcendental explanations of the rose. He still clings, it is evident, to the idea of the lyrical poet even though he has changed and gone over to didacticism. Yet in *Men and Women* the element of song is still present in pro-fusion, and the lyrical element was to find expression in Browning from time to time thereafter. But his tendency was ever more and more toward the moral and didactic; and the real crisis came in the years between the composition of the two parts of *Saul*. With the first version of *Saul*, Brown-ing left Christopher Smart behind him.

In the *Parleyings* as a whole Browning combines the early self-revelatory manner of *Pauline* with his later-acquired but long-practised didactic manner. In the *Parleying With Christopher Smart* in particular, in which he naturally comes to the discussion of the function of poetry, we find him insisting that poetry must instruct. This, as we have seen, was his own view, and he states it as such; but he also attrib-utes it to Christopher Smart, who had no such theory of poetry, and whose verses were spontaneous hymns of praise to God for the beauty of His universe. Yet in a sense Brown-ing is not perverting the views of the mad poet. Between Browning and Smart there is still—in spite of "nearly fifty years" of development by Browning—one great point in common. To both of them poetry has as its end and aim the glorification of God. Smart expressed himself in simple lyrics; Browning developed a highly individualized style, a

[69] *"Transcendentalism: A Poem in Twelve Books,"* ll. 2-4.

tendency to go deeply into human psychology, and a philosophical and moral didacticism. Yet Browning's poetry
ever tended to uphold and to proclaim his belief that God
was in his heaven, and all therefore must be well with the
world. Moreover, Browning had not lost his love of the beauties of the earth: it was only, as he said, that he "loved men
and women better."[70] So in love of beauty in the earth, and
in the belief that poetry should be used to the glory of God,
Browning is still very close to Christopher Smart. And it will
be noticed that it is in exactly these points that Browning
claims kinship with Smart. He says that man needs to have
pointed out to him the beauties of nature

> . . . ere he note by what degrees
> Of strength and beauty to its end Design
> Ever thus operates—(your thought and mine,
> No matter for the many dissident) . . .[71]

And here he and Smart, undeniably, agree. But Browning
goes on to identify Smart with himself in an insistence on the
belief that art should instruct; and *that*, as we have seen, was
scarcely a belief of Smart's.

Browning enlists Smart on his side in order to attack the
position of some of his own contemporaries. For as Browning, full of his own moral purpose, looked about him in 1887,
he saw many poets with whose practice he did not agree.
There were "many dissident." Browning felt the difference
between himself and those who

> . . . judged—as some—
> That who makes poetry must reproduce
> Thus ever and thus only, as they come,
> Each strength, each beauty, everywhere diffuse
> Throughout creation . . .[72]

Poets were intent too much on simply reproducing the beau-

---

[70] See *Fra Lippo Lippi*, ll. 286-290; and Griffin and Minchin, p. 39.
[71] *With Christopher Smart*, ll. 159-162.
[72] *Idem*, ll. 186-190.

ties of the earth without ever going beyond that. It is not the
catalogue of lovely things to which Browning objects; it is
the fact that poets confine themselves to that alone. Smart's
service was genuine,

> —That was effectual service: made aware
> Of strengths and beauties, Man but hears the text,
> Awaits your teaching. Nature? What comes next?
> Why all the strength and beauty?—to be shown
> Thus in one word's flash, thenceforth let alone
> By Man who needs must deal with aught that's known
> Never so lately and so little? Friend,
> First give us knowledge, then appoint its use!
> Strength, beauty are the means: ignore their end?[73]

So Browning comes to the most explicit statement in all his
works, concerning his own theory of poetry:

> Why gains unemployed?
> Nature was made to be by Man enjoyed
> First; followed duly by enjoyment's fruit,
> Instruction—haply leaving joy behind:
> And you, the instructor, would you slack pursuit
> Of the main prize, as poet help mankind
> Just to enjoy, there leave them? Play the fool,
> Abjuring a superior privilege?
> Please simply when your function is to rule—
> By thought incite to deed?[74]

Earth is full of beauty; but must the poet particularize each
and every manifestation of it? Spare us the trouble, as well
as yourself, says Browning; man needs so much of beauty
to teach him life's lesson, and no more. Realizing that about
him is a new generation, whose practice is different from his,

> Oh, yes—
> The other method's favored in our day![75]

73 *With Christopher Smart,* ll. 209-217.
74 *Idem,* ll. 224-233.
75 *Idem,* ll. 239-240.

he nevertheless utters his own message quite clearly: they will avoid all sorts of difficulties if they will only assimilate each thing about them and apply it to the problems of life and living. Only by learning *as* they live, can men make their advance a safe and sure one; and only so will they avoid the anger at the fates that now they feel.

The poets whom Browning was addressing were of course the poets of the Aesthetic Movement, believers in the doctrine of Art for Art's sake. This movement had its origin in England among the Pre-Raphaelite poets, who, strange to say, owed considerable of their art of telling a dramatic story to the example of Browning himself. The Rossettis indeed had a high religious seriousness about them. Discouragement with present conditions led them and William Morris to turn for their subjects to the past,[76] where they found many a colorful story without moral significance.[77] With each succeeding step the movement went further and further away from the Mid-Victorian idea that art should instruct. After Morris, who described himself as the "idle singer of an empty day," the movement was carried on by Swinburne, who was so frankly pagan as to be considered atheistical, and whose verse was often so devoid of moral purpose as to be described as mere verbal melody. Especially through the 'seventies and 'eighties Swinburne was an artistic force to be reckoned with. In the early 'eighties he was joined by Oscar Wilde, and the Aesthetic Movement quickened pace. The Incomparable Max, in his essay "1880" in *The Yellow Book*, tells how the movement swept the town:

Beauty had existed long before 1880. It was Mr. Oscar Wilde who managed her début. To study the period is to admit that to him was due no small part of the social vogue that Beauty began to enjoy . . . Aestheticism (for so they named

[76] This tendency Browning was to criticize in the *Parleying With Gerard de Lairesse*. See below, pp. 232-234.

[77] See the famous *Apology* which Morris prefixed to the first volume of *The Earthly Paradise* (1868-1870).

the movement) did indeed permeate in a manner all classes. But it was to the *haut monde* that its primary appeal was made. The sacred emblems of Chelsea were sold in the fashionable toy-shops, its reverently chanted creeds became the patter of the *boudoirs*. The old Grosvenor Gallery, that stronghold of the few, was verily invaded. Never was such a fusion of delighted folk as at its private views. There was Robert Browning, the philosopher, doffing his hat with a courtly sweep to more than one duchess . . .

Beerbohm does well to call Browning "philosopher" as he notes his attendance at this gathering in which he was so out of place, but of whose existence and character he was so acutely aware. Such an observer as Browning must have foreseen the inevitable culmination of the movement in such a figure as Oscar Wilde. Dilettantism and moral and spiritual degeneracy follow necessarily in the wake of aestheticism when it divorces itself from any moral significance. Already the movement had gone much too far to suit Robert Browning, the philosopher.

In his attack upon the tenets of the Aesthetic School in the *Parleying*, Browning without a doubt had Swinburne in mind. In 1887 Swinburne was still the ostensible leader of the movement and its most famous exponent. His *Atalanta* (1865) and more especially his *Poems and Ballads* (1866) had made him the most talked-of man in England. But besides being the outstanding figure in the movement in 1887, Swinburne was in his nature and tastes utterly incompatible with Browning. He had been a nihilist in religion after his first year at Oxford, and his poems were famous for their atheistical tendencies. He was Bohemian in his manner of living, and Mr. Chesterton has told the world of Browning's hatred of Bohemianism.[78] He and Browning had met at least as early as midsummer in 1871, when Browning went up to Scotland and talked with Jowett concerning the rendition of a phrase from Euripides that Browning had used in *Balaus-*

[78] See Chesterton, *Robert Browning*, New York, 1903, p. 114.

tion's Adventure. To Swinburne, who was present, Euripides was anathema.[79] In 1872 Swinburne had occasion to attack Robert Buchanan, a friend of Browning's. The two poets, however, exchanged copies of their poems during the next few years, but it is not surprising that their acquaintance never ripened into friendship. Then in 1879 Browning mortally offended Swinburne by accepting the presidency of Furnivall's New Shakespeare Society, to which Swinburne was sworn enemy. There was an open conflict between Furnivall and Swinburne—a conflict which became scurrilous, and during which Swinburne was dubbed with the famous appellation of "Pigsbrook." The next year saw the publication of Swinburne's *Heptalogia: or, The Seven against Sense,* which included parodies upon both Browning and Mrs. Browning, the latter being in Gosse's opinion "the very best parody in existence."[80] Swinburne exultantly told a friend that he could parody Robert Browning's discords with impunity, since Browning could never revenge himself by parodying his harmonies.[81]

The contrast between the poetic ideals of the two poets, both outstanding figures, was obvious to everyone. William Michael Rossetti, a friend of both of them, took occasion to compare them in a small volume on Swinburne's *Poems and Ballads* in 1866. It is illuminating to see the lyrical and aesthetic Swinburne, whose "mind appears to be very like a *tabula rasa* on moral and religious subjects, so occupied is it with instincts, feelings, perceptions,"[82] compared so early in his career with Browning. Rossetti pays high tribute to Browning, but he does not fail to point out the absolute contrast between him and Swinburne:

Between Browning and Swinburne (especially as lyric poets)

[79] See Griffin and Minchin, pp. 243-244; and Gosse, *Life of Swinburne,* New York, 1917, pp. 230-232.
[80] Gosse, *Life of Swinburne,* p. 253.
[81] *Ibid.*
[82] William Michael Rossetti, *Swinburne's Poems and Ballads. A Criticism,* London, 1866, p. 17.

there is scarcely any point of contact; the former taking an
incomparably keener and more varied interest in men and their
surroundings, while the latter elicits with a more certain finger
the artistic harmonies of the fewer chords he touches.[83]

And indeed the comparison of the Christian and the pagan,
the teacher and the singer, must have presented itself to
many minds, and above all to the minds of the two men who
were chiefly concerned.

Consequently in the *Parleying With Christopher Smart*,
when Browning comes to sum up his ideas on the theory of
poetry, he cannot neglect to mention Swinburne, the exponent of a creed so different from his own. Swinburne is one of
those "many dissident" who do not believe in a Design oper-
ating through strength and beauty, who are content to
chronicle the lovely things of earth without ever going beyond that. He leads mankind to enjoy beauty, and then
leaves them, abjuring his superior privilege as a poet, the
privilege of ruling mankind through his instruction. Without rancor Browning points out to the younger poet the
error of his ways, and it is significant, both of his own philosophy and of his criticism of Swinburne, that his closing
thought should be a warning against the dangers of atheism.

III

TURNING now to an exegesis of the *Parleying*, we go back
once more to Christopher Smart. Browning addresses the
poet, but his words have a reminiscent rather than a conver-
sational tone:

> It seems as if . . . or did the actual chance
> Startle me and perplex? Let truth be said!
> How might this happen? Dreaming, blindfold led
> By visionary hand, did soul's advance
> Precede my body's, gain inheritance

[83] *Idem,* p. 49. Since the above pages were set up, I have discovered
Swinburne's papers in the *Fortnightly* (which Browning read regularly) in
1868, arguing for the emancipation of Art from Morality.

> Of fact by fancy—so that when I read
> At length with waking eyes your Song, instead
> Of mere bewilderment, with me first glance
> Was but full recognition that in trance
> Or merely thought's adventure some old day
> Of dim and done-with boyishness, or—well,
> Why might it not have been, the miracle
> Broke on me as I took my sober way
> Through veritable regions of our earth
> And made discovery, many a wondrous one?[84]

Browning's first experience with the *Song* had been a strange one, because first glance brought full recognition, as if he had read it all before. Had he himself in fancy conceived the ideas in the *Song?* Or did the miracle break on him in some more sober mood? At any rate, it was all familiar to him, and the experience seemed a sort of miracle.

So he goes on to show by an elaborate simile the place he conceives the *Song* to hold among the other works of Smart —a simile which at the same time recounts his own discovery of the *Song:*

> I was exploring some huge house, had gone
> Through room and room complacently . . .
> The master of the mansion was no fool
> Assuredly, no genius just as sure!
> . . . On and on I went, . . .
> Till lo, I push a door, sudden uplift
> A hanging, enter, chance upon a shift
> Indeed of scene! So—thus it is thou deck'st,
> High heaven, our low earth's brick-and-mortar work?
> It was the Chapel . . .[85]

and Browning is filled with reverent admiration at the sight of it. It is a shrine which from roof to floor is all one evidence "of how far earth may rival heaven." His description

84 *With Christopher Smart*, ll. 1-15.
85 *Idem*, ll. 17-36.

catches beautifully the spirit of Smart's work—work which
is fittingly compared in color to that of a painter:

> No niche
> Where glory was not prisoned to enrich
> Man's gaze with gold and gems, no space but glowed
> With color, gleamed with carving—hues which owed
> Their outburst to a brush the painter fed
> With rainbow-substance . . .[86]

But the great miracle of the place was its marvellous combi-
nation of things old and new. The artist, full of a joyous love
of beauty, had learned his lesson from the lives of older artists. His work gave the impression of a workman whose life
and work was one continual development:

> And all seemed old yet new:
> Youth,—in the marble's curve, the canvas' hue,
> Apparent,—wanted not the crowning thrill
> Of age the consecrator. Hands long still
> Had worked here—could it be, what lent them skill
> Retained a power to supervise, protect,
> Enforce new lessons with the old, connect
> Our life with theirs? No merely modern touch
> Told me that here the artist, doing much,
> Elsewhere did more, perchance does better, lives—
> So needs must learn.[87]

Thus "big with anticipation—well-nigh fear—" of what
should come next, Browning went forth from the Chapel.
What followed? Nothing! Again room succeeded room in
dull commonplace evenness.

With this instance, Browning says, he has attempted to
diagnose the case of Smart. The man was sane to begin with;
all at once the revelation came upon him like fire from
heaven. Then, just as suddenly, he resumed sobriety, and
everything was with him as it had been before. Browning
finds it hard to comprehend how a man can subside to insig-

[86] *With Christopher Smart,* ll. 45-50.
[87] *Idem,* ll. 53-63.

nificance after an experience of this sort. In one respect Smart was the one man able to bear the torch of English poetry between Milton and Keats; if he had the greatness to do this, how did it happen that that greatness showed itself once and once only? The problem engrosses Browning's attention through many lines:

> Now, what I fain would know is—could it be
> That he—whoe'er he was that furnished forth
> The Chapel, making thus, from South to North,
> Rafael touch Leighton, Michelagnolo
> Join Watts, was found but once combining so
> The elder and the younger, taking stand
> On Art's supreme,—or that yourself who sang
> A Song where flute-breath silvers trumpet-clang,
> And stations you for once on either hand
> With Milton and with Keats, empowered to claim
> Affinity on just one point—(or blame
> Or praise my judgment, thus it fronts you full)—
> How came it you resume the void and null,
> Subside to insignificance,—live, die
> —Proved plainly two mere mortals who drew nigh
> One moment—that, to Art's best hierarchy,
> This, to the superhuman poet-pair?[88]

It is the same question that has been troubling Browning all his life, from *Paracelsus* to the *Parleying*. How can such a miracle be explained? Once and only once! He repeats the problem over and over.

But the great fact remains that such a thing did happen. The disguise fell from nature,

> . . . so that Truth remained
> Naked, and whoso saw for once could tell
> Us others of her majesty and might
> In large, her lovelinesses infinite
> In little . . .[89]

[88] *With Christopher Smart,* ll. 87-103.
[89] *Idem,* ll. 141-145.

And while the mad poet was able to see into the heart of
things, his vision was miraculously translated into words, so
that others were able to see too—as if with a new power of
sight—the "old things thus made new." For it is the function of art to point out to man the unsuspected beauties of
the earth, that he may see, through each manifestation of
strength and each evidence of beauty, how Design operates
through it all. Thus at any rate Browning believes, with
Smart, who once in his life

. . . pierced the screen
'Twixt thing and word, lit language straight from soul . . .[90]

Then Smart went back to his old manner of cataloguing
the things of earth, startled himself perhaps at the great
Song which his madness had produced:

Then—back was furled
The robe thus thrown aside, and straight the world
Darkened into the old oft-catalogued
Repository of things that sky, wave, land,
Or show or hide, clear late, accretion-clogged
Now, just as long ago, by tellings and
Re-tellings to satiety, which strike
Muffled upon the ear's drum. Very like
None was so startled as yourself when friends
Came, hailed your fast-returning wits: "Health mends
Importantly, for—to be plain with you—
This scribble on the wall was done—in lieu
Of pen and paper—with—ha, ha!—your key
Denting it on the wainscot! Do you see
How wise our caution was? Thus much we stopped
Of babble that had else grown print: and lopped
From your trim bay-tree this unsightly bough—
Smart's who translated Horace! Write us now" . . .
Why, what Smart did write—never afterward
One line to show that he, who paced the sward,
Had reached the zenith from his madhouse cell.[91]

90 *With Christopher Smart,* ll. 113-114.
91 *Idem,* ll. 164-184.

Then Browning goes back to his questioning. Why did
Smart never afterward write one line equal to the *Song?*
Was it because he judged—Browning knows full well, he
says, that Smart never had such an idea—that poetry ought
to be, as some people think, a mere catalogue of the strengths
and beauties of the earth? The words strength and beauty
are the two words which Browning continually and justly
uses to characterize the material with which Smart deals.
Here they suggest to him a paraphrase of Smart's style, and
he promptly gives an example of each quality, a strength
and a beauty:

> "So, indeed,
> Wallows the whale's bulk in the waste of brine,
> Nor otherwise its feather-tufts make fine
> Wild Virgin's Bower when stars faint off to seed!"[92]

[92] *Idem,* ll. 195-198. The notes in the Florentine edition suggest that
Browning is here quoting from some of the Seatonian prize poems, and cite
a passage from *The Immensity of the Supreme Being* (see *Poems,* 1791, I,
77):

> While high above their heads Leviathan
> The terror and the glory of the main
> His pastime takes with transport, proud to see
> The ocean's vast dominion all his own.

And from *The Power of the Supreme Being* the passage is cited (see
Poems, I, 98):

> 'Twere but the echo of the parting breeze,
> When Zephyr faints upon the lily's breast . . .

These are fairly close to Browning's lines in Smart's manner, but the editors did not see that the subjects were such common ones with Smart (see,
for example, the *Hymn to the Supreme Being,* stanza xvi, in *Poems,* I, 61)
that Browning naturally chose them when he attempted to characterize the
poet. For his aim is to do just that—to characterize and not to quote. The
suggestion for Browning's lines is to be found all through Smart, but more
particularly in *A Song to David,* which he knew best. In stanza lxxvi we
read

> Strong against tide, th' enormous whale
> Emerges as he goes.

And in stanza lxviii,

> But as for pray'r, or ere it faints,
> Far better is the breath of saints
> Than galbanum or myrrh.

All Browning cared for was to characterize Smart's habit of cataloguing
all sorts of things in the earth in order to show their strength and beauty.

But Browning explains hastily that the passage is not meant
as a quotation:

> (My prose—your poetry I dare not give,
> Purpling too much my mere gray argument.)[93]

Then Browning goes back once more to his questions. Did
Smart, realizing that the glory that had come upon him was
fugitive, and that he no longer had the power of depicting
truth vividly, calmly resign himself?

The question remains unanswered. Browning is caught
once more by the words strength and beauty, and turns aside
to say what effectual service he thinks it is to point out the
good things of the earth. But that is only the text, and the
poet should go on to teach mankind the significance of the
beautiful things he has shown them:

> Strengths, beauties, by one word's flash thus laid bare
> —That was effectual service: made aware
> Of strengths and beauties, Man but hears the text,
> Awaits your teaching. Nature? What comes next?
> Why all the strength and beauty?—to be shown
> Thus in one word's flash, thenceforth let alone
> By Man who needs must deal with aught that's known
> Never so lately and so little? Friend,
> First give us knowledge, then appoint its use!
> Strength, beauty are the means: ignore their end?[94]

This, as we have seen, brings Browning to his own matured
theory of poetry, which he expounds at some length. He
knows that it is vastly different from that of most of his contemporaries: hence he contrasts the two views and points out,
in closing, the advantages of his own and the disadvantages
of theirs:

> From edge to edge
> Of earth's round, strength and beauty everywhere
> Pullulate—and must you particularize

[93] *With Christopher Smart*, ll. 199-200.
[94] *Idem*, ll. 208-217.

All, each and every apparition? Spare
Yourself and us the trouble! Ears and eyes
Want so much strength and beauty, and no less
Nor more, to learn life's lesson by. Oh, yes—
The other method's favored in our day!
The end ere the beginning: as you may,
Master the heavens before you study earth,
Make you familiar with the meteor's birth
Ere you descend to scrutinize the rose![95]

Browning is here objecting to the tendency of his age to go
at things in the wrong order. People study the heavens and
formulate laws for the universe, without understanding the
things that touch their own lives most closely. There are
great dangers in this method. If you begin with the heavens
instead of with the earth, and judge things by some law that
you formulate for yourself, there is little wonder that things
seem to you to be getting worse. Such a mistaken procedure,
Browning would probably say, produces such a cry as this
of Swinburne's:

Yea, with thine hate, O God, thou hast covered us . . .[96]

If people are to go far afield in collecting beauties for their
poetry, without ever seeing how these things apply to their
own lives, they are doomed to a bitter disillusionment.

He himself believes in another method. Only by advancing
step by step, slowly and surely, from the known to the unknown, can man arrive at any certainty of knowledge or any
happiness. So he gives his advice to these people who follow
the favored method of the day:

I say, o'erstep no least one of the rows
That lead man from the bottom where he plants

[95] *With Christopher Smart*, ll. 233-244.
[96] *Atalanta in Calydon*, in *The Poems of Algernon Charles Swinburne*,
London, 1904, IV, 288. Rossetti on p. 27 of his *Criticism* says of Swinburne:
"Intellect pitted against a material and moral *pieuvre* appears to be his conception of the state of man; and no wonder that the fight looks to him a
most ghastly one, unconvinced as he is . . . of the justice of the Umpire,
and convinced . . . of the mortality of the soul."

Foot first of all, to life's last ladder-top:
Arrived there, vain enough will seem the vaunts
Of those who say—"We scale the skies, then drop
To earth—to find, how all things there are loth
To answer heavenly law: we understand
The meteor's course, and lo, the rose's growth—
How other than should be by law's command!"[97]

Browning is attempting here to characterize the attitude of
those contemporary thinkers who accept the large generali-
zations of the hasty spokesmen of the scientific movement.[98]
He looks upon Swinburne and his atheistic and bitter beliefs
as the natural outcome of such a method of thinking. He appeals to Christopher Smart:

Would not you tell such—"Friends, beware lest fume
Offuscate sense: learn earth first ere presume
To teach heaven legislation. Law must be
Active in earth or nowhere: earth you see,—
Or there or not at all, Will, Power and Love
Admit discovery,—as below, above
Seek next law's confirmation! But reverse
The order, where's the wonder things grow worse
Than, by the law your fancy formulates,
They should be? Cease from anger at the fates
Which thwart themselves so madly.[99]

And so he reiterates his advice, in a new application of the
old proverb, to make all things teach us lessons to live by:

Live and learn,
Not first learn and then live, is our concern.[100]

[97] *With Christopher Smart,* ll. 245-253.
[98] Compare pp. 194-200 of this volume.
[99] *With Christopher Smart,* ll. 254-264.
[100] *Idem,* ll. 264-265.

CHAPTER IV

THE PARLEYING WITH GEORGE BUBB DODINGTON

I

THE *Parleying With George Bubb Dodington*, self-seeking politician of the reign of George II, is of all the *Parleyings* the one most evidently written for the sake of the attack upon a contemporary. Ostensibly the poem is a description of the political methods of Dodington, whose vanity and overreaching ambition made him little better than a fool in spite of his great powers. With Dodington as a text, however, the *Parleying* turns into an essay upon political self-seeking in which the simple and blundering methods of the eighteenth-century statesman are contrasted with the polished and highly successful methods of Benjamin Disraeli. In parleying with such men as these it is useless to discuss morals, wherefore Browning rules all questions of morality out of court. The poem thus becomes a discussion in sustained irony of the best way to succeed in politics; and Benjamin Disraeli becomes the hero of the piece.

George Bubb Dodington, Lord Melcombe, not only serves as an excellent foil to Disraeli, but he represents one of the major interests of Browning's life. The poet's father, a man of many interests and enthusiasms, was perhaps more deeply interested in memoir, history and biography than in any other subject. Consequently the library in which the poet received his education was filled with books of this nature.[1] To this rich storehouse the father of the poet served as no ordinary guide; for he is thus described by his half-brother, Reuben Browning:

His wonderful store of information might really be compared

[1] See Griffin and Minchin, pp. 17-19.

to an inexhaustible mine. It comprised not merely a thorough
scholastic outline of the world, but the critical points of ancient
and modern history, the lore of the Middle Ages, all political
combinations of parties, their description and consequences.[2]

There were two copies of Dodington's *Diary* in the
Browning library. One had been placed there by the poet's
father, and was there during Browning's boyhood; the other
bears the inscription of the poet's name and the date "Jan.
20. '86," which means perhaps that Browning bought this
second copy in preparation for writing the *Parleying*.[3] It is
undoubtedly this copy which he consulted. Inside the cover
and on the fly-leaves of this volume are inscribed extracts
from Hawkins' *Life of Johnson*, Edgeworth, *On Education*,
and Belsham's *George II*, concerning the political life of
Dodington. The handwriting is that of a previous owner.

The *Diary* was published at Dublin in 1784 by Henry
Penruddocke Wyndham, who had come into possession of
Dodington's papers. In attempting to justify himself for
publishing the *Diary* when Dodington had left explicit in-
structions that none of his papers should be published save
those which would "in some degree do honour to his memory,"[4] Wyndham sketches the nature of the author of the
Diary. This sketch is of great importance, partly because
Browning seems to have been more intimately acquainted
with this *Preface* than with any other part of the *Diary*, and
partly because the sketch helps greatly to an understanding
of the book. For of the *Diary* it may be said, that unless one
is intimately acquainted with the vicissitudes of politics between the years 1749 and 1761, which period the *Diary*

---

[2] This passage is taken from the preface to a small book of sketches by
Robert Browning, senior. It is reprinted by Griffin and Minchin, p. 8.

[3] This copy of the *Diary* is now in the possession of Professor C. B.
Tinker. He graciously allowed me to use it for this study.

[4] See *Diary of George Bubb Dodington, Lord Melcombe,* Dublin, 1784;
Preface, pp. vii, viii. Wyndham might have saved himself much agony if
he could have consulted *The Memoirs of Richard Cumberland,* London,
1856, p. 102. Dodington wished the *Diary* to be published.

covers,[5] it is impossible to make a great deal of the book. The *Diary* is in no sense a picture of the times of George II. It is not even a good objective picture of Dodington himself. It is rather an account of the fears, hopes, indignations, and satisfactions of a fickle, servile, and vain courtier. One must resort to the memoirs of Walpole, Cumberland, Chesterfield, Hervey, and others for the objective view of Dodington which Browning has. The *Parleying*—that is, the part which deals with Dodington—is an essay upon his political career as a whole.

The first entry in the *Diary* is for March 8, 1749. Before this date Dodington had lived a long and eventful life. He was born in 1691, and made his entrance into the political world in 1715 by his election to Parliament from Winchelsea, a borough which was controlled by his family. In May of the same year Dodington succeeded Sir Paul Methuen as envoy extraordinary to Madrid, and stayed there until 1717. By the death of his uncle, George Dodington, he came into the family name—he was born George Bubb—and a huge fortune. At this time (1720) his parliamentary influence was considerable. He could command Winchelsea, Weymouth, and Melcombe Regis, which at that time returned four members, and generally he was in control of Bridgewater, the borough which he represented until 1754. In 1724 he succeeded Henry Pelham as Lord of the Treasury. Dodington was at this time an adherent of Walpole, and in 1726 he addressed complimentary verses to Sir Robert, declaring that he

> To share thy adverse Fate alone pretend;
> In power a servant; out of power a friend.[6]

In thrifty fashion Dodington made the same verses serve a similar occasion in 1761 when he was addressing Lord Bute.[7]

---

[5] Dodington was fifty-eight years old in 1749. The *Diary* covers twelve years. It stops the year before he died.

[6] *Epistle to the Rt. Hon. Sir Robert Walpole,* London, 1726, p. 9.

[7] See Horace Walpole's witty remarks upon this occasion; *Memoirs of the Reign of George II,* London, 1846, I, 438.

Progress evidently was too slow under Walpole, and after
1726 we find Dodington abusing his master to Frederick,
Prince of Wales, who had set up a rival establishment to
George II and the administration. In the next year he went
over to the Prince openly. In 1734 Chesterfield and Lyttle-
ton displaced Dodington in the Prince's favor, and Dodington joined the Duke of Argyle. The Prince applied to Dodington in 1737 before he asked any other statesman in the
ministry for aid in getting his income increased. This was
practically an invitation to change patrons again. Dodington, however, saw the untimeliness and unreasonableness of
the Prince's demands,[8] and voted against the increase. In
1739 the coalition of Argyle and Walpole broke up, and
Dodington went with Argyle. He lost his place at the Treasury and joined the opposition gathered now about the Prince
of Wales. It was at this time that Sir Charles Hanbury Williams ridiculed Dodington's subservience to Argyle in satirical verse.[9] The great debate of 1742 found Dodington attacking the "infamous administration" of Walpole, who in
reply taunted Dodington as "the self-mortifying gentleman"
who for sixteen years had quietly accepted his share of the
infamy. Dodington's attack upon his old friends brought
him into particular contempt.[10] Argyle and the opposition
gradually declined in strength; but in 1744 Pelham, who
had come into power, made Dodington Treasurer of the
Navy, several other members of the Prince's party deserting
also and taking office. In 1749 the Prince made another bid
for Dodington through Ralph,[11] a hack writer in the employ

[8] An account of the affair may be found in the appendix to Dodington's
Diary, pp. 301-323.
[9] See in *The Works of . . . Sir Chas. Hanbury Williams . . .,* London,
1822, 3 vols., *An Ode to The Duke of Argyle* (I, 14 ff.), *Argyle's Decampment* (I, 17 ff.), and *Giles Earle and Geo. Bubb Doddington, . . .* (I, 30
ff.).
[10] *The Letters of Horace Walpole,* ed. Cunningham, London, 1877, I,
137, 217.
[11] See the appendix to Dodington's *Diary,* pp. 325-326.

of Dodington, and after two days' reflection that statesman
accepted, and entered in his *Diary* under March 11,

> This day in the morning I wrote to Mr. Pelham, desiring
> him, as I was not able to go out, to wait upon the King, and in
> my name humbly to resign, into his majesty's hands, my office
> as Treasurer of the Navy.
> The same day I gave Mr. Ralph my answer in writing to the
> Prince's gracious message . . .[12]

To save his reputation Dodington would not receive any
definite promise from the Prince until July 18, when the
Prince promised him "a Peerage with the management of the
House of Lords, and the Seals of Secretary of State, for the
Southern Province."[13] But in 1751 the Prince of Wales unfortunately died, and Dodington was left unattached. He
lost no time in making overtures to Pelham and his brother,
the Duke of Newcastle, while at the same time he abused
them to the Princess of Wales whom he visited quite regularly.[14] At this time he told Pelham

> . . . that, as I was, now, entirely free from engagements, I was
> sincerely desirous of Mr. Pelham's favour and friendship, if he
> would accept of my friendship and attachment: if then he
> would accept of my services, he might, *upon proper conditions*,
> command my interest . . . mine [his disposition] was entirely
> inclined to be his friend and servant, *upon proper conditions*.[15]

Pelham was eager for Dodington's support in the House of
Commons, but the King—so Pelham intimated—could not
forgive Dodington's former desertions.[16] Pelham hit upon
the simple expedient of taking Dodington's support and of
giving him fair promises in return. Pelham, with the vague
promise of lifting the King's proscription, held the votes of

---

12 The *Diary*, p. 2.
13 *Idem*, p. 4.
14 A typical example of Dodington's duplicity in this respect may be observed in the *Diary*, pp. 105-116.
15 *Idem*, p. 86.
16 See *idem*, pp. 91-94.

Dodington's boroughs until March 6, 1754, upon which day
he died. The Duke of Newcastle formed the new ministry
and continued Pelham's policy of promises to Dodington.
He, however, grew impatient and recounted to Newcastle his
own virtues and deserts, after which recital the wily Duke
"took me in his arms, and kissed me twice, with strong assur-
ances of affection and service."[17] Dodington was not deceived
by these manifestations, and in June, 1754, he delivered his
ultimatum to Newcastle in the most sustained flight of elo-
quence in the *Diary*:

. . . till I know it from your Grace, I cannot believe that so
just and generous a Prince would accept a poor subject's offers
of service, and suffer him to carry them into execution, at so
great an expence, with a resolution absolutely to exclude him
from all sorts of common favour. I thought it would be what
never happened before, or to me only. He said, he would do
everything in his power, and did not imagine it could end so. I
told him, that I heartily wished it might not, but it must end
one way or another, it must not remain as it was; for I was determined to make some sort of figure in life: I earnestly wished
it might be under his protection, but if that could not be, I
must make some figure; what it would be, I could not determine
yet; I must look round me a little, and consult my friends, but
some figure I was resolved to make.[18]

This was not the expression of a youth's ambition, for Dodington was sixty-three years of age at this time. He continued his outburst to Newcastle with typical duplicity:

He must think that 2000£. a year would not make my fortune,
with one foot in the grave; that as to rank, I had heard that
the King was odd about titles: that I had as much respect for
the Peerage as any man, but he could not but see, that, in my
situation, without succession or collateral, a Peerage to me,
was not worth the expence of new painting my coach: that I
desired to pass my life as his attached friend and servant, per-

17 The *Diary*, pp. 183-190.
18 *Idem*, pp. 201-202.

suaded that he would, as such, do me favourable justice the first opportunity that offered.[19]

But nothing came of the ultimatum at once, and Dodington spent the next year in bewildering intrigue, chiefly with Lord Halifax. Even Pitt condescended to make proposals to Dodington.[20] At last in December, 1755, Dodington "kissed hands" as Treasurer of the Navy under the Newcastle-Fox government. This action was as sudden as it was base. The Princess of Wales passed him without speaking. The next year he lost his place again. The most creditable performance of his whole life was a "humane and pathetic speech" which he made in the House of Commons in 1757 in behalf of Admiral Byng, who had been sentenced to be executed.[21]

After further intrigues and more fluctuations in his political hopes Dodington joined Lord Bute, and in 1761 was made Baron Melcombe of Melcombe Regis by the new king, George III. He received no further office, however, and died, as Horace Walpole puts it, "of a dropsy in his stomach, just when the views of his life were nearest being realized."[22] Toward the end of his life he seems to have grown desperate of achieving his political aspirations, and like Falstaff lent himself to many undignified procedures. He was one of the "rosy anchorites" of Sir Francis Dashwood's Hell Fire Club, which sacrificed publicly to Venus and Bacchus.[23]

The earlier part of Browning's Parleying With George Bubb Dodington is an essay upon Dodington's political career. It remains for us to see the statesman as his contemporaries saw him and as Browning saw him. The charges which Browning brought against Dodington's character—vanity, self-love, duplicity, obsequiousness, treachery—had been stated in almost every memoir and biography dealing with

[19] The Diary, pp. 199-200.
[20] See idem, pp. 248-257.
[21] See Walpole's Memoirs of the Reign of George II, 1846, II, 320-321.
[22] The Letters of Horace Walpole, 1877, IV, 7.
[23] For an account of these activities see Walpole's Memoirs of the Reign of George III, London, 1894, I, 137-138.

figures of the middle years of the eighteenth century. Richard Cumberland gives a full-length portrait of Dodington—
the vast bulk of his person, the colossal dignity, the wardrobe
loaded with rich and flaring suits. As secretary to Lord
Halifax, Cumberland had many opportunities for observing
the tasteless magnificence of Dodington's villa at Hammer-
smith, or the tremendous mansion at Eastbury which was
constructed by Vanbrugh in the manner of Blenheim.[24]
Chesterfield attempted a final judgment upon Dodington:

> With submission to my Lord Rochester, God made Doding-
> ton the coxcomb he is; mere human means could never have
> brought it about. He is a coxcomb superior to his parts, though
> his parts are superior to almost anybody's. He is thoroughly
> convinced of the beauty of his person, which cannot be worse
> than it is without deformity. His distinguished awkwardness
> he mistakes for a peculiar gracefulness. He thinks himself suc-
> cessful with women, though he has never been tolerated by any,
> except the w—— he keeps, and the wife he married. He talks of
> his ancestors, though no mortal knows that he even had a
> father. And what is difficult for him to do, he even overrates his
> own parts. Common coxcombs hope to impose on others, more
> than they impose upon themselves; Dodington is sincere, nay
> moderate; for he thinks still ten times better of himself than
> he owns. Blest coxcomb![25]

All who comment upon Dodington remark upon his excellent parts. It was the unseemly eagerness to push himself
ahead that betrayed his otherwise intelligent mind into the
foolishness and treachery which defeated his political ambi-
tions. Walpole writes of him:

> This man, with great knowledge of business, much wit, and
> great parts, had, by mere absurdity of judgment, and a dispo-
> sition to finesse, thrown himself out of all estimation, and out
> of all the great views which his large fortune and abilities could

---

[24] *The Memoirs of Richard Cumberland,* London, 1856, pp. 95-102, gives
perhaps the clearest picture we have of Dodington.

[25] *The Letters and Works of Lord Chesterfield,* ed. Mahon, London, 1853,
V, 385.

not have failed to promote, if he but preserved the least shadow of steadiness.[26]

"A great man of excellent parts . . .," he is described, with always the destroying qualification, "unsteady, treacherous, vain, with no regard to truth whenever any purpose was to be answered by it . . ."[27] He epitomized his whole political philosophy when he asked Shelburne, "When did you ever know anybody get out of a great scrape but by a great lye?"[28]

One or two other things must be noticed concerning Dodington. To his peers and superiors he was obsequious. To those not in authority he was

. . . so overbearing, so insolent, and so insupportable, that he seemed to exact that applause as his due which other people solicit, and to think he had a right to make every auditor his admirer . . .[29]

The arrogance of Dodington was genuine enough, but he seems not to have used it toward the poets of the time. To them he attempted to be a Maecenas, and he gathered about himself a group of literary men—Young (of the *Night Thoughts*), Thomson, Fielding, Whitehead, Glover, Welsted—a group not nearly so undistinguished as Pope would lead one to believe.[30] Besides this, Dodington himself possessed a lyre and sang well enough to get one poem in *The Oxford Book of English Verse* (Number 443).

Perhaps Browning read many of the accounts of Doding-

[26] Walpole, *Memoirs of the Reign of George II*, 1846, I, 87-88.

[27] Fitzmaurice, *The Life of William, Earl of Shelburne*, London, 1875, I, 121-122.

[28] *Idem*, I, 121.

[29] Lord Hervey, *Memoirs of the Reign of George the Second*, London, 1884, II, 97. Hervey, Dodington's rival in wit, said that Dodington possessed the absolute *"je ne sais quoi* of displeasing." *Ibid.*

[30] See the *Prologue to the Satires* (*To Arbuthnot*), ll. 229-244. Dodington was originally Bufo. It has not been pointed out before, I believe, that Pope is describing the tasteless splendor of Dodington's villa in this poem.

ton scattered through the memoirs, biographies, and collections of letters in his father's library. It is altogether likely
that Browning heard from his father, who was so complete a
student of history, the story of Dodington's political vaga-
ries. In this way the career of the eighteenth-century politician may have become a memorable and pleasurable experience of Browning's youth.

The Dodington that appears in the *Parleying* is not precisely the Dodington of the court of George II. There are
many similarities; he is still both knave and fool. But Browning has not given the politician credit for any good qualities
or any excellent parts. He represents Dodington as the simplest of liars who is not cunning enough to persuade the
people to elevate him to a place of power. Browning, evidently for the sake of the more effective contrasts with Disraeli and his methods, imposes nineteenth-century conditions
of statesmanship upon Dodington. He makes Dodington dependent upon the wishes of the people. He made Dodington
serve as a type of the perfidious and unsuccessful statesman
because he believed Dodington to be on the intellectual and
spiritual level of the common people,—a knave, a liar, and a
hypocrite without cunning. The crafty people do not obey
their like. This is Browning's interpretation of the failure of
Dodington. It need not be said that it is not historically accurate. Dodington failed because of his unsteadiness and
treachery to his political masters, not because he was unable
to deceive the "rabble-rout."

How, then, did Browning get such a conception of Dodington? The ultimate reason was that the poet determined to
make Dodington's character serve as a perfect contrast in
all points of political management to that of Benjamin Disraeli. But as Browning consulted the *Diary* in preparation
for writing the *Parleying* he found several things which
would make him think his conception of Dodington a just
one. For example, on the fly-leaf of the *Diary* which Brown-

ing used there was copied a passage from Hawkins' *Life of Johnson:*

Whoever is desirous of being acquainted with the intrigues of contending factions, & the methods of exciting popular discontent, may rec[eive] ample information from the perusal of Lord Melcombe's Diary.[31]

This is hardly an accurate description of the *Diary*, but it may well be a source of Browning's opinion of Dodington. Turning to the *Preface* Browning may have found there all the qualities ascribed to Dodington which he ascribed to that statesman. One passage in Wyndham's remarks upon Dodington's nature probably came to Browning's notice, for it seems to have been echoed in the *Parleying:*

However, I cannot patiently forgive the violent declamation of his Lordship [Dodington] against "the low and venal wretches of Bridgewater;" as if a bribe, taken by a miserable voter, and, possibly for the support of a numerous and indigent family, was more dishonourable, than a place or pension, enjoyed or coveted by the opulent, for the sole purposes, either of accumulating riches, or of extending the pomp of pride and power.[32]

Wyndham refers in this passage to Dodington's chagrin upon losing his seat at Bridgewater, a borough which he had sat for for nearly thirty years. The discomfited gentleman calls the voters of Bridgewater "a set of low, worthless fellows, who finding they shall not be bribed without an opposition, have prevailed upon Lord Egmont to lend his name, to whom they will give one vote, that they may be able to sell the other."[33] Browning saw these passages perhaps, and concluded that Dodington depended upon the votes of the people—an idea to which he gives far too prominent a place in his description of Dodington's political career. The as-

[31] This is the copy of the *Diary* referred to above, p. 135. The quotation occurs in the *Life of Johnson*, London, 1787, p. 393.
[32] *Preface* to the *Diary*, p. ix.
[33] This happened in 1754. See the *Diary*, pp. 165-166.

tonishing thing about the *Diary* is that the common people
are mentioned so rarely. When Dodington does mention
them it is to impress Pelham or Newcastle with the completeness of his control over his boroughs.[34] Dodington's political
career depended rather upon the favor of those in authority
—the King, Walpole, Pelham, and Newcastle. It seems that
Browning read no further than the fly-leaves and the *Preface* of the *Diary* when he undertook to parley with Dodington in 1886.

There is one other source for Browning's opinions of Dodington. There were in his father's library three volumes of
the works of Sir Charles Hanbury Williams, annotated by
Horace Walpole, and Browning had looked into them at
least as recently as 1880.[35] In the first part of Volume One
Dodington is assailed again and again in rollicking satirical
verse. This could hardly have failed to interest Browning. In
describing Dodington's desertion of Walpole for Argyle in
1740, and his anomalous position thereafter, one song runs:

> So this great Duke was turned out,
>   Whom no two people follow'd;
> And then the Torys all rejoic'd,
>   And then the Whigs all halloo'd.

> One man [Dodington] alone in all this land,
>   Did not much like this story,
> Whom I did not except, because
>   He's neither Whig nor Tory.

> To no one party, no one man,
>   Not to his ownself tight;
> For what he voted for at noon,
>   He rail'd against at night.

[34] See the *Diary*, p. 91. Dodington controlled Weymouth, Winchelsea, and
Melcombe Regis regularly.

[35] Sotheby, *Catalogue*, item no. 1212, contains the description of Browning's copy of *The Works, of . . . Sir Chas. Hanbury Williams . . .* 3
vols., London, 1822. The poet's inscription supplies the date, Dec. 22, 1880.

A false, suspicious friend was he,
As all the world can tell;
He flatter'd Walpole at Whitehall,
And damn'd him in Pall-mall.

But what he said in either place,
Ne'er answer'd what he meant:
Offensive was his flattery,
His satire innocent.[36]

This passage, I believe, gave Browning his conception of Dodington's perfidy. A more scurrilous and amusing poem supplied the poet with his conception of Dodington's dealings with the common people. This poem was *A Grub upon Bub*, "Written for the use of the Votesmen of Bridgewater, March 1740-1," to the tune of "Packington's Pound." It runs:

Good people draw near, and attend to my song,
And despise not my ballad for being a Grub;
For if 'tis not a good one, at least 'tis not long,
And I'll tell you, in short, the fall of poor Bub:
How he lost his good place,
And is in disgrace,
And does not know where to show his flat face;
For the Torys will never receive such a scrub,
And no Whig at court will be civil to Bub . . .

He's on this grown a patriot, and soon will harangue,
And of Virtue will prate like a saint on a tub;
But I shall leave him for Sir William to bang,
If he 'as but a clear stage, how he'll mumble poor Bub:
Who has never a friend,
That assistance will lend,
Or his cause, tho' his life were at stake, will defend;
Nay, if 'twas not in hopes to give Walpole a rub,
The patriots themselves would p-ss upon Bub.[37]

[36] *The Works, of . . . Sir Charles Hanbury Williams*, I, 18-19. The poem is called *Argyle's Decampment* (*Written in June, 1740*). Besides references in the poem, Dodington is identified by name in a later stanza.
[37] *The Works, of . . . Sir Charles Hanbury Williams*, I, 25, 27. Sir William of the poem is Sir William Yonge, Secretary at War.

From these sources, then, Browning has drawn his conception of the eighteenth-century statesman. The results are that Browning underestimates the abilities of Dodington, and makes him a demagogue of the most hypocrital, simple, and unsuccessful sort. He is both knave and fool, no whit different from those he tries to rule. This is not an accurate picture of Dodington, but it must be remembered that the portrait was designed to serve as a companion-piece and a contrast to that of the successful, but not less knavish, statesman, Benjamin Disraeli.

II

DOUBTLESS, Dodington was chosen as the subject of one of the *Parleyings* because he represented to Browning the world of politics. He represented no less, as we have seen, a world of quackery and unmoral cunning. Politics seems to Browning to be one of the categories of quackery. It is not surprising, therefore, to find Browning casting out all moral considerations in his *Parleying* with the politicians. The discussion is to be upon their own plane, and Dodington and Disraeli are to be judged not by their morality but by their success. In this field, too, Browning finds evidence of progress, though it is a perverse and wayward progress. Man as a political animal grows ever more and more discriminating. Strength, which sufficed at first to rule him, gives way at length to intelligence; in the course of time many men possessing both intelligence and strength are to be found, and the people may choose their rulers, and these rulers must possess some special qualification.[38] The man who would rule must keep ahead of the multitude.

In the *Parleying With George Bubb Dodington* Browning's thought turns upon two great principles of the psychology of politics, both of which are fundamental beliefs with Browning. The first of these is that

[38] See *With George Bubb Dodington*, ll. 135-142.

> No animal—much less our lordly Man—
> Obeys its like . . .[39]

The second principle is the positive side of the first: to state
it baldly, it is the introduction of the supernatural element
which awes men,

> Exact the thing I call
> Man's despot, just the Supernatural . . .[40]

These ideas, which are in reality only the two sides of one
idea, attain their clearest expression in the present *Parleying*, but they had been expressed many times before in
Browning's works. In 1843 in *The Return of the Druses* the
idea is the informing principle of the drama. Djabal sees
that he is powerless to help the Druses unless they believe he
is supernaturally gifted, and therefore declares himself
Hakeem:

> I learn from Europe: all who seek
> Man's good must awe man, by such means as these.
> We two will be divine to them—we are![41]

The same conception of statesmanship occurs in slightly different form in *Colombe's Birthday* written in the next year.[42]
In *Men and Women* (1855) Bishop Blougram recognizes the
value of the supernatural element in ruling his "million im-
beciles."[43] If one of the people's superstitions is destroyed
the whole spell is broken. In *Dramatis Personae* (1864), the
idea attains expression twice. As long as Caliban can convince himself that Setebos is "altogether such a one as himself" he has no fear whatever. It is the monster's belief in the
supernatural quality, invisibility, and omniscience of Setebos, which reduces Caliban to obedience. Sludge knows the
secret of awing men, too;

---

[39] *With George Bubb Dodington*, ll. 134-135.
[40] *Idem*, ll. 309-310.
[41] Act IV, ll. 125-127.
[42] See Act IV, ll. 225-236.
[43] See *Bishop Blougram's Apology*, ll. 749-768.

> And never mind the nods and raps and winks,
> 'T is the pure obvious supernatural
> Steps forward, does its duty: why, of course![44]

All of Sludge's villainy is built upon his knowledge of the one great principle that "Man's nature owns a supernatural." It was by the element of superstition in man that Prince Hohenstiel-Schwangau mounted and ruled.[45] Djabal, Blougram, Sludge, Hohenstiel-Schwangau, and Disraeli, who in the *Parleying* is in possession of the secret, exploit mankind by means of this knowledge.

In the *Parleying* Browning selects Dodington as the perfect example of his theory that man will not obey his like. Dodington's political methods are out of date. Simple lying can no longer deceive such accomplished and crafty liars as the people are themselves. The people realize fully that they might

> . . . fish, from out the mothers' sons
> That welter thus, a dozen Dodingtons![46]

Dodington is proved to be both knave and fool, and naturally the people reject him. There is progress even here, in cunning. Once simple force and simple lying may have ruled men, but now something more than strength and intelligence is needed to make the people bow and worship. Browning has found it:

> . . . this it is,—at any rate
> To-day's conception thus I formulate:
> As simple force has been replaced, just so
> Must simple wit be . . .[47]

To-day's conception of the successful statesman is the magician, the wizard, the complete master of the principle that it

---

[44] *Mr. Sludge, "The Medium,"* ll. 1165-1167.
[45] See *Hohenstiel-Schwangau,* ll. 1501-1514. See also *Halbert and Hob,* l. 50.
[46] *With George Bubb Dodington,* ll. 166-167.
[47] *Idem,* ll. 172-175.

is the supernatural that brings men into subjection, Benjamin Disraeli.

Mrs. Orr in her *Handbook*[48] suggests rather hesitantly that Browning may be describing Lord Beaconsfield in his portrait of to-day's conception of statesmanship. She suggests the name but does nothing more, as if Browning had told her, and she scarcely found it credible.[49] Yet the portrait is the authentic portrait of Disraeli, and no one who reads the *Parleying* carefully and who knows Browning's large design can doubt it. The portrait at almost full length is set before us:

> Once for all,
> His [man's] nature owns a Supernatural
> In fact as well as phrase—which found must be
> —Where, in this doubting age? Old mystery
> Has served its turn—seen through and sent adrift
> To nothingness: new wizard-craft makes shift
> Nowadays shorn of help by robe and book,—
> Otherwise, elsewhere, for success must look
> Than chalked-ring, incantation-gibberish.
> Somebody comes to conjure: that's he? Pish!
> He's like the roomful of rapt gazers,—there's
> No sort of difference in the garb he wears
> From ordinary dressing,—gesture, speech,
> Deportment, just like those of all and each
> That eye their master of the minute. Stay!
> What of the something—call it how you may—
> Uncanny in the—quack? That's easy said!
> Notice how the Professor turns no head
> And yet takes cognizance of who accepts,
> Denies, is puzzled as to the adept's
> Supremacy, yields up or lies in wait
> To trap the trickster! Doubtless, out of date
> Are dealings with the devil: yet, the stir
> Of mouth, its smile half smug half sinister,

[48] Orr, *Handbook*, p. 351.
[49] No other treatment of the *Parleyings* does anything with the suggestion.

Mock-modest boldness masked in diffidence,—
What if the man have—who knows how or whence?—
Confederate potency unguessed by us—
Prove no such cheat as he pretends?[50]

This picture of Disraeli as the charlatan, the master of leg-
erdemain, was a common one in the seventies and eighties of
the last century. *Punch* and many other magazines were in
the habit of referring to Disraeli as the "Professor of mystery." Matthew Arnold constantly called him "the charlatan."[51] Browning, in all likelihood, took his description from
a first-hand impression of Disraeli; yet it is similar to many
descriptions of the statesman. The *Fortnightly Review*, for
example, draws this picture of Disraeli as he appeared at the
height of his power in 1878:

Like the Sorcerer, in Mr. Gilbert's play, he moves about taking
part in all that concerns men's businesses and bosoms, wearing
the dress, speaking the language, using the slang, and not ex-
empt from the other vulgarities of ordinary life. Still you feel
that he has come from another world, and that he is to be
judged by the law of his domicile, wherever that may be, rather
than by the rule according to which Englishmen pass moral
sentence upon each other. Robin Goodfellow, or the Elfin King,
or any other weird or graceful creature of extra-natural superstition, seems to have as much connection with our prosaic world
as the Earl of Beaconsfield. If some fine day he should cast
aside his peer's robes, and the dull vesture of decay which seems
to hem him in less closely and more incongruously than it sits
upon other men, and if he should appear in a blaze of light as
the Genius of the Gardens of Joy, or descend in red fire through
a trap-door, the transformation would not appear more
strange or theatrical than many incidents of his history.[52]

The views taken of the statesman in these two accounts are

---

[50] *With George Bubb Dodington*, ll. 190-217.
[51] See, for example, *The Letters of Matthew Arnold*, ed. Russell, London, 1895, II, 159, 193.
[52] *The Fortnightly Review*, XXIII (N. S.), 477-478. The article is called
The Political Adventures of Lord Beaconsfield. (Anonymous.)

almost identical. But there is more to Browning's picture.
We draw closer to the "quack":

> You see, a little year ago
> They heard him thunder at the thing which, lo,
> To-day he vaunts for unscathed, while what erst
> Heaven-high he lauded, lies hell-low, accursed!
> And yet where's change? Who, awe-struck, cares to point
> Critical finger at a dubious joint
> In armor, true *aes triplex*, breast and back
> Binding about, defiant of attack,
> An imperturbability that's—well,
> Or innocence or impudence—how tell
> One from the other? Could ourselves broach lies,
> Yet brave mankind with those unaltered eyes,
> Those lips that keep the quietude of truth?
> Dare we attempt the like? What quick uncouth
> Disturbance of thy smug economy,
> O coward visage! Straight would all descry
> Back on the man's brow the boy's blush once more!
> No: he goes deeper—could our sense explore—
> Finds conscience beneath conscience such as ours.
> Genius is not so rare,—prodigious powers—
> Well, others boast such,—but a power like this
> Mendacious intrepidity—*quid vis?*[53]

We are accustomed to earnest impostors, or those who seem
in deadly earnest. But here is guile with a difference;

> Here no act wants its qualifying smile,
> Its covert pleasantry to neutralize
> The outward ardor. Can our chief despise
> Even while most he seems to adulate?[54]

The picture is finished by a glimpse at the statesman's methods as he scorns and sneers at what he is most desirous of

[53] *With George Bubb Dodington*, ll. 228-249.
[54] *Idem*, ll. 259-262. Disraeli was commonly called "the chief" by his sup-
porters in the Conservative Party.

bringing to pass, "laughingly careless,—triply cased in brass."

This is the authentic portrait of Disraeli as he was seen by his enemies. Monypenny and Buckle in their monumental work, *The Life of Benjamin Disraeli*, in attempting to give an idea of the statesman's manner, describe him as he was in 1847:

> It would scarcely be tolerated in another; he seems so careless, supercilious, indifferent to the trouble of pleasing . . . His action, where he has any is ungraceful, nay, what is worse, it is studiously careless—even offensively so.[55]

And again Monypenny and Buckle quote a vivid sketch of Disraeli as he appeared to Sir John Skelton in 1867:

> And the potent wizard himself, with his olive complexion and coal-black eyes, and the mighty dome of his forehead (no Christian temple, be sure), is unlike any living creature one has met. I had never seen him in the daylight before, and the daylight accentuates his strangeness. The face is more like a mask than ever, and the division between him and mere mortals more marked. I would as soon have thought of sitting down at table with Hamlet, or Lear, or the Wandering Jew . . .[56]

All accounts of Disraeli bring up finally at the mystery of his personality, and all find again and again the presence of that element which Browning calls the "supernatural." His biographers come to the conclusion that

> There is probably some truth in Fraser's assertion that Disraeli's 'fixed idea' was 'that he was a mysterious wire-puller.'[57]

55 Monypenny and Buckle, *The Life of Benjamin Disraeli*, London, 1912-1920, 6 vols. II, 316.

56 Quoted in *The Life of Benjamin Disraeli*, IV, 558-559. This account of Disraeli was later included in Skelton's *Table Talk of Shirley*, London, 1895, pp. 257-258.

57 Monypenny and Buckle, *The Life of Benjamin Disraeli*, V, 110.

Again, Browning has seen the same thing:

> No use
> In men but to make sport for you, induce
> The puppets now to dance, now stand stockstill,
> Now knock their heads together, at your will
> For will's sake only—while each plays his part
> Submissive: why? through terror at the heart:
> "Can it be—this bold man, whose hand we saw
> Openly pull the wires, obeys some law
> Quite above Man's—nay, God's?"[58]

In this manner, then, has Browning painted the picture of Disraeli, arch-politician and Prime Minister of England, for his gallery of rogues. Already in the gallery were the portraits of several other contemporary figures, Louis Napoleon, Cardinal Wiseman, and Home, the medium.[59] We must add to this group John Callcot Horsley, the object of Browning's vituperation in the *Parleying With Francis Furini*. In this selected group Disraeli attained the bad eminence of being chief rogue, being foremost in unscrupulousness and success. It is worthy of notice that Browning has treated all save Horsley in the same ironical manner, and has allowed each to disclose the depths of his villainy in monologue, and in phrases and words strikingly alike.[60]

There is little use of examining here the truth of Browning's view of Disraeli. The magnificent, though idolatrous, biography of that subtle statesman, begun by Monypenny and completed by Buckle, in six volumes, convinces one that Disraeli is one of the wisest, most earnest, and sincere men that ever ruled England. There were millions who believed that in Disraeli's own day. Likewise, there were just as many

[58] *With George Bubb Dodington*, ll. 332-340.

[59] These are the heroes, respectively, of the poems, *Hohenstiel-Schwangau, Bishop Blougram's Apology* and *Mr. Sludge, "The Medium."*

[60] Compare, for example, *Bishop Blougram's Apology*, ll. 367-380, with the *Parleying*, ll. 263-265. See also in *Bishop Blougram*, ll. 749-768; *Sludge*, ll. 1165-1177; *Hohenstiel-Schwangau*, ll. 1501-1507.

who believed with the poet that he was the greatest charlatan
of modern times, in league with the devil, an outsider and
foreigner, that he never treated either his subjects or the
public seriously, and that the change "of the Jew into the
true Briton would require Ovid's metamorphosis, not Darwin's." Browning's conception of Disraeli was by no means
unique.

One or two points may help us to see why Browning felt
as he did toward Disraeli. The first difference between the
two was political. All his life Browning was a Whig-Lib-
eral,[61] of the great party of Peel and later of Gladstone, and
the party of the middle-class townspeople. Disraeli was, of
course, the leader of the Tory-Conservative party, and naturally almost every great issue that came up in English politics between the years 1843 and 1881 found them on opposite sides. In the very years when Disraeli was beginning to
break from Sir Robert Peel and to make his name known
about England for his abilities, Browning wrote, complain-
ing to his friend Domett, himself a statesman who had gone
overseas,

> Our men scarce seem in earnest now.
> Distinguished names!—but 't is, somehow,
> As if they played at being names
> Still more distinguished, like the games
> Of children. Turn our sport to earnest
> With a visage of the sternest!
> Bring the real times back, confessed
> Still better than our very best![62]

And in 1845, the year in which Disraeli delivered his masterly philippics night after night in the House of Commons
until he finally overthrew Sir Robert Peel, the poet again
voiced his disapproval of Disraeli. This time it was an objec-

[61] See Griffin and Minchin, pp. 289-291.
[62] *Waring* (1842), ll. 201-208.

tion against the statesman's stand in the debates upon the
Corn Laws:

> —"Such trifles!" you say?
> Fortù in my England at home,
>   Men meet gravely to-day
> And debate, if abolishing Corn-laws
>   Be righteous and wise
> —If 't were proper, Scirocco should vanish
>   In black from the skies![63]

Years later, too, Disraeli counselled non-intervention in
Italy when the Italians were struggling with Austria for
their nationality. Disraeli was also the friend, confidant, and
public admirer of Louis Napoleon. These facts were not calculated to make Browning an admirer of the statesman, and
as we have seen Browning became a partisan of Gladstone in
his later years.

Disraeli, on his side, lost little love upon the poet. In a
letter to Lady Bradford from No. 10 Downing Street on
April 4, 1878, he mentioned meeting among the "second-rate
fashionables"

Browning, a noisy, conceited poet; all the talk about pictures
and art, and Raffaelle, and what Sterne calls 'the Correggiosity
of Correggio.'[64]

And in an entry in the *Diary* of Sir Stafford Northcote for
July 11, 1880, we read,

After dinner we talked chiefly Books; the Chief [Disraeli] is always at his best in his library, and seemed thoroughly to enjoy
a good ramble over literature. He was contemptuous over
Browning (of whom, however, he had read very little) and the
other poetasters of the Day . . .[65]

All in all, there was sufficient reason for Browning's attack

[63] *The Englishman in Italy*, ll. 286-292.

[64] Monypenny and Buckle, *Life of Disraeli*, VI, 283.

[65] Quoted by Monypenny and Buckle, *Life of Disraeli*, VI, 583. See also
Lang's *Northcote*, Edinburgh, and London, 1890, II, 177.

upon Disraeli. Browning cared nothing for Disraeli's politics, and Disraeli cared nothing for Browning's poetry. Could a sharper barb have been fashioned for the vanity of either?

III

BROWNING begins in the first lines of the *Parleying* to take the eighteenth-century statesman to task for his way of working:

> Ah, George Bubb Dodington Lord Melcombe,—no,
> Yours was the wrong way![66]

Even if Dodington could reconcile within himself the two conflicting ideals—one, to seem to the world to be spending body and soul for the public good, and the other, a natural desire to feather his own nest in the richest manner—he has gone about it in the most impracticable and shortsighted way. Of course, says Browning ironically, Dodington is right in principle. He has authority from both Scripture and nature. "Laborers deserve their hire," and we have only to glance at the manner in which birds build their nests:

> . . . at outside, roughly wrought,
> Twig knots with twig, loam plasters up each chink,
> Leaving the inmate rudely lodged—you think?
> Peep but inside! That specious rude-and-rough
> Covers a domicile where downy fluff
> Embeds the ease-deserving architect,
> Who toiled and moiled not merely to affect
> 'Twixt sprig and spray a stop-gap in the teeth
> Of wind and weather, guard what swung beneath
> From upset only, but contrived himself
> A snug interior, warm and soft and sleek.[67]

Of course, Browning admits Dodington's contention that the

66 *With George Bubb Dodington*, ll. 1-2.
67 *Idem*, ll. 20-30.

first duty of man is self-aggrandizement—he admits it at
least for the length of the *Parleying*. And thus each bird
lines his nest as nature prompts him: the human mud-lark
prefers pelf; the eagle likes rock, just as some men choose
power; the rook is happy in the companionship of other
rooks; and the morose crow prefers his own company. There
is "no sort of bird but suits his taste somehow."[68] And now
Darwin has given us a feathered parallel to Dodington in
the Bower Birds of Australia[69] and we find that the secret
motor of his mighty mind was nothing but vanity:

> How says the Sage?
> Birds born to strut prepare a platform-stage
> With sparkling stones and speckled shells, all sorts
> Of slimy rubbish, odds and ends and orts,
> Whereon to pose and posture and engage
> The priceless female simper.[70]

Browning has gone thus into detail in order to forestall any
complaints. For Dodington would have complained, says
Browning, and would have asked, "What fool conjectures
that profession means performance?" Or who would expect
to find Othello's face still black or Hamlet in his melancholy
robes once the play is done?[71] Each man resumes his natural
manner of life. Just so is it in statesmanship. All outside appearance is mere acting. It is on this basis, then, that Browning and Dodington are to parley. Morals are ruled out of
court automatically, since Dodington has none:

> Come, we, this night,
> Profess one purpose, hold one principle,
> Are at odds only as to—not the will
> But way of winning solace for ourselves . . .[72]

[68] *With George Bubb Dodington*, l. 39.
[69] See Darwin, *The Descent of Man*, New York, 1871, I, 61; II, 66, 98, 108.
[70] *With George Bubb Dodington*, ll. 49-54.
[71] See *idem*, ll. 59-65. Compare *Bishop Blougram*, ll. 486-489, 70.
[72] *With George Bubb Dodington*, ll. 73-76.

But even granted that Dodington's aim is permissible, his means of attaining that end are at fault. This is how Dodington would like to have statesmanship and himself regarded by the people:

> . . . we do good to men at—whose expense
> But ours? who tire the body, tease the soul,
> Simply that, running, we may reach fame's goal
> And wreathe at last our brows with bay—the State's
> Disinterested slaves, nay—please the Fates—
> Saviours and nothing less: such lot has been!
> Statesmanship triumphs pedestalled, serene,—
> O happy consummation!—brought about
> By managing with skill the rabble-rout
> For which we labor (never mind the name—
> People or populace, for praise or blame)
> Making them understand—their heaven, their hell,
> Their every hope and fear is ours as well.
> Man's cause—what other can we have at heart?
> Whence follows that the necessary part
> High o'er Man's head we play . . . [73]

And while Dodington is playing the game of politics high over the heads of men, the multitude concludes that Dodington's sole purpose is to assist them. By this pretence, says Dodington, we attain the high privilege of bearing the storms for mankind's sake. It is the call to duty:

> Up, then—earn
> Albeit no prize we may but martyrdom! [74]

But the practical question is how to get to "such fit heights to launch salvation from." How can the people be coaxed to coöperate in their salvation? How may they be persuaded to allow us to save them?

[73] *With George Bubb Dodington,* ll. 79-94.
[74] *Idem,* ll. 103-104.

In answering these questions Dodington discloses his whole political method. He counsels the seeker for public office to

> "Make shift
> By sham—the harsh word: preach and teach, persuade
> Somehow the Public—not despising aid
> Of salutary artifice—we seek
> Solely their good: our strength would raise the weak,
> Our cultivated knowledge supplement
> Their rudeness, rawness: why to us were lent
> Ability except to come in use?
> Who loves his kind must by all means induce
> That kind to let his love play freely, press
> In Man's behalf to full performance!"[75]

And upon hearing Dodington speak of his glorious purposes, do the people believe and bend the knee?

> Not so, George!
> Try simple falsehood on shrewd folk who forge
> Lies of superior fashion day by day
> And hour by hour? With craftsmen versed as they
> What chance of competition when the tools
> Only a novice wields?[76]

Dodington, the "disinterested statesman," had better save his pearls, and not cast them before such swine as these. But above all, Dodington must learn the first principle of political psychology, that

> No animal—much less our lordly Man—
> Obeys its like . . .[77]

[75] *With George Bubb Dodington,* ll. 109-119.
[76] *Idem,* ll. 122-127.
[77] *Idem,* ll. 134-135.

At this point in the *Parleying* Browning sketches for Dodington the progress of the art of ruling:

> . . . with strength all rule began,
> The stoutest awes the pasture. Soon succeeds
> Discrimination,—nicer power Man needs
> To rule him than is bred of bone and thew:
> Intelligence must move strength's self. This too
> Lasts but its time: the multitude at length
> Looks inside for intelligence and strength
> And finds them here and there to pick and choose . . .[78]

And as he speaks, he imagines Dodington rushing eagerly forward, "All at your service, mine, see!" But no one is ready to admit that Dodington is foremost in intelligence and strength, and all look with suspicion upon the statesman's "unexampled yearning" to help man. They suspect that he loves himself infinitely better than he loves them; and besides the trick is obsolete. They suggest that he try some other tricks. Humanity is such a composite mixture of sloth-stifled genius, ignorant idealism, misplaced energy—in this mass Dodington is not unusual. A dozen such as he might be found; therefore, why should Dodington be called up as the conquering statesman? His abilities are paralleled on every side. The statesman who rules to-day must have some special gift. It is hardly right to grant privileges to an ordinary simple liar such as Dodington is. Therefore we turn to a more successful statesman, "to-day's conception." And this, as we have seen, is Browning's view of the methods and successes of Benjamin Disraeli.

In Disraeli's case, as in Dodington's, morals are ruled at once out of court, for the reason that they are equally non-existent, according to Browning. At once Disraeli sets about showing the causes for Dodington's failure by explaining his

[78] *With George Bubb Dodington,* ll. 135-142.

own manner of working. In the first place Disraeli is not like other men:

> "I pretend
> No such community with men. Perpend
> My key to domination! Who would use
> Man for his pleasure needs must introduce
> The element that awes Man. Once for all,
> His nature owns a Supernatural
> In fact as well as phrase . . ."[79]

Disraeli has the secret of domination! Dodington knew nothing of the supernatural. But in this doubting age where is the supernatural to be found? People have seen through old mystery. Chalked-ring and incantation-gibberish deceive nobody. The modern conjurer is like the roomful of beholders in dress, gesture, speech, and deportment. Yet there is something uncanny in this modern wizard, Disraeli. He turns not at all, and yet is acutely aware of all men—those who accept his statements, those who are puzzled, and those who lie in wait to trap him. Dealings with the devil are doubtless out of date, yet we are sure that this man has "confederate potency unguessed by us." How else could he be so smug, yet so sinister; so bold, yet so diffident?

If Dodington had played "statesmanship's new card" he would have carried all before him. For we all of us have one human heart, as the bard says.[80] We would have succumbed. Yet whether to call Disraeli god, man, or beast is hard to say. "Quack" he certainly is. He boasts to-day of things which he thundered at only a year ago, and what a little while ago was high in his estimation now lies hell-low, accursed.[81] And yet there is no real change in the nature of those things. But there is none so hardy as to point with critical finger at a

[79] *With George Bubb Dodington,* ll. 186-192.
[80] See *With George Bubb Dodington,* ll. 219-220. This is Browning's faulty rendering of Shakespeare's famous line, "One touch of nature makes the whole world kin," *Troilus and Cressida,* III, iii, 175.
[81] Browning probably had in mind Disraeli's turn against Peel in 1843-1845, his change of front on the Corn Laws, etc.

dubious joint in the armor of the statesman, triply cased in
brass as he is. We could not broach lies with the unaltered
countenance of this man! A blush would betray us. He goes
deeper, and finds a conscience beneath ours. Genius is not so
rare, but a mendacious intrepidity such as Disraeli's transcends credulity. This man, we say, cannot be an impostor.
The impostor admits of no diversion from his aim, is zealous
always, and is ever grave. But here no act wants its qualify-
ing smile and covert pleasantry to neutralize the ostensible
ardor. It is almost as if Disraeli had said,

> "What though it be my fate
> To deal with fools? Among the crowd must lurk
> Some few with faculty to judge my work
> Spite of its way which suits, they understand,
> The crass majority:—the Sacred Band,
> No duping them forsooth!" So tells a touch
> Of subintelligential nod and wink—
> Turning foes friends. Coarse flattery moves the gorge:
> Mine were the mode to awe the many, George![82]

Men guess that Dodington despises them, even when he is
most intent upon showing the people his love for them. If
Dodington would win them he must follow the master's way.
Sneer at them, scorn what you most strain to bring to pass,
laugh at them—pushing strenuously meanwhile to the end
in view. And this is the result:

> Why, you formulate within
> The vulgar headpiece this conception "Win
> A master-mind to serve us needs we must,
> One who, from motives we but take on trust,
> Acts strangelier—haply wiselier than we know—
> Stronglier, for certain . . ."[83]

If Disraeli had declared his motives were entirely altruistic

---

[82] *With George Bubb Dodington*, ll. 263-271. Compare *Bishop Blougram's Apology*, ll. 370-379.
[83] *With George Bubb Dodington*, ll. 279-284.

the common people would have understood and disbelieved. Had he said openly that he laughed at the good of the people while achieving his own ends, the people would again understand, believe, and have none of him. But here it is through the recognition of the people that Disraeli has earned by hard work the place, and by this means he mounts to such a stage above all his competitors that it would be agony for anyone else to maintain it—except Bubb Dodington. They cannot get along without Disraeli:

> ". . . Yet,—here's the rub—
> So slightly does he hold by our esteem
> Which solely fixed him fast there, that we seem
> Mocked every minute to our face, by gibe
> And jest—scorn insuppressive: what ascribe
> The rashness to? Our pay and praise to boot—
> Do these avail him to tread underfoot
> Something inside us all and each, that stands
> Somehow instead of somewhat which commands
> 'Lie not'?"[84]

The mendacious intrepidity of this man is the third casing of brass, the element that awes man; for man hesitates to affront God with lies as a rule, and it is nature's simple instinct to speak truth and walk straight upon the whole. This man has some power to which we are strangers. And this, says Browning, is

> Exact the thing I call
> Man's despot, just the Supernatural
> Which, George, was wholly out of—far beyond
> Your theory and practice.[85]

Disraeli has the great secret of political psychology, which was far beyond the grasp of Dodington. The eighteenth-century statesman had studied in the old school of simple lying. Both school and lie are obsolete now. Disraeli falls back

[84] *With George Bubb Dodington,* ll. 296-305.
[85] *Idem,* ll. 309-312.

on a still working pretext in his lying. He uses such falsities
as

> "Hearth and Home,
> The Altar, love of England, hate of Rome"—
> That's serviceable lying . . .[86]

Such lies as these would have screened Dodington decently.
But the wary statesman has to be ever on his guard, for the
dupes of the statesmen, the people, advance in perspicacity,
and in the course of time they will see through the subtle lies
just as they saw through the simple ones. They will discover
the greed and the selfishness at the source of the lies. Then,

> . . . last resource
> Should be to what but—exquisite disguise
> Disguise-abjuring, truth that looks like lies,
> Frankness so sure to meet with unbelief?
> Say—you hold in contempt—not them in chief—
> But first and foremost your own self! No use
> In men but to make sport for you, induce
> The puppets now to dance, now stand stockstill,
> Now knock their heads together, at your will
> For will's sake only—while each plays his part
> Submissive: why? through terror at the heart:
> "Can it be—this bold man, whose hand we saw
> Openly pull wires, obeys some law
> Quite above Man's—nay, God's? On face fall they.
> This was the secret missed, again I say,
> Out of your power to grasp conception of,
> Much less employ to purpose. Hence the scoff
> That greets your very name: folk see but one
> Fool more, as well as knave, in Dodington.[87]

[86] Browning is probably attacking Disraeli for his well-known ability as
a phrase-maker. These are slogans used by Disraeli in several political
campaigns. The first was used in the Corn Laws debates and in his Labor
reforms of 1874-1875. See Monypenny and Buckle, *Life of Disraeli*, V,
Chap. X. Disraeli made great political capital out of the religious disputes
that arose in the 'sixties. He posed on several occasions as the "Protestant
Hero," and one remembers his phrase "to put down ritualism." See *The
Life of Disraeli*, III, 267, 271, 545; IV, Chap. X; V, 58-59, 205, 315, 321 ff.
[87] *With George Bubb Dodington*, ll. 327-345.

Thus ends the piece of long-drawn-out irony. Dodington has had his lesson in practical politics from Disraeli, and the nineteenth-century statesman has become chief knave in Browning's gallery of rogues.

CHAPTER V

THE PARLEYING WITH FRANCIS FURINI

I

THE *Parleying With Francis Furini*, the Italian painter-priest of the first half of the seventeenth century, is unique among the *Parleyings*. Furini alone of all the men with whom Browning parleyed is not one "whose works connect themselves with the intellectual sympathies and the imaginative pleasures of his very earliest youth."[1] Indeed, it is to be doubted if the paintings of Francis Furini had any real effect upon the mind of Robert Browning at any time during his life. In the Dulwich Gallery, the favorite haunt of Browning's youth, where he first became acquainted with the paintings of Gerard de Lairesse, there were no pictures by the Tuscan priest. Browning may have become acquainted with the name and nature of Furini from the brief account of him given in Pilkington's *Dictionary of Painters*,[2] a book that seems to have been much read in the library in Southampton Street, but it is almost certain that he saw no pictures by the obscure Furini until his long residence in Florence in the years 1847-1855. In these years he visited assiduously the many galleries and churches about Florence, and it is there that most of the pictures by Furini were.[3]

Again in contrast to the other men with whom Browning parleyed, Furini wrote nothing. The poet was able to know the others at first hand. His knowledge of Furini, however, seems to have come to him entirely through Filippo Baldi-

---

[1] Orr, *Handbook*, p. 339.

[2] Browning used the edition of 1805, corrected and revised by Fuseli; see Griffin and Minchin, p. 15, note 1.

[3] A few of Furini's paintings were in Paris, but most of them were in the hands of Roman and Florentine nobles, and were rather inaccessible. See the account of Furini's paintings in Baldinucci, *Delle Notizie De' Professori del Disegno da Cimabue in Qua,* Edizione accresciuta di Annotizioni, in Firenze, 1767-1774, 20 vols., XVI, 3-22; especially pp. 5-10, 20-22.

nucci's *Delle Notizie De' Professori del Disegno da Cimabue in Qua,*[4] a compilation of the lives of Italian painters arranged chronologically. This work he seems to have had steadily by him after his first acquaintance with it in Florence. While Browning refers to the actual pictures by Furini and speaks of them as if he had seen them, Baldinucci's account of the life of the Tuscan painter, whom he knew in person, is avowedly his source of information and his only one. The *Parleying,* as we shall see, really rises from Browning's refusal to accept Baldinucci's interpretation of Furini's character, so that in a sense it becomes a parleying with Filippo Baldinucci.

Since, then, Furini is not only a later acquaintance of Browning's but also an indirect one, we need not be surprised to find that his influence upon the poet is in no way comparable to that of such men as Gerard de Lairesse or Christopher Smart. Furini, indeed, is really little more than a vehicle by which Browning expresses his mature opinions upon the subjects of Darwinian Evolution and the nude in art. Both of these subjects were pertinent questions in the year 1887. I believe that Browning deliberately chose Furini as the subject of a *Parleying* because as both painter and priest he could be made to strike at the enemies of the poet's beliefs in art and in philosophy. Therefore, we may dismiss Furini for the present and turn our attention where it is sorely needed, to Filippo Baldinucci and his compendious *Delle Notizie De' Professori del Disegno.* Little or no attention has been paid to this work hitherto; partly, I suppose, because it has not been translated out of the Italian, and partly because Vasari has occupied the attention of critics as Browning's source-book in art. Yet, as we shall see, the *Notizie* exercised considerable influence upon Browning from the year 1847 to the end of his life.

The nine-year residence of the Brownings in Italy, chiefly

---

[4] Baldinucci was publishing his *Notizie,* 1681-1728. I quote from the edition referred to in note 3.

in Florence, was given over passionately to the study of art. Browning, we learn from the letters of Mrs. Browning to her friends, haunted the galleries and churches of Florence.[5] She records how he found the old paintings of Giotto, Ghirlandajo, Cimabue, in the year 1850,[6] an event which he celebrated himself in *Old Pictures in Florence*. But it is of more importance for us that in these years when he was seeing all the Florentine paintings he was assiduously studying Vasari's *Le Vite Pittori* and Baldinucci's *Notizie*. In all probability he bought Vasari's work on first coming to Florence, for the copy of Vasari offered for sale by Sotheby on the dissolution of Browning's library in 1913[7] bears the inscription in Browning's hand "Florence 1846-1857." A letter, too, from Mrs. Browning to Horne in 1847 proves this: "We live here in the most secluded manner, eschewing English visitors, and reading Vasari, and dreaming dreams of seeing Venice in the summer."[8] We should know Browning's indebtedness in any case from the frank avowal in *Old Pictures in Florence*, and even better from the use he made of Vasari in *Fra Lippo Lippi* and *Andrea del Sarto*.[9] All this study came to an amazing flowering in *Men and Women* in 1855, and we are prone to agree with Browning when he says:

> But at any rate I have loved the season
>> Of Art's spring-birth so dim and dewy;
> My sculptor is Nicolo the Pisan,
>> My painter—who but Cimabue?
> Nor ever was man of them all indeed,
>> From these to Ghiberti and Ghirlandajo,
> Could say that he missed my critic-meed,
>> So, now to my special grievance—heigh-ho![10]

5 See *Letters of E. B. B.*, I, 326, 355, 365, etc.
6 See *idem*, p. 448.
7 Sotheby, *Catalogue*, item no. 1182.
8 Cooke, p. 218.
9 The best account of Browning's indebtedness to Vasari is to be found in Cooke, pp. 11-13, 144-148, 218 ff.
10 *Old Pictures in Florence*, ll. 177-184.

It has been commonly assumed that Vasari was at this period Browning's only guide-book in matters of painting and painters. Undeniably Vasari was the chief source of reference for the poet's study. But to an extent which has not hitherto been realized, Browning was in these years using the *Notizie* of Baldinucci to verify and supplement the more colorful accounts of Vasari. In 1866 in writing to Edward Dowden he acknowledged an indebtedness which was then at least eighteen years old.[11] The first acknowledgment of Baldinucci in the poems did not come until 1876 with *Filippo Baldinucci on the Privilege of Burial*. Commentators upon the poems of Browning have of course realized the influence of Baldinucci upon Browning after 1876. None, however, has seen the significance of Baldinucci for Browning before that date. Therefore it becomes necessary to trace at some length Browning's use of Baldinucci, especially between the years 1847-1866, and to define Browning's attitude toward Baldinucci, in order that we may understand his treatment of him in the *Parleying With Francis Furini*.

Browning's letter to Dowden (1866) shows that Browning has relied on the *Notizie* in his study of Fra Lippo Lippi:

But here I get up from my knee and assure you there is no slip in the other case; at least, I was wide awake when I made Fra Lippo the elder practitioner of Art [than Masaccio], if not, as I believe, the earlier born. I looked into the matter carefully long ago, and long before I thought of my own poem, from my interest in the Brancacci frescoes, indeed in all early Florentine Art. I believe the strange confusions and mistakes of Vasari are set tolerably right now: you may know, he took Lippino the son for Lippo the father. I suppose Lippo to have been born, as Baldinucci says, about 1400 . . .[12]

I grant readily that Browning followed Vasari's account for the greater part of his poem; for the character of Fra Lippo

---

[11] See *Letters from R. B. to Various Correspondents*, 2d Series, I, 18.
[12] *Ibid.*

and the incidents of the poem are most of them from *Le Vite
Pittore*. But a careful comparison of *Fra Lippo Lippi* and
the *Notizie* shows that Browning was indebted to Baldinucci
for several important details. In making "hulking Tom,"
who is of course Masaccio, the disciple and not the master of
Lippo, Browning broke with Vasari, and to set other strange
confusions and mistakes of that author right he resorted to
Baldinucci, who in his life of Fra Lippo Lippi had gone over
the same ground to a different result:

Il Vasari nella prima edizione della vita di questo artefice data
in luce del 1550. afferma che egli morisse di anni sessantasette
l'anno 1438, e così sarebbe stato il suo natale l'anno 1371. e
nella seconda edizione del 1568. dice ch' egli morisse di anni 57.
del 1438. e così sarebbe nato del 1381. Scrive poi che questi da-
tosi a studiare le opere fatte da Masaccio nella Capella de'
Brancacci nel Carmine di Firenze, si facesse valente pittore: e
che giunto all' età di anni diciasette, invanito per le lodi di ogni
persona, lasciato l'abito della Religione si ponesse a operare da
se. In tali supposti prese il Vasari, o lo Stampatore della sua
storia notibile errori . . .[13]

And in setting right the dates of Lippo's birth and achievements Baldinucci draws attention to a detail of the painter's
picture of S. Ambrogio di Firenze which Browning is quick
to use in his poem:

Premieramente non si può dubitare che Fra Filippo non arri-
vasse se non all' età di sessantasette anni, come dice il Vasari
nella prima edizione, almeno alli cinquantasette, per le ragioni
da dirsi: ed anche perchè il ritratto di detto Fra Filippo, che
di sua propria mano si vedo nella sua tavola di S. Ambrogio
di Firenze,[14] lo mostra di non punto minore età. Ma nasce ben
contradizione nell' esaminarsi i tempi del natale, e della morte
sua. Masaccio, secondo quello che erroneamente dici il Vasari,
nacque l'anno 1417. e morì nel 1443. onde dentro a questo tempo,

---

[13] *Notizie*, III, 212-213.
[14] Browning in his poem tells how Lippi put below his own picture in his
great painting the words: *"Iste perfecit opus!"* Baldinucci proves pretty
conclusively that S. Ambrogio was painted in 1447; see *Notizie*, III, 214-215.

e forse all' ultimo, furono fatte le opere della Capella de' Brancacci. Non pote dunque Fra Filippo dell' anno 1388. stando
alla prima, e dell' anno 1398. stando alla seconda edizione della
storia, ne' quali respetivi tempi egli compì il diciassettesimo
anno della sua età, avere studiate le opere di Masaccio, che poi
secondo il Vasari stette o 29, o almeno 19. anni a venire al
mondo; ma perchè e l'autorità del Vasari come pratico professor di pittura, e la maniera medesima di Fra Filippo fanno credere che veramente egli uscisse della scuola di Masaccio, bi-
sogna concludere, che non nascesse altrimenti nè del 1371. nè
del 1381. ma che fosse contemporaneo in tutto e per tutto del
medesimo Masaccio; che egli imparasse l'arte de lui; e che fosse
il suo natale circa all' anno 1400. e che ciò sia la verità, e non
opinione, vedasi da questo.[15]

But in spite of all the evidence that he had amassed Baldinucci would not change the tradition that said that Masaccio
was the master of Lippo, and presently we find that Lippo
was put "di studiar le bellissime opere, conche Masaccio
aveva abbellita la Capella de' Brancacci posta nella lor
Chiesa,"[16] and it is left to Browning to make the next step
and declare that "hulking Tom," Masaccio, was the pupil of
Fra Lippo Lippi. Two other details in Baldinucci's account
of the life of Fra Lippo Lippi seem to have impressed
Browning. The first of these is that Lippi was put into the
Carmine monastery by his aunt Lapaccia when he was eight
years old.[17] The other is the fact that Lippi was one of the
first of the psychologically realistic painters:

. . . perchè nelle stesse sue opere si scorge un giudizio parti-
colarissimo, ed una singolare industria, ch' egli ebbe sempre in
ciò che appartiene all' espressione, non pure delle azioni, ma

15 *Notizie*, III, 213-214.
16 *Notizie*, III, 217. Baldinucci, as it turns out, was wise not to commit
himself further. Browning's contention that Masaccio was the pupil of Fra
Lippo Lippi is generally not believed. Lippo was a disciple of Masaccio,
though Vasari's dates are sadly awry. Baldinucci merely concludes: "Con-
cludasi dunque, che Fra Filippo della scuola di Masaccio nascesse circa i
tempi del natale del medesimo Masaccio, cioè circa il 1400 . . ." p. 216.
17 See *idem*, p. 217.

degli affetti eziandio delle figure rappresentate: qualità che non
già ne dozzinali artefici, ma in quelli solamente si ravvisa, che
già dopo molto lungo studio, a lungo operare si son fatti all'
arte medesima superiori.[18]

The psychological realism of Fra Lippo Lippi's paintings is
much more stressed in Baldinucci than in Vasari. It is interesting to observe in this connection that the passage on realism in Browning's poem has usually been thought to be his
personal contribution to the criticism of Fra Lippo Lippi's
art. But it is possible that Browning developed from Baldinucci's words the following passage on the painter's belief in
realism as the highest expression of art, a passage which as-
sumes a most prominent place in the poem:

> You be judge!
> You speak no Latin more than I, belike;
> However, you're my man, you've seen the world
> —The beauty and the wonder and the power,
> The shapes of things, their colors, lights and shades,
> Changes, surprises,—and God made it all!
> —For what? Do you feel thankful, ay or no,
> For this fair town's face, yonder river's line,
> The mountain round it and the sky above,
> Much more the figures of man, woman, child,
> These are the frame to? What's it all about?
> To be passed over, despised? or dwelt upon,
> Wondered at? oh, this last of course!—you say.
> But why not do as well as say,—paint these
> Just as they are, careless what comes of it?
> God's works—paint any one, and count it crime
> To let a truth slip.[19]

But the influence of the *Notizie* is not confined to this one
poem. *Andrea del Sarto* and *Old Pictures in Florence*, which
are also in *Men and Women* (1855), show the same kind of
influence. Baldinucci takes Vasari's account of the life of

18 *Notizie*, III, 220.
19 *Fra Lippo Lippi*, ll. 280-296.

Andrea del Sarto as his working material. The interest in the *Notizie* lies then in the additions, corrections, and in the emphasis which Baldinucci brings to his work. It is significant indeed that his account should lay so much emphasis upon the greatness and failure of Andrea, but it is no more significant than that he and Browning should give the same causes for that failure. Vasari, to be sure, gives the same causes, but he merely mentions them, and does not dwell upon them in the emphatic manner of Baldinucci. Of particular interest then is Baldinucci's summary of the nature of Andrea del Sarto:

Siccome bene spesso suole avvenire, che gli uomini dotari dalla Natura di grand' animo tuttochè mediocremente instruiti ne' lor mestieri, ponendosi a far gran cose in esse talmente si portino, che in fine ne traggano alcuna lode; cosi all' incontro s' offervera che quelli, che tal dono non posseggono, quantunque di chiaro intelletto e di profondo giudizio siano, con cui possono operar miracoli nell' arte loro; contuttociò *con una certa falsa umilità sempre di se medesimi troppo diffidando*, con non poco danno del mondo e di se stessi lasciano di mettersi a que' cimenti, ne' quali potrebbono *senz' alcun fallo* pervenire a gradi di pregio impareggiabile. Tale appunto fu a mio parere il per altro non mai abbastanza celebrato Andrea del Sarto, gloria de' pennelli Fiorentini: il quale contendandosi di essere arrivato al non plus ultra in tutto quello, che e' volle fare nell' esercizio dell' arte della pittura, a cagione di quanto io dissi, *lasciò di fare in benefizio ed esaltazione di se stesso*, quel molto più che far poteva.[20]

Here, in brief, is Browning's complete conception of "the faultless painter"—at least, of his mind and his art. But Baldinucci is not content to say his mind once and go on. He takes every opportunity to say almost precisely what Browning was to say in his poem a hundred and seventy years later:

Merita questo grand' uomo lode immortale, non solo per essere

20 *Notizie*, IV, 185. The italics are my own.

stato nell' arte della pittura uno de' più sublimi artefici, che
abbia avuto il mondo; ma per la gren prestezza e facilità ch'
egli ebbe nell' operare, con un gusto si perfetto, che si può dire,
col parere de' primi maestri, che nell' infinite opere che e' fece,
non sia chi sappia trovare un errore.[21]

The likeness of this to Browning's estimate of Andrea is at
once apparent and startling.

The idea fascinated Baldinucci. He constantly recurred to
his explanation of Andrea's failure to attain the highest
rank with Raphael, Angelo and Leonardo da Vinci.[22] We
must pick up a few loose details which Browning uses in his
poem, and which are particularly emphasized in Baldinucci's
account. In very short space we get several important ones—
Andrea's manner of living from hand to mouth, and of sell-
ing his pictures for little or nothing, his great work at the
court of Francis I of France, his treachery to that monarch,
and the baneful influence of Lucrezia del Fede, his wife. Baldinucci's account of these things follows:

Fino a questo tempo aveva Andrea atteso ad arricchire il
mondo coll' opere sue di tesoro inestimabile; ma per esser' egli,
come si è accennato da principio, persona tanto timida e di
poco animo, aveva se medesimo tuttavia mantenuto in istato di
povertà, posciachè poco o nulla si faceva pagare i suio lavori;
quando se gli porse occasione di avvantaggiarsi nel posto di
gloria e di fortuna. Tale fu l' esser' egli stato chiamato al proprio servizio dal Re Francesco I. Vi andò Andrea, conducendo
seco Andrea Sguazzilla suo discepolo: e avendo in quel luogo
fatte opere maravigliose per quella Maestà, fu dalla medesima
largamente ricompensato: e avendo il Re conosciuta, non tanto
l' eccellenza de' suoi lavori, quanto la gran pratica, ch' egli
aveva nel maneggiate il pennello, e per l'ottima natura sua, che
sapeva tanto bene accomodarsi ad ogni cosa, posegli tanto
amore, che con doni e con promesse fece ogni opera per fermarlo
quivi al suo servizio: dove al certo sarebbe egli in breve arrivato
a gradi onoratissimi, e ricchissimo diventato, s' egli fosse stato

più uomo di quel che e' fu; perchè non andò molto, che gli furon date alcune lettere, scrittegli di Firenze dalla Lucrezia del Fede sua moglie, della quale (che bellissima era oltre ogni credere) andava egli tanto perduto, con esserne ancora molto geleso, che ella lo guidava a suo talento; onde subito prese licenza dal Re, con promessa di tornare fra certo tempo, e là condurre la moglie, per poter con più quiete attendere all' opere sue. Avuta licenza dal Re con buona somma di dinaro pel viaggio, se ne tornò a Firenze, dove stato parecci mesi spendendo, e nulla nell' arte facendo, diede .fine a' suoi danari. Lasciò passare il tempo, ordinato dal Re pel suo ritorno alla Corte, perchè la donna sua, alla quale più primeva far le comari coll' amiche e colle vicine, di quel che le importasse la necessità del marito, e l' impegno preso col Re; fece tanto colle lagrime e colle preghiere, che che in fine lo condusse a non uscir di Firenze, senza far conto della parola data a quel Monarca, del quale perciò cadde in tanta disgrazia, che maipiù non ne volle sentir parlare: e cosi rimasesi Andrea nella sua solita povertà.[23]

Though Browning, as we know,[24] used Vasari as a source for his poem, there are too many details suggestive of Browning's treatment in the passage from Baldinucci quoted above, for it to be ignored longer.

For *Old Pictures in Florence*, which also came out in *Men and Women*, Browning must have used the *Notizie* somewhat. It is significant, perhaps, that the same volume of the *Notizie* which gives the account of Andrea also contains the lives of Antonio del Pollaiuolo, Domenico del Ghirlandajo, Giovanni Bellini, Rafaello da Urbino, Jacopo Pacchiarotto, Pietro Perugino, Sandro Botticelli, Jacopo Razzi (Bazzi), Domenico Beccafumi—all of whom appear once or many times in Browning. Lorenzo Ghiberti, a favorite of Browning's, appears in the third volume of the *Notizie* with Fra Lippo Lippi and Masaccio.

But in spite of the influence which the *Notizie* seems to have exercised upon Browning, Baldinucci is not acknowl-

---

23 *Notizie*, IV, 193-194.
24 See *Andrea del Sarto*, ll. 106 ff.

edged in the poems themselves until the *Pacchiarotto* volume of 1876. Here the historian of Italian painting appears by name in two poems, *Pacchiarotto and How He Worked in Distemper*, the poem which gives title to the book and moral lesson to the poet's critics; and more particularly the last poem of the volume save the *Epilogue, Filippo Baldinucci on the Privilege of Burial*.

Baldinucci's account of Pacchiarotto is brief, and evidently is not the main source of the poet's information. Yet there is one incident in Pacchiarotto's life which Baldinucci seems to have called to Browning's attention. Vasari gives the same incident, but gives no such prominence and vividness to it as do both Browning and Baldinucci. The *Notizie* says:

Nella parte 3. della Storia di Siena del Cav. Gio. Antonio Pecci, ora passato all' altra vita, si narra, che questo dipintore essendosi intromesso con alcuni suoi compagni nelle fazioni popolari, che l'anno 1535. regnavano in quella Città, per timore di non cadere nelle mani del Bargello si nascose in una sepoltura della Pieve di S. Gio. Batista, dov' era stato sepolto di pochi giorni un cadavero, e standovi una notte, e un giorno intero, nel trarsene fuori si trovò il capo, e la barba piena di vermini.[25]

And it will be remembered that in the same volume of the *Notizie* are the accounts of Beccafumi and Razzi (Bazzi), painters who appear in Browning's poem as rivals to Pacchiarotto.

In *Filippo Baldinucci on the Privilege of Burial* the author of the *Notizie* is the only source. Browning gives the story, save for the characteristic twist at the end where the young Jew comes back for his revenge, almost as Baldinucci tells it in the life of the painter Buti.[26] Of course Browning heightens the unconscious self-satire to suit his purposes in

[25] *Notizie*, IV, 236, note. Compare *Pacchiarotto* . . ., especially ll. 296-344.

[26] *Notizie*, X, 35-41.

the poem. But since the sources of this poem have been adequately treated by Cooke[27] and others, there is no need for us to pause. It is enough to note that Baldinucci comes in this poem into his proper prominence as one of Browning's chief source-books in matters of art.

On two other occasions in Browning's poetry does Filippo Baldinucci appear. The first of these is, of course, in the *Parleying With Francis Furini*, of which I shall speak at length later. The other is in the poem *Beatrice Signorini*, which was published in the *Asolando* volume of 1889. In this poem Baldinucci is again called by name and mentioned as the source of the tale. It is perhaps enough to say that Browning uses the biographies of two painters, Giovanni Francesco Romanelli and Artemisia Genteleschi, almost implicitly for his story.[28] An adequate treatment of Browning's indebtedness to Baldinucci for this particular poem may be found in Cooke,[29] so we need dwell no longer upon it.

One would suppose that Browning would be grateful to the man who had helped him to write *Fra Lippo Lippi*, *Andrea del Sarto*, *Old Pictures in Florence*, *Pacchiarotto*, *Filippo Baldinucci on the Privilege of Burial*, *Francis Furini*, and *Beatrice Signorini*, and who besides this must have given him much of his great information concerning painters and paintings. But he was not. Browning despised Baldinucci; perhaps rightfully so. At every opportunity the historian is described as "blockhead Baldinucci," and "mild moral-monger," and "scruple-splitting, sickly-sensitive" Baldinucci. This is Browning's characteristic attitude toward Baldinucci, especially from 1876 on. In that year Browning had taken exception to Baldinucci's narrow hatred of the Jews, satirizing him with considerable bitterness:

27 Cooke, pp. 139-141.
28 Compare *Notizie*, XII, 3-13, especially pp. 11-13. Also XVIII, 204-230.
29 Cooke, pp. 47-50.

"No, boy, you must not pelt a Jew!
O Lord, how long? How long, O Lord?"[30]

In *Francis Furini* and *Beatrice Signorini* Browning reveals
a hatred of the historian's prudish attitude toward nude
paintings:

If you see Florence, pay that piece your vows
Though blockhead Baldinucci's mind, imbued
With monkish morals, bade folk "Drape the nude
And stop the scandal!"[31]

And indeed the narrowness and littleness of the historian's
mind may be found in almost any page of his *Notizie*. But the
poet is hardly right, I think, when in defending himself for
calling the chief Jew a High Priest instead of a Rabbi in
Filippo Baldinucci on the Privilege of Burial he calls Baldinucci "a typically ignorant Tuscan."[32]

But Browning's vituperation of Baldinucci reached its
crescendo pitch in the *Parleying With Francis Furini*. Baldinucci in the course of his twenty-two-page biography of
Furini had condemned the painter many times. His chief
complaint was Furini's predilection for the feminine nude.[33]
But he attacked him also for using such costly and brilliant
colors,[34] complained of the cost of paints necessary to depict
flesh,[35] cried out against Furini's use of young girls as
models,[36]—expenses which made Furini die in debt. He even
intimated that Furini's predilection for the feminine nude

---

[30] *Filippo Baldinucci on the Privilege of Burial*, ll. 463-464.
[31] *Beatrice Signorini*, ll. 20-23.
[32] See *Letters from R. B. to Various Correspondents*, 2d Series, II, 61.
In spite of Browning's protest that he got the High Priest from the "typically ignorant Tuscan" Baldinucci, the *Notizie* calls the chief Jew "Rab-
bini."
[33] See *Notizie*, XVI, 19-20; also pp. 5-6, 10.
[34] See *idem*, pp. 10, 19-20.
[35] See *ibid*.
[36] See *idem*, pp. 19-20.

was a mask to cloak lasciviousness.[37] Baldinucci, says Browning, thinks all men filthy-minded because he himself is so:

> Nay, I mistake not: wrath that's but lukewarm
> Would boil indeed were such a critic styled
> Himself an artist:[38] artist! Ossa piled
> Topping Olympus—the absurd which crowns
> The extravagant—whereat one laughs, not frowns.
> Paints he? One bids the poor pretender take
> His sorry self, a trouble and disgrace,
> From out the sacred presence, void the place
> Artists claim only. What—not merely wake
> Our pity that suppressed concupiscence—
> A satyr masked as matron—makes pretence
> To the coarse blue-fly's instinct—can perceive
> No better reason why she should exist—
> —God's lily-limbed and blush-rose-bosomed Eve—[39]
> Than as a hot-bed for the sensualist
> To fly-blow with his fancies, make pure stuff
> Breed him back filth—this were not crime enough?
> But further—fly to style itself—nay more—
> To steal among the sacred ones, crouch down
> Though but to where their garments sweep the floor—
> —Still catching some faint sparkle from the crown
> Crowning transcendent Michael, Leonard,
> Rafael,—to sit beside the feet of such,
> Unspurned because unnoticed, then reward
> Their toleration—mercy overmuch—
> By stealing from the throne-step to the fools
> Curious outside the gateway, all a-gape
> To learn by what procedure in the schools
> Of Art, a merest man in outward shape
> May learn to be Correggio![40]

Truly an amazing vituperation! How could one so long dead, and one so mild and small as Baldinucci have evoked

[37] See *Notizie,* XVI, 19-20.

[38] Baldinucci was a painter and styled himself "Accademico Della Crusca," member of the Florentine academy, on his title-page.

[39] A favorite subject with Furini; see *Notizie,* XVI, 6, 7, 16.

[40] *With Francis Furini,* ll. 144-173.

this storm? Furthermore, Baldinucci had some justification
for his adverse criticism, for Furini seems to have sought
particularly subjects which would not only allow the painting of the flesh, but which would also lend themselves to lascivious treatment; for example, Cleopatra, Lot with his
Daughters,—a subject which he treated several times,—
Adam and Eve, Rachel, the Muses, Bacchantes.[41] Furini's
repentance and his dying command that his lascivious pictures be burnt[42] lend color to Baldinucci's view. But after
all, neither hatred of a scrupulous moral-splitting hypocrite
of an age long dead, nor love of a wronged Italian painter
long dead too, inspired this mountain of wrath.

The fact of the matter is that Robert Browning is here defending his son, Robert Wiedemann Barrett Browning, an
artist who, like Furini, had a predilection for the feminine
nude in his paintings, and who also had *his* critic, John Callcot Horsley, treasurer of the Royal Academy during the
years 1882-1897. Read closely, the gigantic vituperation in
the long passage quoted above is seen to be directed definitely against him. Truly it is much more applicable to Horsley than it is to Baldinucci. If we read the names of modern
British painters—Leighton and Watts—into the passage in
place of Rafael and Michael Angelo,[43] the case is complete.

For Horsley, a member of the Royal Academy, patron of
Burlington House, styled himself painter, though in 1887 he
had been long out of fashion. He has his perfect parallel in
the Florentine academician and historian of art. He, too, as
did Baldinucci, crept among the great. He was unofficial
publicist for the Academy in his lifetime, and before his
death was to write his "Recollections." Above all, as we shall
see, he shared Baldinucci's aversion for the feminine nude.
The likeness between these "mild moral-mongers" of Flor-

41 See *Notizie,* XVI, 13-15.
42 See *idem,* pp. 17-18.
43 Browning has openly made this comparison elsewhere in the *Parleyings.* See *With Christopher Smart,* ll. 90-91; quoted above, p. 128.

ence and London came home to Browning with a crash when
the attack was made against his own son. Browning was
never able to bear patiently an attack which touched him
personally, as his notorious sonnet upon Edward Fitzgerald
shows. His invective against Horsley here is another case in
point.

Arthur Symons seems to have been the only critic who sus-
pected that Browning was attacking Horsley.[44] But the case
can be proved to the hilt by an appeal to the events of the
years 1884-1886, if further proof is required than the vehemence of Browning's attack. From the year 1884 onward
the younger Browning exhibited pictures almost every year
in the Royal Academy, the Grosvenor Gallery, and the Paris
Salon. These pictures, the subjects of which were often suggested by his father, the poet,[45] were like Furini's given over
to a study of the nude. One has only to scan the titles of a
few of Pen Browning's pictures to see their character:

Joan of Arc and the Kingfisher[46] (Joan about to bathe).
After the Bath, a nude figure standing, one knee on a couch
covered with a tiger skin, R. B. B. 1887.[47]
A Faun playing Pipe to two Nymphs by a River, nude figures,
1884.[48]
Landscape with Hilly Background, river in middle distance.
Five female nude figures are bathing.[49]
Diana, nude female figure.[50]

[44] See *Browning Society Papers*, London, II, 169-179; *Some Notes on
Mr. Browning's Latest Volume*, a paper delivered on Friday, April 29,
1887. While observing that the attack concerned a contemporary, however,
Symons missed the general autobiographical character of the *Parleyings*.
[45] Sotheby, *Catalogue*, item no. 182, contains Browning's suggestions to
his son for a statue of Dryope, and indicates clearly that such suggestions
were his habit.
[46] Sotheby, *Catalogue*, item no. 182, contains seven lines of verse by the
poet, which were placed below this picture when it was exhibited. For a discussion of these lines, and for a full description of the painting, see below,
pp. 209-211.
[47] Sotheby, *Catalogue*, item no. 29.
[48] *Idem*, item no. 34.
[49] *Idem*, item no. 30.
[50] *Idem*, item no. 37.

Water Lilies and Kingfisher (nude figures).[51]
Dolci far Niente, three nude females bathing.[52]
Dryope (a large bronze).[53]

It is the first of the pictures in the list that particularly concerns us here. It suffered much at the hands of the critics when it was exhibited at the Grosvenor Gallery in 1886. In the same year Browning, who followed with profound interest the fortunes of the various pictures by his son, complained in a letter to Furnivall:

I am ashamed at the objection taken by some of the critics to the Eve-like simplicity of Pen's peasant-girl, who before going on to saintliness (which the Church still withholds from her) was satisfied with the proverbially next step to it—cleanliness. If they knew anything of Joan's habits even when advanced in her saintly career, they would remember she was no prude by any means. Her favored young cavalier, the Duc d' Alençon, mentions that he had frequently seen her undress, and that "aliquando videbat ejus mammas quae pulchrae erant"—in his very words.[54]

The critics who attacked Pen Browning's pictures were led by John Callcot Horsley. He—who, by the way, was responsible to a large extent for the establishment of Burlington House—felt that the spirit of the Paris Salon was invading English art too boldly. He had in 1884 refused to exhibit at Burlington House the statue of Dryope, for which the elder Browning had given suggestions to his son,[55] and it was only upon the intercession of the elder Browning that the bronze was exhibited instead at the Grosvenor Gallery.[56] Horsley carried his objections to the nude in art before the

[51] Sotheby, *Catalogue*, item no. 44.
[52] *Idem*, item no. 74.
[53] *Idem*, item no. 1271. Browning suggested the subject and method of treatment for this statue to his son; see note 45 on preceding page. Browning himself may have got his ideas for Dryope from Gerard de Lairesse; see below, p. 230.
[54] *Letters from R. B. to Various Correspondents*, 1st Series, II, 55-56.
[55] See note 53.
[56] Sotheby, *Catalogue*, item no. 1271.

public in the next year. Above the curious signature of "A British Matron" there was launched[57] in the *Times* of May 20, 1885,[58] an abortive and violent attack against the nude in painting. Horsley seems to have been behind the whole assault. The complaint was that the British galleries were filled with immoral pictures. The letter was answered by "An English Girl." "An Englishwoman," "Senex," and others took up the battle. Finally Horsley appeared in his own person, and his letter of May 25, 1885, is at once the most specific and the longest of the amusing correspondence. Not only does he attack nudes in general, but he singles out definite pictures. Watts, Leighton, Calderon—all friends of the poet —and some few others are the offenders. In the course of the correspondence we learn that a society for the prevention of the paintings of nudes is in process of organization. Gradually, however, the cries die away and nothing more is heard.

That Browning followed the argument in the *Times* goes without saying.[59] Indeed, several echoes of the correspondence found their way into the *Parleying*. Browning's description of Baldinucci as "a satyr masked as matron"[60] must certainly refer to the signer of the letter, "A British Matron." The closing lines of the *Parleying*, too, "no harm is meant," serve as an ironic echo of the letters of May 20 and 21 in the *Times*. Besides these specific likenesses there are many intangible similarities to assure one that Browning had this odd correspondence very much in mind as he wrote the *Parleying*. Horsley, not Baldinucci, is the real object of the attack. That Browning is paying his son's score against the moral-mongering critic will appear still more definitely in the exegesis of the *Parleying*.[61]

[57] See *D. N. B.*, 2d Supplement, under *Horsley*. See also *With Francis Furini*, l. 154.
[58] The article in the *D. N. B.* gives this date erroneously as 2 May, 1885.
[59] The *Times* was read assiduously by Browning. See Griffin and Minchin, p. 290.
[60] *With Francis Furini*, l. 154. Browning seems to think this was Horsley.
[61] See below, pp. 210-211.

II

ALMOST every commentator who has deigned to notice at all the *Parleying With Francis Furini*, has called it, probably following Mrs. Orr,[62] a defence of painting in the nude, and has been quite content to stop there. Undoubtedly the poem is this. The defence of Furini's—and Pen Browning's—manner of painting is the most apparent object of the poem. But this is by no means all, or perhaps even the greater purport of the *Parleying*. Furini is a priest as well as a painter, and it is in his religious capacity that Browning makes most use of him throughout his poem. Because of Furini's double function Browning has some license for passing from the subject of painting to that of Darwinian Evolution. Put baldly the jump seems startling, but in the poem the philosophic problem seems to rise more naturally from the discussion of the nude in painting. Browning has been proving Furini "Good son, good brother, good priest, good painter,"[63] and damning Baldinucci as little-minded and filthy-souled. But suddenly he turns to Furini and commands him to pray, and Furini prays, giving thanks to God for the pure beauty of His works:

> "Bounteous God,
> Deviser and Dispenser of all gifts
> To soul through sense,—in Art the soul uplifts
> Man's best of thanks! What but Thy measuring-rod
> Meted forth heaven and earth? more intimate,
> Thy very hands were busied with the task
> Of making, in this human shape, a mask—
> A match for that divine. Shall love abate
> Man's wonder? Nowise! True—true—all too true—
> No gift but, in the very plenitude
> Of its perfection, goes maimed, misconstrued
> By wickedness or weakness: still, some few

62 Orr, *Handbook,* pp. 351 ff.
63 Browning has authority for these statements from the *Notizie,* XVI, 18-21.

> Have grace to see Thy purpose, strength to mar
> Thy work by no admixture of their own,
> —Limn truth not falsehood, bid us love alone
> The type untampered with, the naked star!"[64]

Indeed, a painter-priest may have prayed such a prayer in splendid justification of his art. But this is not Baldinucci's painter who treated the feminine nude in rather frank fashion, and then, repenting on his death-bed, begged that his pictures be burnt.

Browning has turned the subject to theology, and having got Furini to pray, his next step is to have him preach; and pat it comes like the villain in the old comedy. Furini begins to preach—not indeed as he would preach before his ignorant peasants in Mugello[65]—but (by Browning's invitation) as if he were expounding his views before a cultivated, and hence sceptical, London audience in the year 1887. There is little or no disguise. It is not Furini who is to preach, but Browning, and the sermon is on a text he has often used before. He is once more defining his position as opposed to that of the Evolutionists.

The poem takes up the argument where it was left in the *Parleying With Bernard de Mandeville*. There, it may be remembered, the poet was intent upon proving to the sceptical and pessimistic Carlyle that God was good, kind, all-loving. And he achieved this, to his own satisfaction, not through the medium of the intellect, which he was at great pains to discredit altogether, but through the medium of the feelings. Man instinctively revolts from evil and fights it, hardly knowing why. Browning builds his whole philosophy upon this moral consciousness in man. To him it is the diminutive sun in man which matches the great sun, which is God, outside. In *Furini* the argument takes a different turn

[64] *With Francis Furini*, ll. 232-247.

[65] After his reformation in 1640 at the age of forty Furini became a good and faithful priest at Santo Sano in Mugello. He held this position until his death in 1649. See *Notizie*, XVI, 10-11.

to somewhat the same end. Here the argument is definitely
against the Evolutionists and what Browning conceives to be
their manner of viewing life. It develops into a justification
of his own position in philosophical and metaphysical matters. It has here the virtue of being the most explicit statement in the poetry of the nineteenth century, concerning the
great contemporaneous revolution in thought brought on by
the Darwinian theory of Evolution.

Browning, after his boyish revolt from orthodoxy, spent
the larger part of his life in defending with really amazing
ingenuity the simple and uncritical faith which his mother
had taught him in his earliest days. In the *Parleying With
Francis Furini* he is making a last stand against the greatest
enemy of that faith, and he is making that stand with his
eyes shut. For that peculiar twist to the philosophy of
Browning's later years exhibits itself nowhere so plainly as
here. He has no trust in the intellect. The faculties of the
reason impeach his faith. Therefore he discounts the intellect
altogether. It is his last stand on the narrow rock in pitch
darkness before the sea ingulfs him. Knowledge is nothing to
Browning but

. . . conjecture manifold,
But, as knowledge, this comes only—things may be as I behold,
Or may not be, but, without me and above me, things there are;
I myself am what I know not—ignorance which proves no bar
To the knowledge that I am, and, since I am, can recognize
What to me is pain and pleasure: this is sure, the rest—sur-
    mise.
If my fellows are or are not, what may please them and what
    pain,—
Mere surmise: my own experience—that is knowledge, once
    again![66]

His knowledge, if it may be called such, is entirely subjective. Outside of him he feels there is a God who made him and

[66] *La Saisiaz*, ll. 257-264.

rules him. His own experience, he seems to say, has nothing
in common with the experiences of other men. His own experience is knowledge, but

> . . . all outside its narrow hem,
> Free surmise may sport and welcome! Pleasures, pains affect
>   mankind
> Just as they affect myself? Why, here's my neighbor color-
>   blind,
> Eyes like mine to all appearance: "green as grass" do I affirm?
> "Red as grass" he contradicts me:—which employs the proper
>   term?[67]

This would be ridiculous were the poet not in such dead earnest. Is each man's opinion a criterion? Is truth nothing more
than a majority of opinions? Certainly no universal laws
may be drawn from such a conception of truth. But Browning pushes his doctrine still further in *Furini:*

> All—for myself—seems ordered wise and well
> Inside it,—what reigns outside, who can tell?[68]

This is almost a nescience. Man, according to the poet, can
have no opinion of the world beyond his own experience:

> Ignorance overwraps his moral sense,
> Winds him about, relaxing, as it wraps,
> So much and no more than lets through perhaps
> The murmured knowledge—"Ignorance exists."[69]

It is easy to see that this theory of the worthlessness of human intelligence ends inevitably in absolute scepticism. All
ends in a blank darkness, which nothing can illumine.
Browning's reason for degrading the intellect is of course
that it impeaches what he wishes to believe. His purpose is to
elevate in dignity the testimony that his feelings bring, that

[67] *La Saisiaz,* ll. 272-276.
[68] *With Francis Furini,* ll. 519-520.
[69] *Idem,* ll. 345-348.

God is love and all is well with the world. And so the poet denies knowledge again:

> Thus much at least is clearly understood—
> Of power does Man possess no particle:
> Of knowledge—just so much as shows that still
> It ends in ignorance on every side:[70]

Yet Browning would not have the conditions different. They are perfect now for man's moral struggle uphill. If man knew anything certain either way—that God was or was not good—what would be the good of struggling against evil?

> Think!
> Could I see plain, be somehow certified
> All was illusion,—evil far and wide
> Was good disguised,—why, out with one huge wipe
> Goes knowledge from me. Type needs antitype:
> As night needs day, as shine needs shade, so good
> Needs evil: how were pity understood
> Unless by pain?[71]

But if God hangs an illusory evil before our eyes in order to make us struggle, it is very much like playing a grotesque joke upon mankind; or, to use again Jones' apt description of Browning's conception *de rerum natura*, "The world is a kind of moral gymnasium, crowded with phantoms, wherein by exercise man makes moral muscle."[72] And all this is in preparation for a contest which never happens. This building of moral muscle for no particular end, as I have said, is a characteristic conception of Browning's, and it explains as nothing else does such poems as *Childe Roland* and *How They Brought the Good News* . . .[73].

One may fairly wonder how the *Parleying*, which threat-

[70] *With Francis Furini*, ll. 281-284.
[71] *Idem*, ll. 479-486.
[72] Henry Jones, *Browning as a Philosophical and Religious Teacher*, Glasgow, 1902, p. 234.
[73] See above, p. 32.

ened at one moment to be another discussion of art, and at
another to be a tirade against Darwinian Evolution, has
wandered into these familiar metaphysical regions. But one
must remember with the later Browning that the desperate
struggle to hold to the faith of his early youth was apt to
pitch him headlong into metaphysics at any moment.

Once he felt the need of plunging into metaphysics his ingenuity was quick to find the means. In the *Parleying* chance
played into his hand, for turning over the account of Furini
in the *Notizie*, what caught his eye was the fact that the
painter had painted "una Andromeda per la Maestà dell
Imperadore,"[74] in which the daughter of Cepheus and Cas-
siopeia on her strip of rock awaits the sea-monster. The figure of Andromeda becomes the symbol of all of Browning's
beliefs. The picture of Andromeda which he has in his mind's
eye informs the whole poem. She, of course, is the feminine
nude. Further, as we shall see in a moment, she symbolizes in
herself Browning's philosophical attitude, both in general,
and in particular, toward the Evolutionists, and the presence of evil in the world. But I dare venture that it was not
Furini's *Andromeda* which the poet had in mind as he described her in the *Parleying*. It was rather the precious *Andromeda* of Polidoro di Caravaggio, a copy of which stood
always before him as he wrote his early poems, until his departure for Italy after his marriage.[75] It was this picture
which inspired the fine lines in *Pauline:*

Andromeda!
And she is with me: years roll, I shall change,
But change can touch her not—so beautiful
With her fixed eyes, earnest and still, and hair
Lifted and spread by the salt-sweeping breeze,
And one red beam, all the storm leaves in heaven,
Resting upon her eyes and hair, such hair,

[74] See *Notizie*, XVI, 7.
[75] See *Letters of R. B. and E. B. B.*, I, 28. See also Orr, *Handbook*, p.
21. It is perhaps worthy of notice that Browning's friend, Sir Frederick
Leighton, also painted an *Andromeda*.

As she awaits the snake on the wet beach
By the dark rock and the white wave just breaking
At her feet; *quite naked* and alone; a thing
I doubt not, nor fear for, *secure some god*
To save will come in thunder from the stars.[76]

Sharp describes the poet truly when he says: "The story of
the innocent victim and the divine deliverer was one of which
in his boyhood he never tired of hearing: and as he grew
older the charm of its pictorial presentment had for him a
deeper and more complex significance."[77] Browning was very
fortunate, then, to find that Furini had done an *Andromeda*
also.

In the *Parleying* the sea-monster and the wild confusion
of the waters seem to represent the forces of evil and ignorance respectively. Browning puts himself in the place of
Andromeda upon the rock-spit which represents to him the
consciousness of being:

Just here my solid standing-place amid
The wash and welter, whence all doubts are bid
Back to the ledge they break against in foam . . .[78]

All about is the pitch blackness of sheer ignorance:

All around
Ignorance wraps him,—whence and how and why
Things are,—yet cloud breaks and lets blink the sky
Just overhead, not elsewhere! What assures
His optics that the very blue which lures
Comes not of black outside it, doubly dense?[79]

Browning knows that he exists, and that something outside

[76] *Pauline*, ll. 656-667. The lines I have italicized in the passage quoted,
take on a deep significance in the light of Browning's treatment of the nude,
and his attitude toward faith, expressed in this *Parleying* a half-century
later.
[77] Sharp, p. 25.
[78] *With Francis Furini*, ll. 509-511.
[79] *Idem*, ll. 339-344.

of him which made him, exists. He calls the outside force
God. He has no experience in common with other strugglers:

> . . . how you fare,
> Caught in the whirlpool—that's the Cause's care,
> Strong, wise, good,—this I know at any rate
> In my own self,—but how may operate
> With you—strength, wisdom, goodness—no least blink
> Of knowledge breaks the darkness round me . . .[80]

He knows just one fact, his own consciousness, the narrow
ledge of knowledge between seas of ignorance, and from this
ledge he dares not stir one step:

> . . . soul's first act
> (Call consciousness the soul—some name we need)
> Getting itself aware, through stuff decreed
> Thereto (so call the body)—who has stept
> So far, there let him stand, become adept
> In body ere he shift his station thence
> One single hair's breadth.[81]

And again,

> There did I plant my first foot. And the next?
> Nowhere! 'T was put forth and withdrawn, perplexed
> At touch of what seemed stable and proved stuff
> Such as the colored clouds are . . .[82]

Such is Browning's position as he defines it in *Furini*. It
is the position of Andromeda on her rock as she awaits the
sea-beast. A prince-charming, Perseus, or God, will appear
in the nick of time. The outcome of the whole is the same as it
was for Browning. God is in his heaven, all-good, all-wise,
all-powerful; and evil in this earth is only illusion:

> . . . still wrong must needs seem wrong
> To do right's service, prove men weak or strong,
> Choosers of evil or good.[83]

[80] *With Francis Furini*, ll. 474-479.
[81] *Idem*, ll. 369-375.
[82] *Idem*, ll. 402-405.
[83] *Idem*, ll. 505-507.

It needs only to be added that the arguments Browning used
he had used many times before, and to better purpose. For
the influx of new ideas had changed the face of the whole
problem, and what Browning had to say no longer met the
issue. He who had once been a prophetic voice was now but
the voice of a bygone generation.

Browning had anticipated the theory of Evolution as early
as 1835. He was then well ahead of the thought of his age in
the philosophy of science. He had seen the intellectual necessity of believing in the ordered ranks of creation and in the
development of life. In *Paracelsus* he expressed this idea by
beginning with protoplasmic self-consciousness and looking
upward through long vistas of time to man.[84] The lines in
Paracelsus describing man read like a prophetic glimpse of
the theory of Evolution; for it was man

> Whose attributes had here and there
> Been scattered o'er the visible world before,
> Asking to be combined, dim fragments meant
> To be united in some wondrous whole,
> Imperfect qualities throughout creation,
> Suggesting some one creature yet to make,
> Some point where all those scattered rays should meet
> Convergent in the faculties of man . . .
> Hints and previsions of which faculties,
> Are strewn confusedly everywhere about
> The inferior natures, and all lead up higher,
> All shape out dimly the superior race,
> The heir of hopes too fair to turn out false,
> And man appears at last.[85]

To this conception of progress through all nature up to man
Browning held steadily—always, of course, with his charac-

[84] The idea is of course inherent to a certain extent in Paracelsus, but in
so far as Browning was indebted to anybody for the thoughts he expressed
at length, it was to Pope. The "progressive" view of Evolution is, of course,
Browning's interpretation of the relation between man and the animals.
[85] *Paracelsus,* V, 685-710.

teristic emphasis on the wondrous whole that was man. He
was to attribute the idea to Cleon, twenty years later:

> If, in the morning of philosophy,
> Ere aught had been recorded, nay perceived,
> Thou, with the light now in thee, couldst have looked
> On all earth's tenantry, from worm to bird,
> Ere man, her last, appeared upon the stage—
> Thou wouldst have seen them perfect, and deduced
> The perfectness of others yet unseen.[86]

Once more the idea that man is the last premeditated work,
and the greatest, is Browning's personal link between his
own philosophy of optimism and the theory of Evolution
that he has anticipated.

But when Evolution, as a scientific theory, was put before
the world, Browning seems not at once to show an interest in
it. He was in Italy at the time, and for eight years after his
return to London in 1861 he was deeply engrossed in *The
Ring and the Book*. When that was finished he turned to the
problem which was engrossing all England; and looking,
perhaps, for fresh matter for his thought, he plunged into
the recent works on the subject of Evolution. He read Darwin, and could scarcely have avoided the utterances of Huxley, Spencer, and Tyndall.

But as Browning read the accounts of Evolution written
from a scientific rather than a philosophical point of view, he
began to realize that the Evolutionists' conception of the
origin and nature of man scarcely agreed with his own. Instead of pointing with pride to the great spiritual advances
of mankind, the scientists of the 'seventies and 'eighties were
busily engaged in hunting out the debasing origins of things.
They seemed to Browning to be like Mammon gazing upon
the gold that paved the floor of Heaven. They were concerned with the least important of physical facts rather than
with the great spiritual implications of the new idea. They

[86] *Cleon*, ll. 187-193.

dwelt upon man's humble origin, and insisted upon the "ape-theory" and the "missing link." At least the popular gar-blers of Darwinism did so; and the leaders sought to find a satisfactory explanation of mankind in their study of the simplest and earliest forms of life.

In 1871, in *Prince Hohenstiel-Schwangau*, Browning's study of Evolution becomes evident in his poetry. He refers definitely to modern science,[87] and gives his own conception of the meaning of the ordered ranks of life:

> O you count the links,
> Descry no bar of the unbroken man?
> Yes,—and who welds a lump of ore, suppose
> He likes to make a chain and not a bar,
> And reach by link on link, link small, link large,
> Out to the due length—why, there's forethought still
> Outside o' the series, forging at one end,
> While at the other there's—no matter what
> The kind of critical intelligence
> Believing that last link had last but one
> For parent, and no link was, first of all,
> Fitted to anvil, hammered into shape.
> Else, I accept the doctrine, and deduce
> This duty, that I recognize mankind,
> In all its height and depth and length and breadth.[88]

But the significant thing is not so much that Browning re-veals that he has been reading modern science, as that he is here registering a disagreement with its findings. It takes no account, he says, of a creative intelligence outside the Evo-lutionary scheme of things; in all respects save that he ac-cepts the theory.

At still another point Browning was to disagree with the Evolutionists. The emphasis which they placed upon the purely physical origins of mankind left out of account the moral consciousness, which to Browning symbolized God in

[87] See *Prince Hohenstiel-Schwangau* . . ., l. 986.
[88] *Idem*, ll. 1042-1056.

man. This was of course the natural retreat for those who
found the evidence marshalled by Evolution intellectually
undeniable. Yet the scientists were to push the theory of
Evolution to that very ground of retreat. In the work of
Herbert Spencer and William Graham Sumner, and later in
the work of the psychologists led by William James, the
theory of Evolution was to be carried into the world of customs and *mores*. It is interesting that in this very advance
Browning had again anticipated the scientists. He had realized, recognizing man's relation to the animal world, that
the same theory of Evolution could be applied to man's
habits and morals. But such an explanation, though plau-
sible, failed utterly to convince him. Nothing short of kinship with divinity could really explain the nobility of man's
conception of virtue. And so Browning, in anticipating the
application of the theory of Evolution to the moral consciousness of man, was anticipating it only to contest its
validity. In 1855 he had written:

> Philosophers deduce you chastity
> Or shame, from just the fact that at the first
> Whoso embraced a woman in the field,
> Threw club down and forewent his brains beside,
> So, stood a ready victim in the reach
> Of any brother savage, club in hand;
> Hence saw the use of going out of sight
> In wood or cave to prosecute his loves . . .
> Does law so analyzed coerce you much?[89]

Law so analyzed could never explain, for Browning, the nobility of man's moral nature. This opinion was held un-
changed, to the end of his life, and it finds its most emphatic
expression in this *Parleying*, as we shall see later in the chapter.

As the theory of Evolution gained ground, greater and

[89] *Bishop Blougram's Apology*, ll. 825-834. The only clue to the identity
of the philosophers mentioned is the line, "I read this in a French book
t'other day," omitted from the quotation above.

greater claims were made for it. It threatened to invade the
realms of theology and philosophy. John Tyndall, for example, in the speech delivered in defence of science at Belfast
in 1874, asserted that the whole universe, material and spiritual, was the proper domain of science:

By an intellectual necessity I cross the boundary of the ex-
perimental evidence, and discern in that matter which we, in our
ignorance of its latent powers, and notwithstanding our professed reverence for its Creator, have hitherto covered with op-
probrium, the promise and potency of all terrestrial life . . .
We claim, and we shall wrest, from theology, the entire domain
of cosmological theory. All schemes and systems which thus in-
fringe upon the domain of science, must, *in so far as they do
this*, submit to its control, and relinquish all thought of con-
trolling it.[90]

When we compare this aggressive confidence in the powers
of the intellect to discover ultimate reality, with the poet's
almost absolute lack of faith in the powers of the human
mind, we see that these two men are at opposite poles of
thought.

This extending of the claims of science, and the fact that
as the century went on the popular conception of Evolution
tended more and more to stress the sensational aspects of the
theory, led Browning not only to break with the Evolutionists, but even to withdraw somewhat from his former position. Browning, indeed, was not alone in his shifting attitude
toward science. One remembers at once Tennyson's early
enthusiasm and consequent disappointment. Many literary
men of the age suffered a similar change in feeling. A letter
from Browning to Furnivall in 1881 will show better than
any analysis just what the poet's attitude toward Darwinism became. It will show too, I am afraid, how inadequate

[90] *The Belfast Address,* 1874, included in Tyndall's *Fragments of Science,* 5th ed., New York, 1883. This address is at once a justification and an
able summary of the state of science at that time. Tyndall was an eminent
scientist himself, a friend to Faraday, Huxley, and Spencer; and, after
Huxley, was perhaps the greatest champion of the discoveries of science.

was Browning's conception of Evolution at this late date compared to his grasp of its philosophical significance in 1835. The letter reads:

In reality, all that seems *proved* in Darwin's scheme was a conception familiar to me from the beginning: see in *Paracelsus* the progressive development from senseless matter to organized, until man's appearance (*Part* V). Also in *Cleon*, see the order of "life's mechanics,"—and I daresay in many passages of my poetry: for how can one look at Nature as a whole and doubt that, wherever there is a gap, a "link" must be "missing" —through the limited power and opportunity of the looker? But go back and back, as you please, *at* the back, as Mr. Sludge is made to insist, you find (*my* faith is as constant) creative intelligence, acting as matter but not resulting from it. Once set the balls rolling, and ball may hit ball and send any number in any direction over the table; but I believe in the cue pushed by a hand. When one is taunted (as I notice is often fancied an easy method with the un-Darwinized)—taunted with thinking successive acts of creation credible, metaphysics have been stopped short at, however physics may fare: time and space being purely conceptions of our own, wholly inapplicable to intelligence of another kind—with whom, as I made Luria say, there is an "everlasting moment of creation," if one at all, —past, present, and future, one and the same state. This consideration does not affect Darwinism proper in any degree. But I do not consider that his case as to the changes in organization, brought about by desire and will in the creature, proved. Tortoises never saw their own shells, top or bottom, nor those of their females, and are diversely variegated all over, each species after its own pattern. And the insects; this one is coloured to escape notice, this other to attract it, a third to frighten the foe—all out of one brood of caterpillars hatched in one day? No—I am incredulous—and *you*, dear patron and friend, are abundantly tired.[91]

It is clear from the foregoing quotation that while Browning goes a good way with the Evolutionists, he has little concep-

---

[91] *Letters from R. B. to Various Correspondents,* 1st Series, I, 83-85.

tion of what they mean by natural selection, or by time. He
scarcely comprehended the scientific expression of the very
theory he had anticipated.

His objections to Evolution, and his tendency to withdraw
from his own earlier position, grew as time went on. By
1887, when he wrote the *Parleyings*, he was almost militant
against the scientists. In *Mandeville* he was ready to deny
that one type of animal developed from another:

> Sun penetrates the ore, the plant—
> They feel and grow: perchance with subtler skill
> He interfuses fly, worm, brute, until
> Each favored object pays life's ministrant
> By pressing, in obedience to his will,
> Up to completion of the task prescribed,
> So stands and stays a type.[92]

The last words are the significant ones, if we are to understand Browning's reaction against Evolution. The purport
of them was to contradict the whole theory.

It is in the *Parleying With Francis Furini*, however, that
Browning expresses fully his objection to the theory. The
scientists are "levelling downward," to use a phrase of the
day: this is the essential difference between his point of view
and theirs. They saw ultimately the base origins of life;
Browning, looking upward, saw man reaching toward God.
Following his plan of showing wherein his ideas on pertinent
problems differ from those of eminent contemporaries,
Browning here points out that his manner of approaching
the problem of being is diametrically opposite to theirs:

> Evolutionists!
> At truth I glimpse from depths, you glance from heights,
> Our stations for discovery opposites,—
> How should ensue agreement? . . .[93]

Thus begins Browning's last dictum on Evolution, put—

92 *With Bernard de Mandeville*, ll. 236-242.
93 *With Francis Furini*, ll. 265-268.

quite without license, of course—into the mouth of the Italian painter-priest, Furini.

III

THE twenty-page biography of Furini in the *Notizie*[94] supplies Browning with all the information he needs for his *Par-*

[94] See *Notizie*, XVI, 1-20; esp. 18-20. While Browning used materials here and there from the whole twenty pages of the sketch of Furini's life, nevertheless he got most of his material concerning the nature of Furini from Baldinucci's summary, which I therefore quote almost in full: "Fu il Furino, uomo come noi sogliamo dire di buona pasta, e amico dell' amico: malinconico anzichè nò; ma che volentieri si adattava alle conversazioni sollazzavoli e sestose, nelle quali molto si rallegrava: ebbe genio di poesia bernesca, nel cui stile fece composizioni assai lodevoli. Non fu punto interessato, anzi pochissimo o nulla stimava il danaro: e non parve, che fosse possibile, ch' e' potesse mai tenere in suo potere un quatrino; perchè dall' averlo allo spenderlo, non si frammettea momento di tempo. Egli aveva però un certo suo scrigno nella nappa del pennello, che non gliele lasciava mancar mai; conciofossecosachè quando e' ne restava senza affatto, si metteva a finire una testa (delle quali avea sempre molte abbozzate) e mandavala a' suoi amici che subito gliele pagavano e molto anche il ringraziavano. Gran fatto dunque non fu, che de' gran guadagni, ch' e' fece, e di quegli anche, che egli averia potuti fare col chiedere gran prezzi dell' opere sue, quando egli avesse voluto, non solo non lasciasse roba, ma che rimanesse sua eredità gravata di qualche debito. Fu anche di ciò gran cagione il lungo faticare, ch' e' faceva in sulle pitture: la gran quantità di azzurro oltramarino, che egli usò sempre nelle medesime, dico nelle carni, e fino nelle stesse bozze, e le intollerabili spese, ch' e' fece sempre ne' naturali delle femmine; talmentechè, come egli disse a persona, che a me l' ha raccontato, bene spesso una testa con busto, che a lui era per ordinario pagata dieci doble, gli costò assai più; convenendogli tener naturali a dieci e fino a quattordici lire il giorno, perchè non solamente premeva in aver naturali di ottime parti e proporzioni, ma per ordinario tenne sempre fanciulle: ed a chi talora con bel modo il riprendeva dell' esporre se stesso a tanto pericolo di anima, nel trattenersi, che faceva del continovo nella fissa imitazione di simili oggetti; rispondeva con una certa ragione, che a me non finisce di soddisfare, benchè in esso, e nel temperamento suo potesse aver sussistenza, ed era questa. Se e' conoscessero, diceva egli, questi scrupulosi la gran fatica, anzi la mortale agonia, che prova l' artefice, nel voler soddisfare a se stesso nel dar verità alla sua fattura: conoscerebbero altresì, quanto impossibil cosa sia, che a chi tanto pena e fatica, possano in un tempo stesso essere importuni altri pensieri. Io però, come dissi, non saprei finirla di approvare; anzi pigliano il fatto dall' intera causa, la stimerei un vero inganno; perchè se talle ella non fosse, anche potrebbe dirsi, esser degno di scusa, chi nel compor versi osceni o maledici, suo ingegno affatica, non già per lo piacere, che egli provi nel fargli, ma per lo dannoso effetto, che essi all' umana conversazione producano, poco rilevando, che il pittore nell' operar suo, e' l poeta nel suo

leying with the painter-priest. Very nearly all the facts that are there presented Browning takes at face value. The outlines of Furini's life are simple. He was born at Florence about the year 1600, was early interested in painting, became a pupil of Matteo Rosselli, rapidly distinguished himself as a painter of brilliant but somewhat frank feminine nudes, was much sought after by the nobles of Italy and France, was easy with his money, and generally in debt, though his pictures brought great sums. In his fortieth year he repented his sinful life and became priest of St. Sano in Mugello, Tuscany, which office he administered with great care and generosity until his death in 1649. On his deathbed, Baldinucci asserts, he repented the lascivious pictures he had painted and begged his friends and relatives to collect them and burn them:

Ed è fama, che egli nell' avvicinarsi a quel tremendo passo, non cessasse mai di pregare gli amici e congiunti a operare, che le pitture sue, per quanto fosse stato possibile, fosser date in preda al fuoco e con tal disposizione venne in potere della morte
. . .[95]

Browning's whole *Parleying* turns upon this passage. He is ready enough to follow Baldinucci in calling Furini "good son, good brother, good friend, good painter, good priest." With Baldinucci he praises Furini's liberality to his peasants in Mugello, "pouring profuse God's wine and oil." But that Furini repented having painted his pictures glori-

comporre lascivamente, a cagione del faticare, che fa, non provi stimoli meno che onesti; ogni qualvolta egli applica ogni sua industria in condurre cosa, che in mancanza de' veri oggetti, possa servire a chi con esso non si affaticò, ne dopo di esso si affaticherà mai, per essere abbattuto, e cadere; in quella guisa appunto, che chi scarica le bombarde e i cannoni, chi accende le bombe, e da il fuoco alle mine, potra bene essere, che lo faccia con cautela di se medesimo, ma non già, che nol faccia a rovina ed esterminio di ognuno, che non sia esso. E tanto basti sopra di ciò, mentre io mi dichiaro, che non è mia intenzione in tal cosa di giudicare il Furino, ne l'Interno suo, ma di parlare dell' azione stessa."—

[95] *Notizie,* XVI, 17.

Notizie, XVI, 18-20.

fying the flesh, and begged that they be burnt, is incredible to Browning:

> Nay, *that*, Furini, never I at least
> Mean to believe![96]

He prefers to believe—in spite of Baldinucci's repeated statements to the contrary—that he who was so good in other things would not have been at fault here. By Baldinucci's own admission Furini was a good painter, and the poet believes him to be such. To be sure he is not great in the sense that Michael Angelo is great,

> But the ample gift
> Of gracing walls else blank of this our house
> Of life with imagery, one bright drift
> Poured forth by pencil,—man and woman mere,
> Glorified till half owned for gods,—the dear
> Fleshly perfection of the human shape,—
> This was apportioned you whereby to praise
> Heaven and bless earth.[97]

Browning stakes all his knowledge of human nature on the belief that he who was "good priest, good man, good painter" did not become craven on his death-bed and cry that his pictures be burnt. He turns on Baldinucci as the author of this slander:

> With main and might—
> So fame runs—did the poor soul beg his friends
> To buy and burn his hand-work, make amends
> For having reproduced therein—(Ah me!
> Sighs fame—that's friend Filippo)—nudity![98]

Then Browning makes Baldinucci list the pictures he objected to: "mother Eve . . . naked and unashamed," a nymph bathing, with "no one least kid-skin cast around

96 *With Francis Furini*, ll. 1-2.
97 *Idem*, ll. 51-58.
98 *Idem*, ll. 71-75.

her," "Diana at the chase, with tunic tucked discreetly hunt-
ing-high," "Queen Venus." Where did the painter learn such
skill at painting bodies? Why, says the horrified Baldinucci,
he saw them; and when pressed to acknowledge that this
practice was an abuse of his art, Furini is made to answer
him,

> 'Did you but know, as I,
> —O scruple-splitting sickly-sensitive
> Mild-moral-monger, what the agony
> Of Art is ere Art satisfy herself
> In imitating Nature—(Man, poor elf,
> Striving to match the finger-mark of Him
> The immeasurably matchless)—gay or grim,
> Pray, would your smile be? Leave mere fools to tax
> Art's high-strung brain's intentness as so lax
> That, in its mid-throe, idle fancy sees
> The moment for admittance!'[99]

Baldinucci thinks that these excuses are specious; but who,
asks Browning, dares hope that the truth will convince
blockheads like Baldinucci?

The poet refuses once more to accept Baldinucci's statement that Furini begged that his pictures be burnt. The artist could not have been so blind to the value of his works:

> I trust
> Rather, Furini, dying breath had vent
> In some fine fervor of thanksgiving just
> For this—that soul and body's power you spent—
> Agonized to adumbrate, trace in dust
> That marvel which we dream the firmament
> Copies in star-device when fancies stray
> Outlining, orb by orb Andromeda—
> God's best of beauteous and magnificent
> Revealed to earth—the naked female form.[100]

[99] *With Francis Furini*, ll. 106-116.
[100] *With Francis Furini*, ll. 134-143. For Furini's *Andromeda* see *Notizie*,
XVI, 7.

The thought that people should be so prudish as to attack
naked beauty—as Baldinucci and Horsley both do—drives
Browning into paroxysms of rage. He launches into a tirade
against such critics, mere pretenders to art—a tirade directed, as we have seen, against Horsley in the guise of Baldinucci.[101] The prudish moralists' suspicion that the nude in
art is lust-born leads Browning to point to Michael Angelo
as an example of the absurdity of their claims:

> Art was just
> A safety-screen—(Art, which Correggio's tongue
> Calls "Virtue")—for a skulking vice: mere lust
> Inspired the artist when his Night and Morn
> Slept and awoke in marble on that edge
> Of heaven above our awe-struck earth: lust-born
> His Eve low bending took the privilege
> Of life from what our eyes saw—God's own palm
> That put the flame forth—to the love and thanks
> Of all creation save this recreant![102]

Baldinucci is only an interloper who has crept in among the
great, and crouched down "to where their garments sweep
the floor." Well, after all, little better could have been expected of Baldinucci. There are folk in the world who admire
the fog more than the star it enwraps. But the worst of it is
that Baldinucci dares to think that the artist mind must be
like his own. He with his impure mind cannot see pictures in
the nude without wanting to be lascivious. He therefore
thinks others must be like himself. He admits

> "I dare not look on diadems
> Without an itch to pick out, purloin gems
> Others contentedly leave sparkling"—gruff
> Answers the guard of the regalia: "Why—

---

101 See above, pp. 181-184.

102 *With Francis Furini,* ll. 174-183. Michael Angelo's *Night* and *Morn,*
colossal figures, are in a chapel of San Lorenzo at Rome; *The Creation of
Eve,* a great favorite of Browning's, is a painting on the ceiling of the Sistine Chapel. See *With Charles Avison,* ll. 232 ff., where the latter work is
used as the supreme example of what painting can achieve.

Consciously kleptomaniac—thrust yourself
Where your illicit craving after pelf
Is tempted most—in the King's treasury?"[103]

What is Baldinucci doing in the world of art, if he does not revere her treasures?

With a sudden impatience Browning breaks off. He turns to Furini and begs him to pray—such a prayer as a painter-priest would pray, extolling art as a man's best praise to God, and showing that "the dear fleshly perfection of the human shape" is the highest form of art as it is the noblest work of God. It is good, says Furini, that

. . . still, some few
Have grace to see Thy purpose, strength to mar
Thy work by no admixture of their own,
—Limn truth not falsehood, bid us love alone
The type untampered with, the naked star![104]

And of such, Browning thinks, is Furini.

Then, the prayer done, Browning begs the painter-priest to preach, not as he would to his simple-witted country folk, but rather as he would were he in London in the year 1887. For, says Browning, Furini has his word to say in behalf of faith; and one and all will listen. Science herself

Encourages the meanest who has racked
Nature until he gains from her some fact,
To state what truth is from his point of view,
Mere pin-point though it be:[105]

So the painter begins Browning's answer to the Evolutionists, which we have already considered at some length earlier in this chapter. It is therefore necessary to add very little more here. It is enough, perhaps, to refer to two points. In the first place, Browning analyzes the point of difference

103 *With Francis Furini*, ll. 221-227.
104 *Idem*, ll. 243-247.
105 *Idem*, ll. 257-260.

between himself and the Evolutionists. It is again the accusation that they are "levelling downward";

> You strain
> Your vision, until atoms, protoplasm,
> And what and whence and how may be the spasm
> Which sets all going, stop you: down perforce
> Needs must your observation take its course,
> Since there's no moving upwards: link by link
> You drop to where the atoms somehow think,
> Feel, know themselves to be: the world's begun,
> Such as we recognize it.[106]

In the second place, we must notice that Browning, driven from the field by the undeniable truth of Evolution in the physical world, appeals or rather retreats to the world of mind and spirit:

> Have you done
> Descending? Here's ourself,—Man, known to-day,
> Duly evolved at last . . .[107]

So he begins his own theory, and soon comes to his favorite theme:

> Where began
> Righteousness, moral sense except in Man?[108]

In spite of Browning's anticipation that science may attempt to explain the moral sense by Evolution,[109] he proceeds with his own argument. The moral sense is a vital factor, showing itself in an intense dissatisfaction with things as they are:

> What does Man see or feel or apprehend
> Here, there, and everywhere, but faults to mend,

106 *With Francis Furini*, ll. 269-277. For the general discussion of Browning's disagreement with the Evolutionists see above, pp. 193-200.

107 *With Francis Furini*, ll. 277-280.

108 *Idem*, ll. 298-299.

109 See above, pp. 195-196.

Omissions to supply,—one wide disease
Of things that are, which Man at once would ease
Had will but power and knowledge? failing both—
Things must take will for deed—Man, nowise loth,
Accepts pre-eminency . . .[110]

The evil which had daunted Browning's intellect until he shut his eyes upon it, is made in this ingenious fashion to be the basis of his moral optimism. Man's pity, love, and yearning after the right, reveal God in little, within him. Man is nothing intellectually and physically, says the poet; yet the fact that man would if he could make the world a better place deifies him, makes him akin to God.

So Browning, asserting again man's ignorance, advises the Evolutionists to begin at the bottom. He knows nothing but his self-consciousness, and how from that can knowledge explain the universe? He explains *his* method:

Well, my attempt to make the cloud disperse
Begins—not from above but underneath:
I climb, you soar,—who soars soon loses breath
And sinks, who climbs keeps one foot firm on fact
Ere hazarding the next step:[111]

Thus, defining his position " 'Twixt ignorance and ignorance enisled," Browning is fully launched in the long metaphysical discussion analyzed at length earlier in the chapter.[112] At the outset, however, he reminds us that Furini has a right to instruct us:

Do I make pretence
To teach, myself unskilled in learning? Lo,
My life's work! Let my pictures prove I know
Somewhat of what this fleshly frame of ours
Or is or should be, how the soul empowers
The body to reveal its every mood

[110] *With Francis Furini,* ll. 304-310.
[111] *Idem,* ll. 365-369.
[112] See above, pp. 185-193.

Of love and hate, pour forth its plenitude
Of passion. If my hand attained to give
Thus permanence to truth else fugitive,
Did not I also fix each fleeting grace
Of form and feature—save the beauteous face—
Arrest decay in transitory might
Of bone and muscle—cause the world to bless
Forever each transcendent nakedness
Of man and woman?[113]

And he directs our attention to his *Andromeda* as an example of his work, realizing that it might have been done
better by a greater artist:

Who proffers help of hand
To weak Andromeda exposed on strand
At mercy of the monster? Were all true,
Help were not wanting: 'But 't is false,' cry you,
'Mere fancy-work of paint and brush!' No less,
Were mine the skill, the magic, to impress
Beholders with a confidence they saw
Life,—veritable flesh and blood in awe
Of just as true a sea-beast,—would they stare
Simply as now, or cry out, curse and swear,
Or call the gods to help, or catch up stick
And stone, according as their hearts were quick
Or sluggish? Well, some old artificer
Could do as much,—at least, so books aver,—
Able to make-believe, while I, poor wight,
Make fancy, nothing more.[114]

Then follows Browning's application of the picture he has
been describing, to the question in his mind. The comparison, implied before, is now worked out in detail. Evil in this
world may be as much make-believe as the picture of An-

[113] *With Francis Furini*, ll. 375-389. The observation that Furini was incapable of painting successfully the human face is Browning's own.
[114] *Idem*, ll. 489-504. Browning refers in this passage to the Greek
painter, Zeuxis; see Orr, *Handbook*, p. 355.

dromeda. God may be confronting us with evil just as Furini confronts us with his painting—for the purpose of seeing how we react toward it. And this is the ultimate position taken by the preacher:

> . . . just the same
> Be feigning or be fact the teacher,—blame
> Diffidence nowise if, from this I judge
> My point of vantage, not an inch I budge.
> All—for myself—seems ordered wise and well
> Inside it,—what reigns outside, who can tell?[115]

Art is the earnest of God's presence in the earth, and

> Though Master keep aloof,
> Signs of His presence multiply from roof
> To basement of the building.[116]

The sermon is ended at last, and there is little left of the *Parleying*. But before Furini is dismissed, he is to have one more chance to express himself—this time with his painter's pencil and brush. "Now praise with pencil, Painter!" And just as Browning equipped the priest with a sermon that seemed to him timely for 1887, so now he gives the artist a subject that is not only made to his hand, but also very pertinent to the poet's purpose:

> Let my spark
> Quicken your tinder! Burn with—Joan of Arc!
> Not at the end, nor midway when there grew
> The brave delusions, when rare fancies flew
> Before the eyes, and in the ears of her
> Strange voices woke imperiously astir:
> No,—paint the peasant girl all peasant-like,
> Spirit and flesh—the hour about to strike
> When this should be transfigured . . .[117]

Here is a subject for Furini—such a one as Sainte-Beuve would approve, or Quicherat,[118] "the downright-digger into truth." And this fact greatly concerns Furini, that D'Alençon, the fast friend of Joan, and her chronicler, says

> . . . "of prudishness no touch
> From first to last defaced the maid; anon,
> Camp-use compelling . . . though I saw while she undressed
> How fair she was—especially her breast—
> Never had I a wild thought!"[119]

Then the poet goes on with his own description:

> Much less would she take heed—
> When eve came, and the lake, the hills around
> Were all one solitude and silence,—found
> Barriered impenetrably safe about,—
> Take heed of interloping eyes shut out,
> But quietly permit the air imbibe
> Her naked beauty till . . . but hear the scribe!
> *Now as she fain would bathe, one even-tide*
> *God's maid, this Joan, from the pool's edge she spied*
> *The fair bluebird clowns call the Fisher-king:*
> *And " 'Las," sighed she, "my Liege is such a thing*
> *As thou, lord but of one poor lonely place*
> *Out of his whole wide France: were mine the grace*
> *To set my Dauphin free as thou, blue bird!"*
> . . . Paint this! Only, turn
> Her face away—that face about to burn
> Into an angel's when the time is ripe!
> That task's beyond you.[120]

Beautiful! But the amazing fact is that the passage is an exact description of Robert Barrett Browning's picture of

---

[118] Jules Joseph Etienne Quicherat, *Procès de Condamnation et de Réhabilitation de Jeanne d'Arc* . . ., Paris, 1841-1849, 5 vols.

[119] D'Alençon's account is given in Quicherat, IV, 1-30. See pp. 4-5 for the quotations Browning uses.

[120] *With Francis Furini*, ll. 594-607, 611-614.

Joan of Arc and the Kingfisher, exhibited at the Grosvenor
Gallery in 1886![121] Furthermore, the seven lines of the poem
italicized by Browning are very evidently the seven lines he
had written to be placed under the picture.[122] The year in
which the *Joan* was exhibited was, it will be recalled, the year
following the controversy over the nude in art, in the *Times.*
The novel treatment of the *Joan* was thus, in a sense, the
Brownings' rejoinder to Horsley and his ilk. But as we have
seen, the picture was objected to by some of the critics;[123] and
the *Parleying,* written in the next year, is the elder Browning's pointed answer to those critics. His praise of his son's
picture of the naked Joan is his reply to the prudish moraliz-
ing of Horsley. With this specific example of how beautiful
the nude in art can be—an example drawn by his son—the
poem closes; just as it began with a defence of the nude in
general.

For this text, Furini and his critic Baldinucci serve admirably. Browning may actually have chosen the Italian
painter for the very reason that his case applied so well to
conditions in England in 1887. Certainly Browning's description of Furini's *Nymph Bathing* applies equally well to
the younger Browning's picture upon the same theme:

> Yes, rosed from top to toe in flush of youth,
> One foot upon the moss-fringe, would some Nymph
> Try, with its venturous fellow, if the lymph
> Were chillier than the slab-stepped fountain-edge;
> The while a-heap her garments on its ledge
> Of boulder lay within hand's easy reach . . .[124]

[121] This fact has not been pointed out before, I think. Orr, *Handbook,* p.
355, gives the place and date of exhibition.

[122] This suggestion is my own. It was Browning's custom to write lines
for pictures by his friends; he had done this service for Woollner in *Deaf
and Dumb,* for Leighton in *Orpheus and Eurydice,* and for Maclise in the
first lines of *In a Gondola.* Sotheby, *Catalogue,* item no. 182, refers to the
seven lines which Browning wrote describing the picture.

[123] See above, p. 183.

[124] *With Francis Furini,* ll. 84-89. Compare *Notizie,* XVI, 6.

And now the long *Parleying* ends, and Furini, his beautiful
Joan finished, is dismissed:

> Finished, Francis? Wipe
> Pencil, scrape palette, and retire content!
> "*Omnia non omnibus*"—no harm is meant![125]

Thus ends what is perhaps the strangest medley of theology,
art, science, argument, vituperation, and poetry that was
ever crowded into so little space.

[125] *With Francis Furini*, ll. 614–616. See above, p. 184.

CHAPTER VI

THE PARLEYING WITH GERARD
DE LAIRESSE

I

FOR the greater part of Browning's life painting was one of his major interests; hence when he came to express, in this work of his maturity, his "accumulated convictions" upon many subjects, it is not surprising to find two parleyings, instead of one, devoted to painting. After discussing in *Furini* a painter of the human figure, Browning turns at once to a painter of landscapes, a man who had been a vital as well as a lasting influence in his education.

The Parleying With Gerard de Lairesse quickly became the most popular of the seven.[1] For in spite of the fact that it contains the usual metaphysical argument of the later Browning, it also contains a wealth of descriptive beauty called into being by Browning's reminiscence of landscapes typical of Lairesse. Browning was not given to lengthy descriptions of nature. It was his peculiarity that in an age interested primarily in nature, both in science and in literature, he was interested consistently in men and women. Nature with him was merely a background for the human drama. It was not, as he himself said, that he had not a great love for nature, but that he loved men and women better.[2] Yet the passages descriptive of nature in Browning's poetry were always popular; and it is significant for our present purposes that he seemed to learn his characteristic conceptions of what was beautiful in nature, and what was ugly, from Gerard de Lairesse.

Browning's interest in painting dates back to his earliest

[1] See *Browning Society Papers*, London, II, 177: Symons, *Some Notes on Mr. Browning's Latest Volume.*
[2] See Griffin and Minchin, p. 39.

youth. His father had given up a very lucrative position in
the West Indies and returned to England with "the intention of devoting himself to art, for which he had many quali-
fications and abundant love,"[3] but family circumstances pre-
vented him from carrying out his purpose. But though
thwarted in his ambition to become a painter, the poet's
father never lost his interest in art. He continued to draw all
his life, and was known for his very amusing caricatures. It
was not strange then that he should encourage his son's interest in painting and painters, and be proud of his efforts
in drawing. And Browning was, it must be remembered, "a
young wonder" at drawing; recalling, in later years, how his
father proudly wrote "R. B. aetat. two years and three
months," beneath a little picture of a "certain cottage and
rocks in lead pencil and black currant juice—paint being
rank poison, as they said when I sucked my brushes."[4] But
perhaps the chief service that the father of the poet rendered
to his son's education in art and its history was in providing
him with a library. Following his own interests he had collected all sorts of books on art, which were of course fully
accessible to his son. In the library in Southampton Street
the young Browning read avidly. His natural inclination
carried him to art. In Pilkington's *Dictionary of Painters*[5]
he found many names that were to become significant to him
later; and he learned much about the history of art from
Vasari's *Lives of the Painters*.[6] But the book on art that he
read most faithfully, and with the greatest pleasure, was one
by Gerard de Lairesse.

This was an English translation from the Dutch *Het
Groot Schilderboek*,[7] which the painter, after blindness came
upon him, dictated to his sons. With the aid of seventy illus-

[3] *Letters of R. B. and E. B. B.,* II, 477.
[4] Griffin and Minchin, p. 11.
[5] Browning read the 1805 edition, revised and enlarged by Fuseli.
[6] This was an abridged English edition of *Le Vite Pittori,* referred to in
the preceding chapter. See Griffin and Minchin, p. 15.
[7] First published in Amsterdam in 1707.

trative plates, which he also managed to dictate,[8] the author
in five hundred pages of technical matter attempted to comprehend the whole art of painting. It took thirteen books to
treat the whole subject.[9] The volume was perhaps the most
ambitious text-book of painting that had been written at the
time, and it was immensely popular. Besides going through
many Dutch editions, it was translated into French and
German,[10] and into English. There were three English editions by 1817; and in that year it still held its position as the
foremost book of its kind.[11] The edition which Browning read
was the second English edition, translated from the Dutch
by John Frederick Fritsch, himself a painter, and published
in 1778.[12] It was called *The Art of Painting in All its
Branches*, a title which indicates the comprehensive plan of
the work.

To this book Browning acknowledges no small indebtedness. He loved Lairesse, he says in the *Parleying*,

> Because of that prodigious book he wrote
> On Artistry's Ideal.[13]

And he read the book again and again, delighting in both the
text and the prints, so that in his later years he still remembered the work. In the very copy which he had read as a
child he wrote in 1874:

I read this book more often and with greater delight when I

[8] *Het Groot Schilderboek*, Amsterdam, 1712, *Preface*, p. ii.
[9] One gets some idea of the scope of Lairesse's work from the titles of
the thirteen books: Book I, *Of Pencilling, second Tint and Beauty;* Book
II, *Of Ordonnance, or Composition;* Book III, *Of Things Antique and Modern;* Book IV, *Of Colouring;* Book V, *Of Lights and Shades;* Book VI, *Of
Landscapes;* Book VII, *Of Portraiture;* Book VIII, *Of Architecture;* Book
IX, *Of the Painting of Cielings* [sic] *or Plafonds;* Book X, *Of Statuary;*
Book XI, *Of Still-Life;* Book XII, *Of Flowers;* Book XIII, *Of Engraving.*
[10] Nagler, *Künstler Lexicon*, 1839, VII, 243, under *Lairesse.*
[11] See *The Art of Painting* . . ., London, 1817, W. M. Craig, *Editor's
Essay.* Craig, who was painter to the Queen, says there, "I have repeatedly
recommended it in my lectures at the Royal Institution as the best work on
art that my auditors could consult."
[12] See the footnote to a mention of Lairesse's book in the first edition of
the *Parleyings*, p. 168.
[13] *With Gerard de Lairesse*, ll. 33-34.

was a child than any other: and still remember the main of it
most gratefully for the good I seem to have got from the prints
and wonderful text.[14]

The work thus singled out as the favorite book of such a vo-
racious reader as the boy Browning attains at once a position of great significance in his education.

Deeply interested as he was in Lairesse's prodigious book,
Browning the boy determined to "pay due homage" to the
artist by making an expedition to see some of his pictures.
From Camberwell, where the Brownings lived, it was just a
"green half-hour's walk over the fields" to the Dulwich Gallery, of which the poet was to speak in later days as "the gallery I so love and so am grateful to—having been used to go
there when a child, far under the age allowed by the regula-
tions."[15] He had, he went on to say, "sate before one, some
one of those pictures I had predetermined to see, a good hour
and then gone away."[16] There he must have seen examples of
all the schools of painting, for the gallery was very representative. From its opening in 1814 it had pictures by
Raphael, Guercino, Titian, Giorgione, Andrea del Sarto,
Guido, and many other Italians. Browning particularly
mentions having seen there "those two Guidos, the wonderful
Rembrandt of Jacob's vision, such a Watteau, the triumphant three Murillo pictures, a Giorgione music-lesson
group, all the Poussins with the 'Armida' and 'Jupiter's
nursing.' "[17] Poussin was very well represented there. But the
gallery was particularly strong in Dutch paintings; and
among the Ostade, Teniers, and Brouwer pictures there
hung three by Gerard de Lairesse. These were *Pan and
Syrinx in a Landscape, Apollo and Daphne in a Landscape*,
and *Apollo flaying Marsyas*.[18] In his later years Browning
could well recall—probably having studied the pictures he

14 Griffin and Minchin, pp. 9-10.
15 *Letters of R. B. and E. B. B.*, I, 524.
16 *Ibid.*
17 *Ibid.*
18 See Summerly, *Hand-book for the Dulwich Gallery*, 1842.

had gone to see, in accordance with his custom—the characteristic manner of Lairesse, how his skies were

> Traversed by flying shapes, earth stocked with brood
> Of monsters,—centaurs bestial, satyrs lewd,—
> Not without much Olympian glory, shapes
> Of god and goddess in their gay escapes
> From the severe serene.[19]

But Browning's pilgrimage which was to have paid his
homage to the painter whose book he loved so well, resulted
in nothing but disappointment. Perhaps he had hoped too
much from the wonderful book. At any rate he has to admit,
in the *Parleying*:

> So my youth's piety obtained success
> Of all-too dubious sort: for though it irk
> To tell the issue, few or none would guess
> From extant lines and colors, De Lairesse,
> Your faculty . . .[20]

So while he is eternally grateful for the service done him by
the prodigious book, he is more than dubious about the value
of the artist's own pictures:

> I lack
> Somehow the heart to wish your practice back
> Which boasted hand's achievement in a score
> Of veritable pictures, less or more,
> Still to be seen: myself have seen them . . .[21]

Thus we learn that gratitude led Browning to see in all some
score of Lairesse's pictures during his lifetime; but we see
no less definitely that the poet's early disappointment in
the painter's artistry persisted.

When as a boy Browning turned in disappointment from
Lairesse's pictures, he was expressing at the same time the

19 *With Gerard de Lairesse*, ll. 11-15.
20 *Idem*, ll. 36-40.
21 *Idem*, ll. 27-31.

world's judgment upon that artist. For though hailed as the
particular glory of Holland, assured by all the leading poets
of his time of a glorious immortality, and even mourned at
his death as a "second Raphael,"[22] Lairesse was not even a
name in London in 1887. And though in 1707, the year in
which *Het Groot Schilderboek* came out in Amsterdam,

> . . . each deftly-grouped
> And aptly-ordered figure-piece was judged
> Worthy a prince's purchase in its day . . .[23]

yet at Paris in 1907 Lairesse's *Amour Tenant des Guir-
landes* sold for no more than two hundred francs.[24] It was
through his book that Lairesse's memory lived, and that his
influence was extended, as we have seen.[25]

Perhaps the most salient characteristic of Lairesse, both
as a painter and as an instructor, is his insistence upon the
beauty and perfection of the classic antique, contrasted with
the sordidness and "deformed ugliness" of the modern subject. This one idea informs the whole of Lairesse's work. This
is all the more remarkable when we consider that he was in
the midst of such stalwart Dutch realists as Teniers, Ostade,
Brouwer and Moller. Lairesse, however, was a pseudo-classi-
cist, and abhorred the modern and the realistic. He realized
well enough that he was out of key with his contemporaries:

> For my part, I believe that the difference between the fine
> and the ugly, is too great not to make a distinction between
> them. I am well pleased, that some call the works of *Bamboccio*,
> *Brouwer*, and *Moller*, and the landscapes of *Brueghel*, *Bril*,
> *Bloemart Savry*, *Berchem*, and such masters painter-like: but I
> oppose to them, *Raphael*, *Correggio*, *Poussin*, *Le Brun*, &c.,
> and in landscape, *Albani*, *Genouille*, *Poussin*, the *German Poly-
> dore*, and such as follow them in their choices.[26]

[22] See commendatory verses prefixed to *Het Groot Schilderboek*, 2d edition, Amsterdam, 1712.
[23] *With Gerard de Lairesse*, ll. 40-42.
[24] See Benezit, *Dictionnaire des Peintures* . . ., under *Lairesse*.
[25] See above, pp. 214-216.
[26] *The Art of Painting* . . ., London, 1778, p. 252.

Lairesse took for his great master Poussin, who in the para-
phernalia of the pseudo-classical school—tombs, temples,
statuary, satyrs, and gods—could tell a story better than
any other painter. Lairesse too tells stories. There is scarcely
a picture of his which does not attempt to portray some fable
from Ovid, or some tale from classical history. His genius
exercises itself upon such subjects as the metamorphosis of
Dryope into a tree as she plucks the lotos twig,[27] or Apollo
pursuing Daphne until she is fixed to the earth,[28] or Jupiter
wooing the hapless Calisto.[29] Lairesse seldom condescends to
treat a subject that is later than Ovid, for he believes
strongly in the superiority of the ancient over the modern
subject:

> But let us reflect on two arts, noble and ignoble or *antique*
> and *modern,* and see how much they differ both in objects and
> execution. *The antique is unlimited,* that is, it can handle *his-*
> *tory,* sacred as well as profane, *fables* and *emblems* both moral
> and spiritual; under which three heads it comprehends, *all that*
> *ever was, is, and shall be;* the *past, present,* and *to come; and*
> *that, after an excellent manner, which never alters, but remains*
> *always the same: The modern, contrarily, is so far from being*
> *free, that it is limited within certain narrow bounds; and is of*
> *small power; for it may or can represent no more than what is*
> *present, and that too in a manner which is always changing:*
> *What is past and to come is without its power; as also histories,*
> *fables and emblems, as well poetical and philosophic as moral.*
> Hence we may judge what the *modern* art of painting is, and
> why it cannot be called *noble;* much less of any harmony with
> the *antique.*[30]

This then is Lairesse: he abjures the modern and the realistic, and clings to the emblematic and allegorical. He must
embellish his flat Holland with god and goddess, nymph and
satyr. He must find sepulchre and temple and statuary until

---

[27] See *The Art of Painting,* pp. 239-240.
[28] See *idem,* pp. 58-62. See also above, p. 216.
[29] See *idem,* pp. 339-342.
[30] *Idem,* p. 99.

it is indeed "Holland turned Dreamland." Browning in characterizing him has caught his spirit; nothing is simple:

> The rose? No rose unless it disentwine
> From Venus' wreath the while she bends to kiss
> Her deathly love . . .[31]

Nor does Browning exaggerate when he tells how Lairesse shows the sky traversed by flying shapes, and the earth stocked with brood of monsters—centaurs and satyrs—not omitting, on the other hand, the shapes of gods and goddesses.[32] For the painter, in his discussion of the theory of his art, drew constantly for his illustrations upon the great body of fable and history that a diligent study of the Latin writers had stored in his mind.

But as Browning had turned, as a boy, from the actual paintings of Lairesse, he was to turn, in his more mature years, from Lairesse's theories of art. He tells us in the *Parleying* that

> Bearded experience bears not to be duped
> Like boyish fancy . . .[33]

The poet cannot be satisfied with unreal fancies spun from ancient and fabulous lore. The sense of actuality is too strong in him. This difference in point of view between the seventeenth-century painter and the nineteenth-century poet is, indeed, the crux of the whole *Parleying*. Browning, who sees things without the embellishments of fancy, can in his later days scarcely comprehend Lairesse's fanciful vision. He addresses Lairesse:

> . . . make it plain to me,
> Who, bee-like, sate sense with the simply true,
> Nor seek to heighten that sufficiency . . .[34]

[31] *With Gerard de Lairesse*, ll. 163-165.
[32] See *idem*, ll. 10-17. For Browning's justification in this characterization see *The Art of Painting*, pp. 245, 249-251, 58-62, 72-76, 228, 239, 339-342; and Plates 22, 23, etc. For Lairesse's justification of his use of emblematic figures see Book II, Ch. 11.
[33] *With Gerard de Lairesse*, ll. 43-44.
[34] *Idem*, ll. 129-131.

Browning was too much captivated by his love of realism to be able to follow any longer Lairesse's fancies.

But in one essential respect Browning did not reject Lairesse. One part of the painter's teaching had been so thoroughly assimilated by the poet in those early days of their acquaintance that it had become an integral part of his own thought. This was the conception of what was beautiful, and what was horrible, in landscape.

Landscape was, in Lairesse, the least fanciful of his creations. He would, it is true, sprinkle his canvases or his descriptions of pictures with many strange figures, but he never failed to fill in an appropriate background of landscape. He has a certain very definite conception of what is appropriate material for the artist and what is not. In fact, Lairesse has a very typical favorite landscape; and while he strongly recommends diversity, it is after all diversity within rather narrow limits. He admires

. . . woods with vistos, wherein the eye may lose itself; rocks, rivers, and water-falls, green fields, &c. delightful to the eye. Herein lies the stress of a landscape. . . . However, this variety consists not only in the difference or irregularity of the objects, as trees, hills, fountains, and the like, but in the diversity of each of them; for instance, bending and strait trees, large and small hills, . . . green and russet lands, &c. The same diversity is to be observed in colouring, according to the seasons of the year; that lovers may not be cloyed by producing, with the cockoo, always the same thing; as stir and motion, crooked and mis-shapen bodies of trees, waving branches, barren grounds, blue mountains, or beasts, birds, huntings and the like; or, contrarily, always repose and quietness . . .[35]

Lairesse was especially fond of urging his readers to suit the action to the time of day in their pictures, or the time of day to the action. Thus he points out that sunshine is proper for "jovial occurrences and histories, which require great bustle; but very improper and obstructing in councils, pleadings

[35] *The Art of Painting*, pp. 203-204. (Book VI, *Of Landscapes*, Ch. I.)

. . . and other such circumstances." Cloud light gives an
uncommon decorum and naturalness, he points out, in solemn
affairs. Torchlight is proper for mournful occasions. He
carefully lists the times of day, with the actions appropriate
to them, so that his followers may not make any mistakes. To
give examples of some of these:

Day-break.

This first-born time of the day favours the enterprizes of
great generals in besieging or storming a town; no time more
proper for it, by the example of *Joshua* in taking *Jericho*. This
rule, though not without exception, has been observed by all nations . . . It is also the proper time for hunting; as in the
representation of a *Diana, Cephalus, Adonis,* or any such subject. . . .

The Morning.

This time principally rejoices nature; even inanimate things
are sensible of it: the glittering light takes the tops of high
mountains, and causes, both in buildings and landscape, great
shades, appearing very delightful. This light, at breaking out,
gives uncommon sweetness when the objects shine in the water;
as also a certain freshness mixed with vapours, which bind the
parts of things so well together, as entirely to please the eye of
the knowing.

At this time the *Heathens* offered their sacrifices; . . . the
Children of Israel had . . . their *morning oblations* . . . The
Jews retain those customs to this day; as also did the ancient
Christians . . . The *Persians* moreover honoured the morning
by their offerings . . .[36]

So he goes through *The Light between Morning and Noon,
Noon, The Afternoon,* and *The Evening.* The light at noon
he considers difficult to represent; wherefore he recommends
hiding the sun's light behind mountains or buildings, and,

[36] *The Art of Painting,* p. 180. (Book V, *Of Lights and Shades,* Ch.
XVII.) The sections quoted, besides illustrating Lairesse's ideas, form a
valuable basis for comparison with certain passages in the *Parleying.* Notice
there, for instance, that Browning describes a battle at dusk, an Artemis in
the morning, and that the description of morning in ll. 210-215 generally resembles Lairesse's.

since this hour gives rest to human labor, suggests subjects
dealing with rest and retirement from the bright sunlight.
Of *The Afternoon* he remarks that as this season is liable to
overcast skies, it is "very proper in the representation of
bacchanals and licentious actions."[37]

Reading *The Art of Painting* over and over until he knew
it almost by heart, as we have seen that Browning did as a
boy, he unconsciously took over the artist's conceptions of
the beautiful and the appropriate in landscape. They became part of the very warp and weft of Browning's intellectual character. To such an extent is this true that we may
observe that whenever, in the poet's works, the necessity for
description is upon him, he seems to revert naturally to Lairesse's judgment concerning what is "painter-like" or "un-
painter-like." Like Lairesse he has a feeling for the appropriate scenery for the particular time of day. His love for
the Alpine and the wild savors often of Byron, rather than
of Lairesse. Nevertheless, the Dutch painter seems to have
left his mark. So generally dispersed through *The Art of
Painting* are Lairesse's landscapes that it is impossible to
select any one long description for quotation; but perhaps
the reader has caught sufficiently the spirit of Lairesse's
scenes to enable him to observe the resemblance between his
landscapes and Browning's. In *Pauline*, for example, in describing morning, noon, and night in that perfect land to
which the lovers are to fly, Browning leans naturally toward
the artist's conception of what a landscape ought to be:

> Night, and one single ridge of narrow path
> Between the sullen river and the woods
> Waving and muttering, for the moonless night
> Has shaped them into images of life,
> . . . No, we will pass to morning—
> Morning, the rocks and valleys and old woods.
> How the sun brightens in the mist, and here,

[37] *The Art of Painting*, pp. 180-181. Compare Browning's description of
Lyda and the satyr in the *Parleying*, with this suggestion.

Half in the air, like creatures of the place,
Trusting the element, living on high boughs
That swing in the wind—look at the silver spray
Flung from the foam-sheet of the cataract
Amid the broken rocks! Shall we stay here
With the wild hawks? No, ere the hot noon come,
Dive we down—safe! See this our new retreat
Walled in with a sloped mound of matted shrubs,
Dark, tangled, old and green, still sloping down
To a small pool whose waters lie asleep
Amid the trailing boughs turned water-plants:
And tall trees overarch to keep us in,
Breaking the sunbeams into emerald shafts,
And in the dreamy water one small group
Of two or three strange trees are got together
Wondering at all around, as strange beasts herd
Together far from their own land: all wildness,
No turf nor moss, for boughs and plants pave all,
And tongues of bank go shelving in the lymph,
Where the pale-throated snake reclines his head,
And old gray stones lie making eddies there,
The wild-mice cross them dry-shod. Deeper in!
Shut thy soft eyes—now look—still deeper in!
This is the very heart of the woods all round
Mountain-like heaped above us; yet even here
One pond of water gleams; far off the river
Sweeps like a sea, barred out from land; but one—
One thin clear sheet has overleaped and wound
Into this silent depth, which gained, it lies
Still, as but let by sufferance; the trees bend
O'er it as wild men watch a sleeping girl,
And through their roots long creeping plants outstretch
Their twined hair, steeped and sparkling; farther on,
Tall rushes and thick flag-knots have combined
To narrow it; so, at length, a silver thread,
It winds, all noiselessly through the deep wood
Till through a cleft-way, through the moss and stone,
It joins its parent-river with a shout . . .[38]

[38] *Pauline*, ll. 732-780.

This is the longest unbroken description of landscape in Browning, with the exception of the present *Parleying;* and it is decidedly typical. The same details recur to some extent in *Paracelsus,* in *Sordello,* in *By the Fireside,* in *Love Among the Ruins,* and many other poems. They combine with the description of the actual country of the Saleve in *La Saisiaz;* and when Browning comes to parley with Gerard de Lairesse, they occur in full purity and directness once more. These countries of Browning's mind are not mere Lairesse; their scenery is richer and more luxuriant. But Lairesse was nevertheless the starting-point for the poet's imagination, and that Browning recognized this fact is clear from the space given to landscape in the *Parleying.* Moreover, the descriptions in the poem, avowedly modelled upon those of Lairesse, reveal how closely Browning has followed the blind painter's conception of the beautiful in landscape, throughout his life.

The same thing, it may be said in passing, is true concerning what Browning conceived to be ugly and repulsive in landscape. Lairesse's discussion of things that were unpainter-like had made a profound impression upon him:

. . . All these, I say, may claim the title of painter-like: but a piece with deformed trees, widely branched and leaved, and disorderly spreading from east towards west, crooked bodied, old and rent, full of knots and hollowness; also rugged grounds without roads or ways, sharp hills, and monstrous mountains filling the off-scape, rough or ruined buildings with their parts lying up and down in confusion; likewise muddy brooks, a gloomy sky, abounding with heavy clouds; the field furnished with lean cattle and vagabonds of gypsies: such a piece, I say, is not to be called a fine landscape. Can any one, without reason, assert him to be a painter-like object, who appears as a lame and dirty beggar, cloathed in rags, splay-footed, bound about the head with a nasty clout, having a skin as yellow as a backed pudding, killing vermin; or in fine, any such paltry figure?[39]

[39] *The Art of Painting,* p. 252.

Whenever Browning had occasion to describe a desolate and wild country, as in *Childe Roland*,[40] such scenes as this sketched by Lairesse in his *Art of Painting* supplied the details. Of course the imagination of the poet has in almost every case heightened the effectiveness of Lairesse's descriptions. The poet was probably not actually conscious that he was drawing upon Lairesse; for such descriptions came to him so early in his life that they became a part of his own imaginative experience. It was as if they had always been his very own. Nevertheless the poet's debt to the Dutch painter remains a great one.

II

IN spite of the fact that Browning revolted against much that Lairesse had taught him, he still has, in the *Parleying*, words of high praise for the painter:

> Beyond
> The ugly actual, lo, on every side
> Imagination's limitless domain
> Displayed a wealth of wondrous sounds and sights
> Ripe to be realized by poet's brain
> Acting on painter's brush![41]

And for the painter's powers of imagination Browning has nothing but praise. In fact that quality is possessed in common by the poet and the painter; and, as we have seen, Lairesse taught Browning how to create landscapes in imagination. We can see easily how this practice in seeing beyond the actual may have had a great part in developing the imagination of Browning as a boy. The fact that his praise of the painter's procedure says much that might be construed

---

[40] See my article on *The Landscape of Browning's Childe Roland*, in *Publications of the Modern Language Association*, XL, 426-432. For other examples of Browning's use of Lairesse in creating an atmosphere of horror see *Easter-Day*, pp. 597-653; *The Ring and the Book, Giuseppe Caponsacchi*, ll. 1879-1889; *Sordello*, Book IV, ll. 120-140; *Paracelsus*, III, 1030-1041.

[41] *With Gerard de Lairesse*, ll. 57-62.

as a description of his own poetic art, leads to the conclusion
that Browning was indebted to the artist for other things
than his conceptions of landscape:

> Faustus' robe,
> And Fortunatus' cap were gifts of price:
> But—oh, your piece of sober sound advice
> That artists should descry abundant worth
> In trivial commonplace . . .[42]

Town and country are to be transformed by the imagination
of the artist, a recommendation in which Browning finds
much virtue.

But there is nevertheless a decided difference between
Lairesse's treatment of the trivial commonplace, and Browning's. Lairesse uses it only as a starting-point, until by his
method "Holland becomes Dreamland." He puts his visions
in place of reality. Browning takes the trivial commonplace
and turns on it the light of his imaginative insight, in an attempt to find the deeper reality. So while his appreciation of
Lairesse's powers of imagination is great, he must differ with
him on the question of what is the proper use of those powers.
To Browning, fancy can never approach in value to realism.
It is one of the axioms of his artistic creed. That of course is
the reason for his love of "Art's spring-birth so dim and
dewy." He saw the Greek art as a form that had taught its
lesson concerning the dignity and beauty of the human body
to the world, yet which now had nothing more to offer. The
early Christian painters, setting aside the Greek forms which
had stagnated, perceived the value of realism. They introduced a subtler kind of painting—a realistic depiction of
man that revealed the soul within the body. So Browning describes their advance over the Greeks:

> On which I conclude, that the early painters,
>   To cries of "Greek Art and what more wish you?"—
> Replied, "To become now self-acquainters,

---

[42] *With Gerard de Lairesse*, ll. 50-54.

228 BROWNING'S PARLEYINGS

And paint man, man, whatever the issue!
Make new hopes shine through the flesh they fray,
  New fears aggrandize the rags and tatters:
To bring the invisible full into play!
  Let the visible go to the dogs—what matters?"[43]

That is, they want to see beyond the obvious to the essential truth; it is the invisible which is important.

To Browning, Fra Lippo Lippi is the exponent of this realism which descries abundant worth in trivial commonplace because it sees beyond the externals. When Lippi painted his realistic and familiar figures on the wall, it will be remembered, the monks "closed in a circle and praised loud," until they were reminded that realism was not the function of art:

  The Prior and the learned pulled a face
  And stopped all that in no time. "How? what's here?
  Quite from the mark of painting, bless us all! . . .
  Your business is not to catch men with show,
  With homage to the perishable clay,
  But lift them over it, ignore it all,
  Make them forget there's such a thing as flesh . . ."[44]

So they rubbed out Lippi's pictures and told him it was art's decline. Yet Lippi goes on enunciating his belief concerning the true function of art:

  God's works—paint any one, and count it crime
  To let a truth slip. Don't object, "His works
  Are here already; nature is complete:
  Suppose you reproduce her—(which you can't)
  There's no advantage! You must beat her, then."
  For, don't you mark? we're made so that we love
  First when we see them painted, things we have passed
  Perhaps a hundred times nor cared to see;
  And so they are better, painted—better to us,

[43] *Old Pictures in Florence*, ll. 145-152.
[44] *Fra Lippo Lippi*, ll. 174-182.

Which is the same thing. Art was given for that;
God uses us to help each other so,
Lending our minds out. Have you noticed, now,
Your cullion's hanging face? A bit of chalk,
And trust me but you should, though! How much more
If I drew higher things with the same truth![45]

Thus Lippi is to Browning the first of the realists in art.
Man as he is, is the subject; paint him as he is, and the soul
will shine through the flesh. This was a discovery indeed, and
Browning continually celebrates the great advance made by
the realists in art. They made the contribution of artistic insight.

But Browning had gone further. Not only did he cele-
brate this progress in artistic insight in the field of art; he
also applied the principle to his own poetry. He showed a
growing tendency to deal with modern subjects in a realistic
fashion. Contemporary figures, such as Bishop Blougram,
Mr. Sludge, Hohenstiel-Schwangau, and the characters in
Red Cotton Night-Cap Country and *The Inn Album*, become increasingly frequent in Browning's poems as the
years go on.

So, looking back on Lairesse and his theories, Browning
sees how far he has advanced over the old painter. He himself has taken the same step in poetry that constituted Fra
Lippo Lippi's advance over the Greeks and their followers.
So his *Parleying* is largely occupied with a comparison of
the two attitudes. He defines the difference between his
method and that of Lairesse precisely as Fra Lippo Lippi
had defined his advance in realism, thirty-two years earlier:

If we no longer see as you of old,
'T is we see deeper. Progress for the bold!
You saw the body, 't is the soul we see,[46]

he says to Lairesse. Naturally Browning feels that this dif-

45 *Fra Lippo Lippi*, ll. 295-309.
46 *With Gerard de Lairesse*, ll. 171-173.

ference indicates a gain. But another question arises. Has he
—have the realists—suffered a corresponding loss? Are the
powers of fancy and of imaginative insight mutually exclu-
sive? Relatively, Browning prefers the latter gift; but according to his doctrine of progress man ought not to lose, in
the course of his development, any good thing.

> Not one of man's acquists
> Ought he resignedly to lose, methinks . . .[47]

Thus the question becomes a vital one:

> How were it could I mingle false with true,
> Boast, with the sights I see, your vision too?
> Advantage would it prove or detriment
> If I saw double? Could I gaze intent
> On Dryope plucking the blossoms red,
> As you, whereat her lote-tree writhed and bled,[48]
> Yet lose no gain, no hard fast wide-awake
> Having and holding nature for the sake
> Of nature only—nymph and lote-tree thus
> Gained by the loss of fruit not fabulous,
> Apple of English homesteads . . .[49]

In order to test the general question, Browning next puts a
specific one. He recalls with delight a walk which Lairesse

[47] *With Gerard de Lairesse*, ll. 143-144.

[48] Browning is here drawing a typical incident from Lairesse; see *The Art of Painting*, pp. 239-240: "I exhibit the subject . . . in a delightful valley (according to the testimony of the poet), planted with myrtles, and encompassed by a brook. In the middle of the piece, I place, as the princi-pal, the tree *Lotos*, full of red blossoms and thickly leaved. From this tree *Dryope* broke off the sprig. I make it to shake and move so violently, that the trunk of it by that means becomes distorted and winding. On the left side, I place the rash *Dryope*, of a beautiful air, and black haired, having her son *Amphisus* about the middle in her left arm. She advances with her left foot towards the tree, a little drawing back the right: her upper parts fall back still more. In her right hand, lifted up, she holds the bloody sprig, at which she stares in confusion. Her left thigh comes forward. Her upper parts sway to the left; her breast is almost fronting directly against the light; her face in profile more or less turns back and her feet are by this time fixed in the ground . . ."

[49] *With Gerard de Lairesse*, ll. 116-126.

had described in his book, an imaginary walk in which he pointed out to his pupils what was painter-like and what un-painter-like, in the open air. Can he, Browning, take such a walk, using the "freakish brain" to supplement nature? He is sure he can:

> . . . we poets go not back at all:
> What you did we could do—from great to small
> Sinking assuredly . . .[50]

So he challenges Lairesse to a contest, in which he is to match Lairesse's famous walk with one of his own. The issue is not only the superiority of the newer imaginative insight over the old fancy. Browning claims for the moderns the gift of keener insight; it remains to prove that they are still gifted with the power of fancy:

> Try now! Bear witness while you walk with me,
> I see as you: if we loose arms, stop pace,
> 'T is that you stand still, I conclude the race
> Without your company.[51]

Then follows a long descriptive passage, comprising a series of scenes which are avowedly modelled on Lairesse. Browning describes several scenes, going through the day and choosing for each time of day an action and setting which Lairesse would consider appropriate.

But even in his attempt at reproducing such a walk as Lairesse's, Browning achieves a different result. The landscapes and the actions described are to be sure word-pictures that Lairesse might well have envied. But there is in them a strong suggestion of Browning. To mention the minor difference first, Browning unconsciously draws for his material upon the ancient Greek sources rather than upon Ovid.[52] But much more important is the fact that the treatment of the material is typical of Browning. Instead of crowding his

---

[50] *With Gerard de Lairesse,* ll. 166-168.
[51] *Idem,* ll. 174-177.
[52] For Browning's intermediate sources see below, pp. 244-249.

canvas with figures as Lairesse does, Browning has, in every
case save one, just one or two figures; and in that one case
there are two outstanding figures, each backed by his army.
Still more important, Browning manages to infuse into his
descriptions something of his own psychological method.
The best example of this is the description of noon, in which
he tells a story of a satyr and a nymph such as Lairesse
might have told, but into which he weaves a subtlety of interpretation such as Lairesse never dreamed of. His habit of
imaginative insight made him discontented with mere picture, and led him to enter dramatically into the passions of
his characters.[53]

The result of the contest between Browning and Lairesse
is of course a foregone conclusion. The decision is left to the
reader, but there can be but one judgment. Browning proves
completely that he can outdo Lairesse in Lairesse's own
chosen field. The point is that Browning believes that, relatively speaking, that sort of thing is not worth doing. He
loved men and women, as he said, better than he loved nature;[54] and in dealing with men and women he could not be
content with mere narrative and pictorial representation. He
had put that sort of thing aside with his boyhood. Consequently he feels that people who are still content to do that
sort of thing are in the earlier stage of development out of
which he has grown.

Thus it is that in this *Parleying*, as in most of the others,
Browning has his word to say concerning his contemporaries.
And the theories of Lairesse apply very aptly to the practice
of most of Browning's fellow-poets. Almost alone of the
poets of the latter half of the nineteenth century, Browning
chose subjects for his poetry from the life that he saw about
him. The Pre-Raphaelites avowedly sought the past for their
inspiration. The popular fame of Tennyson rested upon the

[53] For the full discussion of this passage see the exegesis of the poem,
below, pp. 247-248.
[54] See above, p. 213.

Idylls and other poems that went to the past for their origins. Matthew Arnold was writing *Empedocles* (1852) and *Merope* (1858). By comparison with these men Browning's debt to the Middle Ages, and even to Greece, seems small indeed. And as he grew older, he turned more and more to modern subjects.[55] So, filled with his conviction of the value of the realistic treatment of modern subjects, Browning finds in Lairesse, with his fanciful treatment of ancient fables, an apt analogy to modern conditions. He addresses the artist:

> Fancy's rainbow-birth
> Conceived mid clouds in Greece, could glance along
> Your passage o'er Dutch veritable earth,
> As with ourselves, who see, familiar throng
> About our pacings men and women worth
> Nowise a glance—so poets apprehend—
> Since naught avails portraying them in verse:
> While painters turn upon the heel, intend
> To spare their work the critic's ready curse
> Due to the daily and undignified.[56]

Although Browning seems here to include himself among the poets whom he censures, his next lines indicate definitely what his position is:

> I who myself contentedly abide
> Awake, nor want the wings of dream,—who tramp
> Earth's common surface, rough, smooth, dry or damp,
> —I understand alternatives, no less
> —Conceive your soul's leap, Gerard de Lairesse![57]

He understands both attitudes; but for himself, he does not want the wings of dream.

His criticism, in its coupling of poets and painters, seems to be directed at the Pre-Raphaelite Brotherhood and its followers. In reading his lines one thinks almost immediately

[55] See above, p. 229.
[56] *With Gerard de Lairesse*, ll. 101-110.
[57] *Idem*, ll. 111-115.

of the Rossettis, Morris, Burne-Jones, Millais, Madox
Brown, Holman-Hunt, and Swinburne. In the light of this
criticism in the *Parleying*, Browning's selection of *Fra
Lippo Lippi* for reading aloud at that memorable gathering
of poets at his home in Dorset Street on September 27,
1855,[58] becomes distinctly significant; for Browning's artistic creed, expressed in that poem, runs directly counter to
the practice of the Pre-Raphaelites.[59]

This criticism of contemporaries who do not consider modern subjects worth dealing with is, however, a general one.
There occurs, some two hundred and fifty lines later, a more
specific criticism of contemporary practice and a more definite objection on Browning's part. Here too Lairesse suggests the grounds of criticism, for the passage deals with the
choice of subjects from *classical* lore:

> Wherefore glozed
> The poets—"Dream afresh old godlike shapes,
> Recapture ancient fable that escapes,
> Push back reality, repeople earth
> With vanished falseness, recognize no worth
> In fact new-born unless 't is rendered back
> Pallid by fancy, as the western rack
> Of fading cloud bequeaths the lake some gleam
> Of its gone glory!"
>
> Let things be—not seem,
> I counsel rather,—do, and nowise dream!
> Earth's young significance is all to learn:
> The dead Greek lore lies buried in the urn
> Where who seeks fire finds ashes. Ghost, forsooth!
> What was the best Greece babbled of as truth?[60]

58 See *Letters of E. B. B.*, II, 213.
59 For the analysis of the significance of *Fra Lippo Lippi* from this point
of view see above, pp. 228-229. The disagreement in principle between
Browning and Rossetti may well have been an underlying factor in the
subsequent coolness between the two men. See *Dante Gabriel Rossetti,
Family Letters and Memoir*, London, 1895, pp. 334-335; also W. M. Rossetti, *Some Reminiscences*, I, 245-246.
60 *With Gerard de Lairesse*, ll. 381-394.

Here the reference is plainly pointed toward poets who were dealing with Greek themes, for there are three mentions of Hellenism within as many lines.[61] There are of course several poets whom Browning might have had in mind. His old friend Walter Savage Landor had been at the mid-century the leading exponent of Hellenism; but the fact that he had at the time of the *Parleyings* been dead for over twenty years, whereas Browning usually preferred to contrast his opinions with those of contemporaries, makes it seem likely that the criticism applies only incidentally to Landor. Swinburne and Morris had been devoting themselves to Greek subjects, and Browning may well have had them in mind.

But whoever were the minor figures involved in Browning's criticism of the tendency to deal with Hellenistic subjects, it is certain that he could not have made such a criticism without having in mind the leading Hellenist of the age, Matthew Arnold. Partly because the two men were friends, and partly because Browning himself had shared Arnold's interest in Greek themes, the reference in the lines quoted above lacks the animus that would serve to identify Arnold without question, by its personalities. Nevertheless, Arnold's admitted position as the leading Hellenist of the time makes the criticism point very clearly to him.

Furthermore, the common interest that the two men had had in Greek themes must have brought Arnold first of all to Browning's mind as he contemplated the tendency toward Hellenistic subjects. Arnold, writing of his *Merope* to Madame du Quaire in 1858, says:

Make Browning look at it, if he is at Florence; one of the very best antique fragments I know is a fragment of a Hippolytus by him.[62]

---

61 The reference to the ghost is the third reference to the Greek, as is made clear by Mrs. Orr. See below, p. 249.

62 *Letters of Matthew Arnold*, ed. Russell, London and New York, 1895, I, 69 ff. The "fragment of a Hippolytus" is known as *Artemis Prologizes* (1842).

And from a letter from Matthew Arnold to his brother, in
July, 1867, we learn that Browning was actually responsible
for the reprinting of one of Arnold's Hellenistic poems:

> I shall be interested in hearing what you think of the poems
> [*New Poems*]; some of them I feel sure, will interest you. There
> are two or three bad faults of punctuation which you will ob-
> serve and correct. "Empedocles" takes up much room, but
> Browning's desire that I should reprint "Empedocles" was
> really the cause of the volume appearing at all.[63]

This interchange of attention to each other's work was due
to an actual common interest in the subjects involved. The
objections of Browning to ancient themes were comparatively recent. He had dealt with Greek subjects himself, occasionally. He had helped Elizabeth Barrett with her *Prometheus* in 1845.[64] Particularly during the 'seventies he had
busied himself with such themes; for *Balaustion's Adventure,
Aristophanes' Apology*, and *The Agamemnon of Aeschylus*
came out in that decade. His interest in Greek subjects
waned very late; yet while it lasted it was so closely associated with Matthew Arnold that he could not have written of
poets who loved the "dead Greek lore" without thinking primarily of him.

Furthermore, the whole passage in which Browning deals
with the Hellenists is almost a direct answer to Arnold's dictum on the very same subject, in his famous *Preface to
Poems*, 1853. There, in the defence of *Empedocles*—which
he was omitting in that edition and which Browning was
later to persuade him to reprint—Arnold began:

> I intended to delineate the feelings of one of the last of the
> Greek religious philosophers, one of the family of Orpheus and
> Musaeus, having survived his fellows, living on into a time when
> the habits of Greek thought and feeling had begun fast to
> change . . .

63 *Letters of Matthew Arnold*, I, 429.
64 *Letters of R. B. and E. B. B.*, I, 37-41.

Throughout the *Preface* Arnold had upheld the desirability
of dreaming afresh "old godlike shapes." A few passages will
show how clearly the issue was joined between him and the
Browning of 1887:

"The Poet," it is said, and by an intelligent critic, "the Poet
who would really fix the public attention must leave the exhausted past, and draw his subjects from matters of present
import, and *therefore* both of interest and novelty."

Now this view I believe to be completely false. It is worth examining, inasmuch as it is a fair sample of a class of critical
dicta everywhere current at the present day, having a philosophical form and air, but no real basis in fact; and which are
calculated to vitiate the judgment of readers of poetry, while
they exert, so far as they are adopted, a misleading influence on
the practice of those who write it.

. . . .

A great human action of a thousand years ago is more interesting to it [the elementary part of our nature, our passions] than
a smaller human action of to-day, even though upon the representation of this last the most consummate skill may have been
expended, and though it has the advantage of appealing by its
modern language, familiar manners, and contemporary allusions, to all our transient feelings and interests.

. . . .

Achilles, Prometheus, Clytemnestra, Dido—what modern
poem presents personages as interesting, even to us moderns, as
these personages of an "exhausted past"?[65]

Thus by precept as well as by practice Arnold is on the opposite side from Browning on this question of the proper
subject for poetry. Browning was, in the passage quoted
above,[66] clearly interpreting the spirit of Arnold as represented in the *Preface* of 1853, and answering it in his line,

Earth's young significance is all to learn . . .[67]

---

[65] These passages, as well as the passage quoted on the preceding page,
are to be found in *Poems: A New Edition*, London, 1853, *Preface*. I quote
from the 1854 edition, pp. ix-xvi.
[66] See above, p. 234.
[67] *With Gerard de Lairesse*, l. 391.

The question arises, Why should Browning, once so vitally interested in Hellenism that he pictured himself spending his old age reading the ancient Greeks, have turned finally against these things that he had loved? The answer to this question is to be found in Browning's general philosophy. It is another case of Browning's shutting his eyes to the evidence of his intellect and the dictates of his own tastes. As he grew older one idea grew more and more fixed in his mind, and the necessity for insisting upon it more and more vital. It was the idea of progress in all human things. Whatever was inconsistent with that axiom Browning was ready to cast ruthlessly away. He shut his eyes on the achievements of Greece in order to point clearly the progress of man. When Matthew Arnold and other Hellenists proclaimed the Greek civilization the greatest mankind had yet evolved, Browning's whole nature revolted. If their statement was true, where was progress? He had preferred the early Christian painters, in all their crudity, to the perfect work of the Greeks. This preference, incidentally, upheld his theory of progress. He himself had developed a realistic method in poetry, and that again seemed to him a sign of advance. But he carried the idea to its ultimate conclusions: the meanest modern subject was superior to the noblest of Greek themes. In this way the *Parleying With Gerard de Lairesse* joins the current of Browning's general philosophy. He proves to his own satisfaction that the moderns have developed a deeper insight into the soul of man; and this, to Browning, was the highest virtue of poetry. That his beloved Greeks should go by the board was unfortunate but necessary. He was once more rigidly applying his favorite idea that

> The first of the new, in our race's story,
> Beats the last of the old . . .[68]

[68] *Old Pictures in Florence*, ll. 155-156. In connection with this whole point it is interesting to compare an early letter from Elizabeth Barrett to the poet, in which she discusses Greek themes and philosophy: "Ah! you tempt me with a grand vision of Prometheus! . . . No, *I do not dare*. And

Having found it necessary to attack the Greek themes, Browning registered a double objection. Having objected to the use of Hellenistic subjects because they made use of the poet's fancy instead of the modern gift of imaginative insight, he went on to object to the Greek philosophy. Here again the underlying reason is his desire to prove a case for progress. As he had demonstrated an advance in artistic method, so he insisted on an advance in philosophy. Progress in all things!

> What was the best Greece babbled of as truth?
> "A shade, a wretched nothing,—sad, thin, drear,
> Cold, dark, it holds on to the lost loves here,
> If hand have haply sprinkled o'er the dead
> Three charitable dust-heaps, made mouth red
> One moment by the sip of sacrifice:
> Just so much comfort thaws the stubborn ice
> Slow-thickening upward till it choke at length
> The last faint flutter craving—not for strength,
> Not beauty, not the riches and the rule
> O'er men that made life life indeed." Sad school
> Was Hades! Gladly,—might the dead but slink
> To life back,—to the dregs once more would drink
> Each interloper, drain the humblest cup
> Fate mixes for humanity.[69]

The Greek philosophy offered no hope whatsoever, beyond a shadowy after-life, to which the greatest hero would prefer

besides . . . I am inclined to think that we want new *forms*, as well as thoughts. The old gods are dethroned. Why should we go back to the antique moulds, classical moulds, as they are so improperly called? If it is a necessity of Art to do so, why then those critics are right who hold that Art is exhausted and the world too worn out for poetry. I do not, for my part, believe this: and I believe the so-called necessity of Art to be the mere feebleness of the artist. Let us all aspire rather to *Life*, and let the dead bury their dead. If we have but courage to face these conventions, to touch this low ground, we shall take strength from it instead of losing it; and of that, I am intimately persuaded. For there is poetry *everywhere*: the 'treasure' . . . lies all over the field. And then Christianity is a worthy *myth*, and poetically acceptable." *Letters of R. B. and E. B. B.*, I, 45-46.
[69] *With Gerard de Lairesse*, ll. 394-408.

the meanest sort of fate on earth. Browning proceeds to
show how philosophy has progressed. Men to-day have
higher hopes. They go on and on, still progressing. Browning asserts it in answer to the Greek stoicism—asserts it with
all his old optimism:

> By proved potency that still
> Makes perfect, be assured, come what come will,
> What once lives never dies—what here attains
> To a beginning, has no end, still gains
> And never loses aught: when, where, and how—
> Lies in Law's lap. What's death then? Even now
> With so much knowledge is it hard to bear
> Brief interposing ignorance? Is care
> For a creation found at fault just there—
> There where the heart breaks bond and outruns time,
> To reach, not follow what shall be?[70]

The hopefulness of his religion is another sign of progress.

III

THE way is now cleared for a consideration of the *Parleying*
itself. Browning begins with an apostrophe to the blind
painter:

> Ah, but—because you were struck blind, could bless
> Your sense no longer with the actual view
> Of man and woman, those fair forms you drew
> In happier days so duteously and true,—
> Must I account my Gerard de Lairesse
> All sorrow-smitten? He was hindered too
> —Was this no hardship?—from producing, plain
> To us who still have eyes, the pageantry
> Which passed and passed before his busy brain . . .[71]

Until blindness came upon him, he captured all this pag-
eantry upon his canvas. Yet Browning, remembering his
early love of Lairesse's "prodigious book," is thankful that,

[70] *With Gerard de Lairesse,* ll. 411-421.
[71] *Idem,* ll. 1-9.

if affliction had to come to Lairesse, it was blindness rather
than the loss of speech:

> Blind—not dumb,
> Else, Gerard, were my inmost bowels stirred
> With pity beyond pity: no, the word
> Was left upon your unmolested lips:
> Your mouth unsealed, despite of eyes' eclipse,
> Talked all brain's yearning into birth . . . [72]

Browning does not wish the artist's practice back; he recalls
his early disappointment at the pictures by Lairesse in the
Dulwich Gallery. But the book, and especially that section in
which Lairesse conducts his pupils on an imaginary walk in
order to show them what is painter-like and what is un-
painter-like, Browning remembers with pleasure:

> . . . 't was a boy that budged
> No foot's breadth from your visioned steps away
> The while that memorable "Walk" he trudged
> In your companionship,—the Book must say
> Where, when and whither,—"Walk," come what come may,
> No measurer of steps on this our globe
> Shall ever match for marvels . . . [73]

For Lairesse turned his imagination on the common sights
about him until "Holland turned Dreamland." In a few
words Browning sums up the wonders of the blind painter's
imagination:

> So commenced
> That "Walk" amid true wonders—none to you,
> But huge to us ignobly common-sensed,
> Purblind, while plain could proper optics view
> In that old sepulchre by lightning split,
> Whereof the lid bore carven,—any dolt
> Imagines why,—Jove's very thunderbolt:
> You who could straight perceive, by glance at it,

[72] *With Gerard de Lairesse,* ll. 22-27.
[73] *Idem,* ll. 44-50.

This tomb must needs be Phaeton's! In a trice,
Confirming that conjecture, close on hand,
Behold, half out, half in the ploughed-up sand,
A chariot-wheel explained its bolt-device:
What other than the Chariot of the Sun
Ever let drop the like?[74]

Browning has in this passage lifted to the level of poetry
Lairesse's prosaic account. His imagination has played upon
the original, and endowed it with a new richness. He shows
too the resourcefulness of Lairesse in imagining the wonders
of ancient lore even in prosaic Holland. And, the poet adds,
this is only part of the walk, which was full of revelations,
every one as wondrous.

Browning next tries to account for this richness of imagination in Lairesse. Was it that the painter's mind was free to
create unhampered by the sense of reality which his sight

[74] *Idem,* ll. 67-80. The walk, which occurs in Chs. 16 and 17 of Book VI
(*Of Landscapes*), is easily the finest part of *The Art of Painting.* The passage Browning paraphrases runs as follows: "Stepping a little further, I
saw another sight as fine as the former; I say, fine with respect to art. It
was an ancient tomb or sepulcher of light red marble, intermixed with dark
grey, and white eyes and veins, with a lid or cover of lapis lazuli. This tomb
was supported by four white marble sphinxes without wings, resting on a
large black marble plinth, which, through its dustiness, seemed to be light-
ish grey. The ground under it was rugged, yet level for three or four feet
round the plinth. This work was generally encompassed with sand extending
to the sea-shore, which it faced; and, ten or twelve steps further, the sea
was seen foaming. In the middle of the belly of the tomb, was a round bass-
relief within a compartment of oak leaves; it exhibited a flying eagle, with
thunder in its bill; whence I conjectured it might be *Phaeton's* grave; and
the rather, because there stood, near the corners, three very old and large
cypresses; of which the hindmost was as yet whole and sound, but the forward ones, by weather or otherwise, so damaged, that one had lost its top,
and the other was on one side half unbranched and bare. Behind this tomb,
stood a large pedestal of greyish-blue stone, on which had formerly, as it
seemed, been set an urn, now flung down, and lying near it half buried in
the ground: it was somewhat broken and damaged: I could make but little
of the carving upon it, since that was underneath, and the ear or handle of
the urn lay upwards; wherefore, in order to see what it was, I began to
clear the ground away from it; but had hardly dug a foot deep, before I
perceived a piece of a chariot, and half a wheel in the shape of a star; this,
I thought, must be the chariot of the sun, as being not much unlike it."
The Art of Painting, p. 255. Browning depends largely, in the *Parleying,*
on his favorite sections of Lairesse, Books V and VI.

would have given him? He could create beautiful things, and
banish everything unbeautiful.

> And bent on banishing was mind, be sure,
> All except beauty from its mustered tribe
> Of objects apparitional which lure
> Painter to show and poet to describe . . .[75]

This is like the practice of modern painters and poets,
Browning says; they find no worth in the things about them.
For himself, he does not want the wings of dream. But he understands alternatives no less, and he understands the blind
painter's "soul's leap." Would it be an advantage or a detri-
ment to Browning himself if with his own vision he could
combine the sort that Lairesse has? He believes very strongly
that man should keep every good gift of mind; and he believes that he still has the gift of fancy:

> Oh, we can fancy too! but somehow fact
> Has got to—say, not so much push aside
> Fancy, as to declare its place supplied
> By fact unseen but no less fact the same,
> Which mind bids sense accept. Is mind to blame,
> Or sense,—does that usurp, this abdicate?
> First of all, as you "walked"—were it too late
> For us to walk, if so we willed? Confess
> We have the sober feet still, De Lairesse!
> Why not the freakish brain too, that must needs
> Supplement nature—not see flowers and weeds
> Simply as such, but link with each and all
> The ultimate perfection . . .?[76]

Not to possess Lairesse's type of art, as well as our own,
Browning says, would be retrogression. And retrogression is
unthinkable:

> No, no: we poets go not back at all:
> What you did we could do—from great to small

75 *With Gerard de Lairesse*, ll. 96-99.
76 *Idem*, ll. 149-161.

> Sinking assuredly: if this world last
> One moment longer when Man finds its Past
> Exceed its Present—blame the Protoplast!
> If we no longer see as you of old,
> 'T is we see deeper. Progress for the bold!
> You saw the body, 't is the soul we see.[77]

Then comes the challenge to Lairesse. Browning will test the powers of the moderns: he will prove that he can equal Lairesse in his own manner. And if Lairesse fails to follow him all the way, then Browning has gone beyond him.

> Come, walk once more
> The "Walk": if I to-day as you of yore
> See just like you the blind—then sight shall cry
> —The whole long day quite gone through—victory![78]

This challenge to the painter is of course a challenge to Browning himself. In reality it is he who must prove that not only can he see in the newer, deeper, more realistic way, but that he can see in the old fanciful way, as well. He will use the very scheme of Lairesse, which he learned from Book V (*Of Lights and Shades*),[79] and which he has made use of before in his poetry[80]—the scheme of dividing his pictures into groups according to the time of day. So the poet begins on his series of scenes, going from daybreak and morning to noon, and then on to late afternoon and finally to evening. In a succession of beautiful pictures Browning does very much what Lairesse might have done, yet something that Lairesse never did do. There is all the difference between the work of the plodder and the work of the genius.

Browning's walk begins amid thunder and sharp white lightning at daybreak. It is a wild, magnificent mountain country of firs and pines, crags and granite ridges. Then suddenly the walkers discover by the lightning "the motive

---

[77] *With Gerard de Lairesse*, ll. 166-173.
[78] *Idem*, ll. 177-180.
[79] See above, pp. 222-223.
[80] See above, pp. 224-226.

of the malice." They see that it is Prometheus who is here groaning, chained by Jove's orders to the rock:

> Circled with flame there yawned a sudden rift
> I' the rock-face, and I saw a form erect
> Front and defy the outrage, while—as checked,
> Chidden, beside him dauntless in the drift—
> Cowered a heaped creature, wing and wing outspread
> In deprecation o'er the crouching head
> Still hungry for the feast foregone awhile.[81]

For this picture of the dauntless Prometheus Browning went back to the days when Elizabeth Barrett, with his help, was rewriting her *Prometheus Bound*.[82] One needs only to remember the heroic utterance of the fire-bringer as she made him speak:

> For the rest
> Let him now hurl his blenching lightnings down,
> And with his white-winged snows, and mutterings deep
> Of subterranean thunders, mix all things:
> Confound them in disorder: none of this
> Shall bend my sturdy will, and make me speak . . .,

or to remember the picture that she gives of him in the dread terrors that are to come:

> For at first
> The Father will split up this jut of rock
> With the great thunder and the bolted flame,
> And hide thy body where the hinge of stone
> Shall catch it like an arm—and when thou hast passed
> A long black time within, thou shalt come out
> To front the sun: and Zeus's winged-hound,
> The strong carnivorous eagle, shall wheel down
> To meet thee . . .[83]

81 *With Gerard de Lairesse*, ll. 188-194.
82 *Letters of R. B. and E. B. B.*, I, 37-41.
83 This and the preceding quotation are taken from the very end of Elizabeth Barrett's translation of Aeschylus' *Prometheus Bound*. (The lines are not numbered.)

It is interesting to note that Browning also calls the vulture
"eagle-hound," and that his language and his picture both
resemble Mrs. Browning more than they do Aeschylus.[84]

But the picture is flashed upon us only for a moment.
Browning leaves the magnificent Prometheus,

> Hate on, love ever! Morn is breaking there—
> The granite ridge pricks through the mist, turns gold
> As wrong turns right. O laughters manifold
> Of ocean's ripple at dull earth's despair![85]

And with the morning come new sights.

After the night's storm the great trees stir themselves
from the stupor of the darkness, and are glorious in the
light. The torrents plunge down the mountain-side; the
earth smokes up mistily. The whole world is a-glitter in the
light. But turn! See Artemis, ἐλαφηζόλος, she who armed
with bow and arrow sends plague and sudden death among
men and animals,[86] and whose arrows are fatal to the maid
about to be married:

> Rather turn
> Whither, upon the upland, pedestalled
> Into the broad day-splendor, whom discern
> These eyes but thee, supreme one, rightly called
> Moon-maid in heaven above and, here below,
> Earth's huntress-queen?[87]

And then follows the most lucid, clear and perfect passage of
this *Parleying*. One must look far back in Browning to find
an equal to it:

[84] I am not unaware that Mrs. Orr says that certain bits of Browning's
picture come directly from Aeschylus; see *Handbook*, p. 356. A note in the
Florentine edition rightly suggests Mrs. Browning's *Prometheus* as the
source for this passage.
[85] *With Gerard de Lairesse*, ll. 206-209.
[86] Browning's image is Homeric; see *Iliad*, VI, 205; XIX, 59; XXI, 483;
and *Odyssey*, XI, 172, 324; XV, 478; XVIII, 202; XX, 61 ff.
[87] *With Gerard de Lairesse*, ll. 226-231.

What hope along the hillside, what far bliss
Lets the crisp hair-plaits fall so low they kiss
Those lucid shoulders? Must a morn so blithe,
Needs have its sorrow when the twang and hiss
Tell that from out thy sheaf one shaft makes writhe
Its victim, thou unerring Artemis?
Why did the chamois stand so fair a mark
Arrested by the novel shape he dreamed
Was bred of liquid marble in the dark
Depths of the mountain's womb which ever teemed
With novel births of wonder? Not one spark
Of pity in that steel-gray glance which gleamed
At the poor hoof's protesting as it stamped
Idly the granite? Let me glide unseen
From thy proud presence: well mayst thou be queen
Of all those strange and sudden deaths which damped
So oft Love's torch and Hymen's taper lit
For happy marriage till the maidens paled
And perished on the temple-step . . .[88]

This is Homer, not Ovid; Lairesse had never seen this **Diana**. The Diana that the Flemish painter knew was the sensual lover of Endymion.[89]

Now noon is the conqueror; the mists have gone, and the fierce blue sky blazes overhead. So the poet retreats to shade:

Deep in the hollow, rather, where combine
Tree, shrub and briar to roof with shade and cool
The remnant of some lily-strangled pool,
Edged round with mossy fringing soft and fine.[90]

Overhead are trees of different kinds. Here the poet sees a picture that Lairesse might have envied him, for it is a picture of a nymph and a satyr. It is the story that Moschus told, of the satyr pining away for the love of the stony-hearted Lyda. Shelley had translated it,[91] and it is likely

[88] *With Gerard de Lairesse*, ll. 240-258.
[89] See *The Art of Painting*, pp. 74-76.
[90] *With Gerard de Lairesse*, ll. 275-278.
[91] His translation is called *Pan, Echo, and the Satyr*.

that Browning knew it in his well-loved Shelley rather than
in the original. But Browning does something to the story
that neither Moschus nor Shelley had done, and something
that Lairesse could never have done. It is here that Browning breaks stride with the blind painter, and in his own dramatic manner throws himself into the feelings of the satyr:

> O Satyr, well I know
> How sad thy case, and what a world of woe
> Was hid by the brown visage furry-framed
> Only for mirth: who otherwise could think—
> Marking thy mouth gape still on laughter's brink,
> Thine eyes a-swim with merriment unnamed
> But haply guessed at by their furtive wink?
> And all the while a heart was panting sick
> Behind that shaggy bulwark of thy breast—
> Passion it was that made those breath-bursts thick
> I took for mirth subsiding into rest.
> So, it was Lyda—she of all the train
> Of forest-thridding nymphs,—'t was only she
> Turned from thy rustic homage in disdain,
> Saw but that poor uncouth outside of thee,
> And, from her circling sisters, mocked a pain
> Echo had pitied—whom Pan loved in vain—
> For she was wishful to partake thy glee,
> Mimic thy mirth—who loved her not again,
> Savage for Lyda's sake. She crouches there—
> Thy cruel beauty, slumberously laid
> Supine on heaped-up beast-skins, unaware
> Thy steps have traced her to the briery glade . . .[92]

The picture is one that Lairesse might have envied, but the
psychology is purely Browning's own.

But now it is afternoon, and the sun seems to linger in the
west as if fearful of missing some dread and decisive act
upon which the fate of the world depends. There is a huge
plain, and to it come trooping silently, and range themselves,

[92] *With Gerard de Lairesse*, ll. 283-305.

two vast powers. They are bent on a battle, and stand there

> . . . host fronting host,
> As statue statue fronts—wrath-molten each,
> Solidified by hate,—earth halved almost,
> To close once more in chaos. Yet two shapes
> Show prominent, each from the universe
> Of minions round about him, that disperse
> Like cloud-obstruction when a bolt escapes.[93]

The leaders are King Darius III and Alexander the Great. They face each other at dusk, each waiting for the other to strike:

> Who flames first? Macedonian is it thou?[94]

The whole scene is ominous and silent.

But darkness comes down upon us. The western crags are black; Caucasus, where Prometheus was chained, is lost now in the night, and Greece too is far away. Human heroes are gone from the world:

> Yet I dimly see almost—
> Yes, for my last adventure! 'T is a ghost.
> So drops away the beauty! There he stands
> Voiceless, scarce strives with deprecating hands.[95]

The ghost, the solitary figure in the scene of night, is symbolical of the emptiness of the Greek philosophy. As Mrs. Orr explains it, "The pallid vision which he repels speaks dumbly of pagan regret for what is past, of pagan hopelessness of the to-come."[96] And with this symbolical figure Browning breaks off his walk.

Then he turns back to Lairesse, for the ghost has re-

---

[93] *With Gerard de Lairesse,* ll. 325-331. With this, and with the preceding scenes, compare what Lairesse says about appropriate actions for certain times of day; above, pp. 221-223. He suggests a battle, an Artemis, and a scene of retirement for noon.

[94] *Idem,* l. 332. The details of this battle at dusk are singularly like Arrian of Nicomedia's *Anabasis of Alexander,* which Browning probably consulted. See Rooke's *Arrian,* 1814, Book III, Chs. 8-16.

[95] *With Gerard de Lairesse,* ll. 359-362.

[96] Orr, *Handbook,* p. 357.

minded him of the theme of progress which the very walk was
taken to uphold:

> Enough! Stop further fooling, De Lairesse!
> My fault, not yours! Some fitter way express
> Heart's satisfaction that the Past indeed
> Is past, gives way before Life's best and last,
> The all-including future! What were life
> Did soul stand still therein, forego her strife
> Through the ambiguous Present to the goal
> Of some all-reconciling Future? Soul,
> Nothing has been which shall not bettered be
> Hereafter . . .[97]

Then with a suddenness that we have hardly been prepared
for, Browning, thinking of the necessity for progress in all
things, turns upon the poets who dwell intellectually in the
past. He adds, after his description of their theories,[98] his
own advice:

> Let things be—not seem,
> I counsel rather,—do, and nowise dream!
> Earth's young significance is all to learn . . .[99]

And in the concluding lines are fused Browning's double set
of objection to such poets. Their method of dream and fancy
is out of date compared to the new development of imaginative insight; and they are turning their backs on all the
young significance of modern life, for the sake of attending
the sad school of Greece. And this was the chief of Browning's objections to the Hellenistic tendency of his fellow-
poets, that they were appealing to a hopeless philosophy.
Death was a hard thing for the Greeks to bear, because for
them it was the end. Browning *can* be resigned with Achilles:

> Be death with me, as with Achilles erst,
> Of Man's calamities the last and worst:
> Take it so . . .[100]

[97] *With Gerard de Lairesse*, ll. 363-372.
[98] See above, p. 233.
[99] *With Gerard de Lairesse*, ll. 389-391.
[100] *Idem*, ll. 409-411. See *Odyssey*, XI, 488-491.

but he has something far more than Achilles had. There is
for him a life beyond the grave. There's spring! And once
more Browning breaks into the old triumphant strain of *Abt
Vogler* and *Rabbi Ben Ezra*—in a beautiful little lyric in
which his voice breaks in spite of his assurance. The walk
proved something of progress, in showing how man had not
lost the old powers in gaining new ones; but this demonstra-
tion of the hopefulness of our new philosophy is the deeper
proof. It is the "fitter way" in which Browning wanted to
express "Heart's satisfaction that the Past indeed is past."
So he ends the *Parleying* with his own lyrical answer to the
greatest ancient bard of them all:

> Here's rhyme
> Such as one makes now,—say, when Spring repeats
> That miracle the Greek Bard sadly greets:
> "Spring for the tree and herb—no Spring for us!"[101]
> Let Spring come: why, a man salutes her thus:
>
> Dance, yellows and whites and reds,—
> Lead your gay orgy, leaves, stalks, heads
> Astir with the wind in the tulip-beds!
>
> There's sunshine; scarcely a wind at all
> Disturbs starved grass and daisies small
> On a certain mound by a churchyard wall.
>
> Daisies and grass be my heart's bedfellows
> On the mound wind spares and sunshine mellows:
> Dance you, reds and whites and yellows![102]

[101] This seems to be Browning's paraphrase of the *Iliad,* VI, 146-149.
[102] *With Gerard de Lairesse,* ll. 421-434. This lyric was first published in
The New Amphion, a small magazine published at Edinburgh University,
in 1886.

CHAPTER VII

THE PARLEYING WITH
CHARLES AVISON

I

THE *Parleying With Charles Avison,* organist of New-castle, is from the point of view of poetry, artistry, and general interest one of the best of the seven. This is quite natural, for Browning's personal interest, which has been growing steadily through the last few *Parleyings,* is here most strongly aroused. Avison, whose *March* was one of the earliest musical recollections of the poet's life, is chosen to represent the art which was not only one of Browning's favorites, but which he considered the greatest of all the arts. The *Parleying* therefore becomes a summation of all the poet's ideas about music. It is filled, consequently, with more colorful imagery and warm emotion than most of the other *Parleyings.* The verse too has a high level of melodious smoothness which none of the other *Parleyings* can quite equal, though they may surpass it in purple patches.

Browning's love of music was marked even from his earliest childhood, perhaps even as early as his practice in painting.[1] In one way it is almost unique. All his other enthusiasms Browning seems to have inherited from his father, or to have acquired from him. But his love of music, together with his religious tendency, came directly from his mother, who was a "sympathetic and accomplished musician."[2] Browning was all his life a music-lover, from

. . . the days when as a mere child he stole downstairs from bed to listen to his mother at the piano, and as she ceased,

---

[1] See above, p. 214.
[2] Griffin and Minchin, pp. 15-16.

flung himself into her arms, whispering, amid sobs, "Play, play" . . .³

And with those days of his early and passionate love of music Browning associated the *Grand March* of Avison, for his mother

. . . loved to sit at the piano in the gloaming when, perhaps, music is most subtle and most potent: and one of his earliest memories was of her playing Avison's once popular Grand March in C Major . . .⁴

This was, as he tells us in the *Parleying*, before his "hand could stretch an octave."⁵

Avison's *March*, styled "Grand," is primitive and simple to a degree. And yet, as Browning remembered, by the very persistence of its melody, when it was played it

> Did veritably seem to grow, expand,
> And greaten up to title as, unchecked,
> Dream-marchers marched, kept marching, slow and sure,
> In time, to tune, unchangeably the same,
> From nowhere into nowhere,—out they came,
> Onward they passed, and in they went.⁶

In this simple melody there was no novel modulation, no discord lurking beneath to be resolved. Yet there was something magical about it:

> Yet, such the might
> Of quietude's immutability,
> That somehow coldness gathered warmth, well nigh
> Quickened—which could not be!—grew burning-bright
> With fife-shriek, cymbal-clash and trumpet-blare,
> To drum-accentuation: pacing turned
> Striding, and striding grew gigantic, spurned
> At last the narrow space 'twixt earth and air,
> So shook me back into my sober self.⁷

³ Griffin and Minchin, p. 17.
⁴ *Idem,* pp. 15-16.
⁵ *With Charles Avison,* ll. 51-52.
⁶ *Idem,* ll. 60-65.
⁷ *Idem,* ll. 70-78.

Such was Browning's recollection of the *March;* and it is
significant that even from the beginning he seems to have
had this habit of peopling a melody with dream-figures, just
as he was later to repeople Galuppi's Venice, or Schumann's,
Master Hugues' church, and the improvisations of the Abbé
Vogler.[8] So it was entirely appropriate that he should have
attached the music of Avison's *March* as he got it from a
manuscript copy in the possession of his father, to the *Parleying* some seventy years later;[9] and still more appropriate
that he should have written as the conclusion for the *Parleying* words for those dream-marchers to sing as they marched.

Browning's early interest in and love of music was encouraged as he grew older. In the irregular education which he
received at his father's house in Southampton Street, music
seems to have been his chief study. At least, he had two regular instructors in that subject—which was two more than
any other subject save French, which had one, attained.
Abel, a pupil of Moscheles, was his instructor in technique.
But what is more important for our purpose is that Browning was, he tells us, an "all unworthy pupil" of

Great John Relfe,
Master of mine, learned, redoubtable . . .[10]

Relfe, musician in ordinary to George III, was one of the
best teachers of pianoforte in London. He was also a composer of sorts. But he attained his greatest distinction as a
writer on musical theory. It was from this learned author of
The Principles of Harmony, "a complete and compendious
illustration of the theory of music," and of *Lucidus Ordo,*
"an attempt to divest thorough-bass and composition of
their intricacies," that Browning learned the elements of
music. Relfe was a learned man, a master of counterpoint
and thorough-bass—a technician above all else. He under-

[8] See below, pp. 267-268.
[9] See Orr, *Handbook,* p. 360. A copy of the *March* is appended at the
end of this chapter.
[10] *With Charles Avison,* ll. 81-82.

took to teach his pupils "not only Thorough Bass, but the whole arcana of the science, so as completely to analyze any regular composition."[11] Under this rigorous master Browning acquired the technical mastery of music which always distinguished him. "I was studying the Grammar of Music," he said in the later years of his life, "when most children are learning the multiplication table, and I know what I am talking about when I speak of music."[12] This mastery of technique not only exhibits itself in every poem that Browning wrote concerning music and musicians, but it inspired him to set to music such songs as Donne's *Goe and Catch a Falling Star*, Hood's *I Will not have the mad Clytie*, and Peacock's *The Mountain Sheep are Sweeter*.[13] It was such able instruction as Relfe's which emboldened him to contemplate writing an opera before he was twenty-one.[14]

But Relfe's most valuable gift to the young poet has not as yet been chronicled. Relfe's books are so technical in their nature that they reveal only incidentally his great knowledge of the history of music and musicians; but his oral instruction to his eager young pupil must have been full of references to the great names of musical history. Through him Browning's knowledge of Abt Vogler must certainly have come, for as Fétis, the compiler of the excellent *Biographie Universelle des Musiciens* (Paris, 1875) points out, "La base de ce [Relfe's] système est puisée dans les livres de l'abbé Vogler et de Schicht." Browning's knowledge of Hudl, Greene, Pepusch, Buononcini, and all the lesser orders of musicians—not to mention Handel, Purcell, Bach and the giants—may well have come from the mouth of his learned master. Moreover, in spite of the technical character of his books, Relfe was fully cognizant of the emotional qualities of

[11] J. Relfe, *Remarks on the Present State of Musical Instruction with the Prospectus of an Improved Plan* . . ., London, 1819, p. 31.
[12] Quoted by Griffin and Minchin, p. 16, from the *Manchester Examiner and Times,* December 18, 1889.
[13] See Orr, *Life,* p. 41.
[14] See Griffin and Minchin, p. 16.

music, of the highly individualized styles of the different composers, and of the general trend of musical style at different periods—all of which must have been highly interesting to the young Browning.

It would be odd, too, if the unusual library of the elder Browning did not contain several books on music and its history. It is hard to imagine that Sir John Hawkins' *History of Music* with all the additions by Burney and Busby was missing. The book that here primarily concerns us, however, is the "little book" by Charles Avison, of which there were two copies in the library.

This was the *Essay on Musical Expression,* published in London in 1752. Browning was perhaps more indebted to Avison's "little book," as he calls it, than anyone has hitherto imagined. The *Essay* takes the reader at once to the world of English music as it was in Handel's day, and plunges him abruptly into the quarrel that was then going on between the rival opera-writers, Handel and Buononcini. The former is commented on many times and at length;[15] and the latter, the "frequent delicacy of whose airs is so striking that we almost forget the defect of Harmony under which they often labour,"[16] comes in for his share of praise and blame. Geminiani, Avison's master, calls forth great enthusiasm:

To this illustrious Example in *vocal* [Marcello], I shall add another, the greatest in *instrumental Music;* I mean the admirable Geminiani; whose Elegance and Spirit of Composition ought to have been much more our Pattern; and from whom the public Taste might have received the highest Improvement, had we thought proper to lay hold of those opportunities which his long Residence in this Kingdom has given us.[17]

For Avison cared more for the Italian musicians than he did for "our illustrious Handel . . . who hath supplied the Town with musical Entertainments of every Kind, for thirty

---

[15] See, for example, *Essay on Musical Expression,* pp. 53-54.
[16] See *idem,* p. 43.
[17] *Idem,* pp. 86-87. See also pp. 88, 97, 109-111.

Years together."[18] In short, Avison in all likelihood supple-
mented Relfe's instruction with a detailed history of the
music of this period. From him Browning may likewise have
first learned of Palestrina and the mode which the poet was
to prefer to the fugues of Master Hugues of Saxe-Gotha.[19]
From Avison, too, Browning may have got the idea of com-
paring music with the other arts—a favorite habit with Avison.[20]

To be sure, Browning's knowledge of music and musical
history is a great deal more comprehensive than that exhibited in Avison's *Essay*. For example, some of the contemporaries of Avison mentioned in the *Parleying* are not to be
found in Avison. The famed Dr. John Christopher Pepusch
(1667-1752), who wrote the *Alexis*—a song which held its
own well into the nineteenth century—who was a prominent
figure in the Academy of Ancient Music, and who so graciously gave way to Handel as organist to the Duke of
Chandos, is not mentioned by Avison. Nor is Greenway, who
trilled the *Alexis*. I suspect that the Greenway whom Browning mentions may be Maurice Greene (1696-1755), the acquaintance of all the musicians mentioned here by Browning,
since I can nowhere in the annals of music discover this
Greenway. But though Browning went beyond Avison, there
is little doubt that it was through the organist of Newcastle
that he first came into vital contact with the musicians of the
eighteenth century.

There was also in the library of the house in Southampton
Street a nameless French memoir of Claude le Jeune[21] which
likewise performed a very important service in the poet's
musical development. It impressed him rather later in his life
than Avison did, but it encouraged in him a conception of

18 *Essay on Musical Expression*, p. 53.
19 See *idem*, pp. 45 note, 46 note, 49-51, 81.
20 See *idem*, pp. 23-31, 44-45, and 74 note.
21 This memoir was in all probability *Esquisse biographique sur Claude
Lejeune, natif de Valenciennes, surnommé le Phénix des musiciens, com-
positeur de la musique des rois Henri III et Henri IV;* Valenciennes, 1845.

music for which he had been groping when he wrote *Pauline*.[22] This conception persisted all through his life, and he was to apply it most fully in the *Parleying With Charles Avison*. He recounts the whole history of his interest in the memoir, in a letter to Elizabeth Barrett on March 7, 1846:

For music, I made myself melancholy just now with some 'Concertos for the Harpsichord by Mr. Handel'—brought home by my father the day before yesterday;—what were light, modern things once! Now I read not very long ago a French Memoir of 'Claude le Jeune' called in his time the Prince of Musicians,— no '*Phoenix*'—the unapproachable wonder to all time—that is, twenty years after his death about—and to this pamphlet was prefixed as motto this startling axiom—'In Music, the Beau Ideal changes every thirty years'—well, is not that *true?* The *Idea*, mind, changes—the general standard . . . so that it is no answer that a single air, such as many one knows, may strike as freshly as ever—they were *not* according to the Ideal of their own time—just now, they drop into the ready ear,—next hundred years, who will be the Rossini? who is no longer the Rossini even I remember—his early overtures are as purely Rococo as Cimarosa's or more. The sounds remain, keep their character perhaps—the scale's proportioned notes affect the same, that is,—the major third, or minor seventh—but the arrangement of these, the sequence the law—for them, if it *should* change every thirty years! To Corelli nothing seemed so conclusive in Heaven or earth as this

I don't believe there is one of his sonatas wherein that formula does not do duty. In these things of Handel that seems replaced by

22 See below, pp. 264-265.

—that was the only true consummation! Then,—to go over a hundred years,—came Rossini's unanswerable coda:

which serves as base to the infinity of songs, gone, gone—*so* gone by! From all of which Ba draws *this* 'conclusion' that there may be worse things than Bartoli's Tuscan to cover a page with!—yet the pity of it! Le Jeune, the Phoenix, and Rossini who directed his letters to his mother as 'mother of the famous composer'—and Henry Lawes, and Dowland's Lute, ah me![23]

The idea of the passing of old music and musicians underlies almost every passage and poem in Browning written about music—*Abt Vogler*, *A Toccata of Galuppi's*, *Master Hugues*, the extended discussion of music in *Fifine at the Fair*, and finally the full theory of music and its relation to his philosophy as a whole in the *Parleying With Charles Avison*, have this axiom of change as one of their basic ideas.

From these books, then, and from the learned Relfe, Browning acquired his conception of music and its history. Yet his passion for this art was subject to ebb and flow. His interest was undoubtedly heightened by his boyish love for Eliza Flower, herself a musical composer of moderate ability, and the "onlie begetter" of *Pauline*, according to Mrs. Orr.[24] His affair with her began when he was thirteen or fourteen, and his interest continued. In *Pauline* Browning shows us the great part that this art played in his thought:

> . . . music, my life,
> Nourished me more than ever . . .[25]

and it is instructive to find that among his associates in 1833, Browning was known as a musician and artist rather than as

23 *Letters of R. B. and E. B. B.*, I, 539-540.
24 Orr, *Life*, p. 35.
25 *Pauline*, ll. 565-566.

a poet.[26] In 1837 we find Browning composing a crooning
measure for Strafford's children to sing in his play of that
name. It was music suitable for children, and music that was
historically accurate, but it was not used in Macready's pro-
duction because the child actors preferred something more
pretentious.[27] This is all the more significant for our purpose
when we consider that Avison and Strafford seemed to be intimately connected in the poet's mind.[28] The *Cavalier Tunes*,
hewn as they were from the same quarry as *Strafford*, are in
matter and spirit strikingly like the song for Pym at the end
of the *Parleying With Charles Avison*.

As long as Browning was in England his musical nature
seems to have been well nourished. Through *Pauline, Paracelsus*, the dramas and early poems, come almost constant allusions or apostrophes to music. Typical of these is the one
in *Waring* (1845), where, wishing Domett back for the sake
of this and that, he says:

> Or Music means this land of ours
> Some favor yet, to pity won
> By Purcell from his Rosy Bowers . . .,

showing an intimacy with past English music. Toward the
end of his stay in England, music seems to have been rivalled
by a returning love for painting.[29] Still his letters to Elizabeth Barrett are full of references to music.[30] But with the
flight to Italy the facilities for music were left behind. Music,
too, to Elizabeth Barrett Browning was rather a closed
book.[31] Thus gradually music went out of Browning's life
and painting came in to take its place. Even so, he was not
entirely willing to give up his youthful passion, and a

26 See Sharp, *Life*, p. 54.
27 See *Poet Lore*, IX, 236 (May, 1889).
28 See below, pp. 268, 281-282.
29 See Orr, *Life*, p. 124.
30 See *Letters of R. B. and E. B. B.*, I, 33, 195, 539, 540; II, 131.
31 See *idem*, I, 519.

glimpse of him here and there shows that he played whenever the chance presented itself. In 1847 we see him:

> Mrs. Browning . . . was still too much of an invalid to walk, but she sat under the great trees upon the lawn-like hillsides near the convent, or in the seats of the dusky convent chapel, while Robert Browning at the organ chased a fugue, or dreamed out upon the twilight keys a faint throbbing *toccata* of Galuppi.[32]

In the next few years music seems to have occupied a comparatively small space in the thoughts of the poet. In *Men and Women* (1855) it is represented by only two poems, *Master Hugues of Saxe-Gotha* and *A Toccata of Galuppi's*. These compare neither in number nor quality with the poems upon the sister art of painting. His heart was otherwise; he was modelling with Gibson and Story, or finding old pictures in Florence. Perhaps, too, the opportunities for music in Florence were none too good, as a passage in *Bishop Blougram's Apology* hints:

> Like Verdi, when, at his worst opera's end
> (The thing they gave at Florence,—what's its name?)
> While the mad houseful's plaudits near outbang
> His orchestra of salt-box, tongs and bones,
> He looks through all the roaring and the wreaths
> Where sits Rossini patient in his stall.[33]

Yet when an opportunity for good music presented itself, Browning took advantage of it. We find him breaking away once a week to the excellent music at Mrs. Sartoris' at Rome in 1854.[34] By 1857 the Brownings had a piano in their Casa Guidi apartments, and the poet was to be seen any morning in the next three years giving music lessons to his son, Pen.[35] In 1860 we find him evincing an enthusiasm in the old man-

[32] Cooke, p. 416.
[33] *Bishop Blougram's Apology*, ll. 381-386.
[34] Orr, *Life*, pp. 190-191.
[35] *Letters of R. B. to Isa Blagden*, pp. 10, 20.

ner for the music of Frederick Hiller.[36] An occasional reference or illustration from music in these years—the one from *Bishop Blougram's Apology*, for example—shows that the poet's interest in musical matters was only dormant. But in all, there can be little doubt, Browning's love for music was starved in Italy. Italy was the natural home of the other arts, and while he was there they filled his life.

On his return to England after Mrs. Browning's death in 1861, the poet, when the arduous task of completing *The Ring and the Book* would allow him, plunged into the world of music at London. Mrs. Orr thus describes Browning's love of music for the next decade of his life:

. . . it had now grown into a passion, from the indulgence of which he derived, as he always declared, some of the most beneficent influences of his life. It would scarcely be an exaggeration to say that he attended every important concert of the season, whether isolated or given in a course. There was no engagement possible or actual, which did not yield to the discovery of its clashing with the day and hour fixed for one of these.[37]

His almost constant companion on such occasions was Miss Egerton-Smith, with whom Browning and his sister spent several summers, and to whom *La Saisiaz* is dedicated. After her death in the autumn of 1877, "he almost mechanically renounced all the musical entertainments to which she had so regularly accompanied him." A "first appearance of Joachim or Sarasate, a first concert of Richter or Henschel or Hallé" at which he had formerly appeared so regularly now had no appeal for him.[38] Music seems to have dropped suddenly from his life:

. . . its almost sudden eclipse was striking in the case of one who not only had been so deeply susceptible to its emotional influences, so conversant with its scientific construction and its

[36] See W. M. Rossetti, *Reminiscences*, p. 189.
[37] Orr, *Life*, p. 290.
[38] Sharp, p. 178.

multitudinous forms, but who was acknowledged as "musical" by those who best knew the subtle and complex meaning of that often misused term.[39]

It is quite natural, therefore, that the poetry of the years 1861-1877 should be richer in musical illustration and reference than Browning's other poetry. Musical terms and illustrations abound in *Balaustion's Adventure, Prince Hohenstiel-Schwangau, Fifine at the Fair, Red Cotton Night-Cap Country.*[40] In this period, too, comes the finest of Browning's poems on music, *Abt Vogler.* And in the faint march music of *St. Martin's Summer* it is hard not to see a forerunner of Avison and his *Grand March* as they appear in the *Parleying.*

After 1877 Browning returned ever more frequently to Italy. The concert music of London, accordingly, passed from his life. But music itself was too deeply rooted in his nature to be cast aside thus lightly; and in his last years we see it blossoming again. We catch a glimpse of Browning stopping at Chambéry, visiting Les Charmettes, the famous abode of Rousseau, and attempting to play Rousseau's *Dream* on the antique harpsichord there, just as he had done twenty-five years before when he passed on his way to Italy with his wife.[41] On another occasion Browning assisted in a performance of the *Barbiere* of Paisello in the Rossini theatre in Venice, an event which was made the more significant by the presence of Richard Wagner.[42] A new acquaintance of the poet's later days, a young lady, said to him, "I don't know whether you care for music, Mr. Browning, . . . but if you do, my mother is having some on Monday." "Why, my dear," he answered, perhaps only half jestingly, "I care for nothing else."[43]

[39] Orr, *Life,* p. 291.
[40] See, for example, *Dis Aliter Visum; Youth and Art; Fifine,* stanzas xlii, lxi, lxii, xci, xcii, cxvi; *The Ring and the Book,* I, 1208; VI, 1176-1178; VII, 958, 1504; X, 1699; XII, 860.
[41] Orr, *Life,* p. 316.
[42] *Idem,* p. 317.
[43] Griffin and Minchin, p. 287.

In the last few years of his life we catch occasional
glimpses of Browning in Venice, at Casa Alvisi, the home of
his friend Mrs. Katherine Bronson, playing upon the spinet
a fugue of Bach's, or singing for the sake of a new Russian
friend folk-songs and airs that he had picked up in his visit
to Russia over fifty years before.[44] His memory for music was
indeed great. Again we see him at Mrs. Bronson's villa in
Asolo in 1889, the last few weeks before his death. In the
loggia of an evening Browning would play upon the tinkling
little spinet made by Fernandino Ferrari at Ravenna in
1522. His taste ran to the old songs of his youth, the Chan-
son de Roland, old English ballads, perhaps Avison's *Grand
March*. These he would play in dreamy fashion.[45] Browning
was very evidently returning in his old age to his full passion
for music, one of the loves of his youth, of which return the
Parleying With Charles Avison is a most fitting manifestation.

II

BROWNING's characteristic conceptions of music and its purposes, its relation to the other arts, its efficacy and power,
seem to be almost complete and established by the time that
he published *Paracelsus* (1835). After this time his ideas
were developed and elaborated, ordered and summed up—as
they are in the *Parleying With Avison*—and illustrated pro-
fusely; nevertheless the germ of the idea was always to be
found in the earlier poems. In *Pauline* Browning delineated
his conception of music and its office:

> For music (which is earnest of a heaven,
> Seeing we know emotions strange by it,
> Not else to be revealed) is like a voice,
> A low voice calling fancy, as a friend,

[44] See Mrs. K. deK. Bronson, *Browning in Venice*, in *Century Magazine*,
XLI, 572-584 (N.S.).

[45] See Mrs. Bronson, *Browning in Asolo*, in *Century Magazine*, XXXVII,
920-931 (N.S.).

To the green woods in the gay summer time:
And she fills all the way with dancing shapes
Which have made painters pale, and they go on
Till stars look at them and winds call to them
As they leave life's path for the twilight world
Where the dead gather.[46]

In this passage we get a suggestion of all the ideas which
made up Browning's characteristic conception of music.
Here is hinted the comparison with the other arts; here is
music's superiority of expression already noted; here is suggested Browning's lifelong conception that the business of
music is to call back "from the twilight world where the dead
gather," those dead men and their emotions; here is even implied the idea which the young poet was to get more explic-
itly a few years later from the French memoir of Claude le
Jeune, that the fashion in music and musicians changes.

That Browning could never forbear a comparison of the
efficacy of the several arts of expression is a commonplace.[47]
No less well known is the fact that Browning always accorded
music first place among the arts in all his utterances, from
Pauline to *Asolando*. Music is capable of a richer, stranger,
deeper, and more direct expression of the passions of mankind than the other arts. Therefore it is music upon which he
calls in *Paracelsus:*

    . . . to perfect and consummate all,
Even as a luminous haze links star to star,
I would supply all chasms with music, breathing
Mysterious motions of the soul, no way
To be defined save in strange melodies.[48]

This comparison of the arts occurs again in *Balaustion's
Adventure;*[49] receives its baldest expression in *Fifine at the*

[46] *Pauline*, ll. 365-374.
[47] He may have learned this trick from Avison. See the *Essay on Musical
Expression*, pp. 23-31. Avison lists many analogies between music and
painting.
[48] *Paracelsus*, II, ll. 475-479.
[49] See especially ll. 318-335.

Fair;[50] and is resorted to finally and settled decisively, as we shall see, in the *Parleying With Charles Avison.* The most poetic and famous statement of the battle of the arts is to be found in *Abt Vogler:*

> . . . for think, had I painted the whole,
> Why, there it had stood, to see, not the process so wonder-
>   worth:
> Had I written the same, made verse—still, effect proceeds from
>   cause,
> Ye know why the forms are fair, ye hear how the tale is told;
> It is all triumphant art, but art in obedience to laws,
> Painter and poet are proud in the artist-list enrolled:—
>
> But here is the finger of God, a flash of the will that can,
> Existent behind all laws, that made them and, lo, they are!
> And I know not if, save in this, such gift be allowed to man,
> That out of three sounds he frame, not a fourth sound, but a
>   star. . . .
>
> But God has a few of us whom he whispers in the ear;
> The rest may reason and welcome: 'tis we musicians know.[51]

Music is eminent in catching "mysterious motions of the soul," "emotions not else to be revealed." It casts its nets in deeper seas than the other arts, and brings to the upper world emotions too profound and elemental to be apprehended by the shallower arts. This becomes one of the chief themes of the *Parleying With Charles Avison.*

We have seen also in the passage from *Pauline* the germ of Browning's characteristic conception of the business and purpose of music. The transient truth must be caught—and this is the business of all the arts—in some permanent form, as flies may be caught in amber. In the end even music is incapable of attaining permanent perfection, for the fashion changes all too often. Truth escapes "time's insufficient gar-

---

50 See especially stanza xc, ll. 1565-1588.

51 *Abt Vogler,* ll. 43-52, 87-88. Professor William Lyon Phelps thinks the poet got his philosophy of music from Schopenhauer's *Die Welt als Wille und Vorstellung,* which was published in 1819. See his *Browning, Schopenhauer and Music,* in *North Amerian Review,* CCVI, 622-627.

niture," and music that moved men once is no longer able to stir the heart. In this respect, indeed, painting and poetry almost outstrip music. They often wear better; yet music is more poignant:

> . . . some musician dead
> And gone, who feeling once what I feel now, instead
> Of words, sought sounds, and saved forever, in the same,
> Truth that escapes prose,—nay, puts poetry to shame.[52]

More precisely, Browning conceives it to be the service of music that it recreates the mood, the life, the times, and the figures in the mind of the composer of the music. Music is like "a low voice calling" to the fancy until it conjures back from "the twilight world" the dancing shapes or the moving emotions of a dead and gone musician. Thus indeed does Galuppi's *Toccata* call up to the poet's mind the gaiety and the tragedy of the "dead and done with" Venice. Life crowds back eagerly from that limbo to which it has gone. The soul of Venice is imprisoned in a bar or two of music. And Galuppi too, "good alike at grave and gay," may be seen sitting "stately at his clavi-chord."

> Here you come with your old music, and here's all the good it
>   brings.
> What, they lived once thus at Venice where the merchants were
>   the kings,
> Where Saint Mark's is, where the Doges used to wed the sea
>   with rings?[53]

Schumann's *Carnival*, which the husband of Elvire plays in *Fifine at the Fair*, gives to Browning the same vivid insight into the dissolute soul of Venice at Carnival time.[54] The music of the imaginary Master Hugues of Saxe-Gotha not only calls back the composer, but—and here is a peculiar working out of Browning's idea—the saints of the church walk through nave, transept, and aisle once more. In the glow of

[52] *Fifine at the Fair*, ll. 1569-1572.
[53] *A Toccata of Galuppi's*, ll. 4-6.
[54] See *Fifine at the Fair*, ll. 1588-1611.

Abt Vogler's music presences walk, and his "house not built
by hands" is peopled by souls yet unborn or by the "wonderful dead":

Nay more; for there wanted not who walked in the glare and
the glow,
Presences plain in the place: or, fresh from the Protoplast,
Furnished for ages to come, when a kindlier wind should blow,
Lured now to begin and live, in a house to their liking at
last;
Or else the wonderful Dead who have passed through the body
and gone,
But were back once more to breathe in an old world worth
their new:
What never had been, was now; what was, as it shall be anon;
And what is,—shall I say, matched both? for I was made
perfect too.[55]

And finally, in the *Parleying With Charles Avison* the
idea receives its most explicit expression. Avison's *Grand
March* calls back to Browning the spirit of the Common-
wealth; Strafford, Hollis, Haselrig, Strode, Hampden, Pym,
come marching with the mob to the stirring tune. More than
this, the musicians of Avison's own day, too,—Handel, Buononcini, Geminiani, Pepusch, and Greene,—come. The idea
of these ghostly figures crowding back toward full life ever
carries with it in Browning a gentle melancholy. It is just a
turn from this melancholy to that which Browning voiced in
his letter to Elizabeth Barrett; the pity that "in Music, the
Beau Ideal changes every thirty years." This last idea was
always in Browning's mind when he thought of music and
musicians. It may be said to be the informing idea of the
Parleying With Charles Avison. Toward the end of the poem
we find Browning considering the state of music in the year
1886, when the *Parleying* was written; and there is more
than a hint that these great names—Brahms, Wagner,
Dvorak, Liszt—shall pass as the name of Avison has.[56]

[55] *Abt Vogler*, ll. 33-40.
[56] See Orr, *Handbook*, p. 358.

It is especially interesting to observe the way in which
Browning turns all his conceptions of music to the delineation of his general philosophy. In this *Parleying* with Avison, he repeats a preachment which he has expounded many
times before. The only difference now is that he uses music to
illustrate his doctrine.[57] This it does most effectively. One of
the most characteristic and striking features of Browning's
philosophical system, as we have seen in the *Parleyings With
Bernard de Mandeville* and *Francis Furini*, is his denial of
any efficacy whatever, or any value, to man's mind and its
products. This, as we have seen, was necessary because the
findings of the intellect had impeached Browning's faith in
an all-loving, all-righteous and all-powerful God. Therefore
Browning repudiates the mind, and turns to the emotions
and instincts of man, and there builds back his faith. Music
deals in this very region of emotions, fears, joys, griefs; and
therefore music is the most effective of the arts, though
poetry and painting may often claim more permanence.
Thus it is that Browning once more gives expression to his
belief, and thus it is that Avison joins the general body of
Browning's philosophy. The poet inveighs against knowledge again:

> Of all the lamentable debts incurred
> By Man through buying knowledge, this were worst:
> That he should find his last gain prove his first
> Was futile—merely nescience absolute,
> Not knowledge in the bud which holds a fruit
> Haply undreamed of in the soul's Spring-tide,
> Pursed in the petals Summer opens wide,
> And Autumn, withering, rounds to perfect ripe,—
> Not this,—but ignorance, a blur to wipe
> From human records, late it graced so much.
> "Truth—this attainment? Ah, but such and such

[57] It is especially interesting to see how the two influences of his mother
—a simple religious faith and a love of music—meet at this point. Browning's attitude toward the intellect was ultimately due to his desire to uphold
the faith she taught him.

> Beliefs of yore seemed inexpugnable
> When we attained them! E'en as they, so will
> This their successor have the due morn, noon,
> Evening and night—just as an old-world tune
> Wears out and drops away, until who hears
> Smilingly questions—'This it was brought tears
> Once to all eyes,—this roused heart's rapture once?'
> So will it be with truth that, for the nonce,
> Styles itself truth perennial: 'ware its wile!
> Knowledge turns nescience,—foremost on the file,
> Simply proves first of our delusions."[58]

The true greatness of music then lies in the fact that it deals in those elemental things of life, the emotions and passions of mankind, rather than with the treacherous intellect. Thus does the *Parleying With Charles Avison* join the main stream of Browning's philosophical thought.

There is in the *Avison* one other characteristic bit of Browning's general philosophy—his notion of progress. For in spite of the fact that the history of music, as the poet sees it, affords no justification for a belief in progress, he sees hope in the contribution which music makes to mankind's advancement. The multiplication and variation of musical appliances did not impress him as being such epoch-making advances. The essential subjects of music were the same in earlier days:

> As Hope,
> Fear, Joy, and Grief,—though ampler stretch and scope
> They seek and find in novel rhythm, fresh phrase,—
> Were equally existent in far days
> Of Music's dim beginning—even so,
> Truth was at full within thee long ago,
> Alive as now it takes what latest shape
> May startle thee by strangeness.[59]

[58] *With Charles Avison*, ll. 339-360.
[59] *With Charles Avison*, ll. 364-371. This idea had been expressed before in *Fifine at the Fair*, ll. 1612-1668.

Yet by its ability to express emotion, music champions the
cause of man, and thus the cause of progress. It has ever
done so; and though it does not advance itself, it encourages
and marks the marching forward of humankind.

III

MRS. SUTHERLAND ORR, Arthur Symons, Nettleship, and
practically every other critic of the *Parleyings* has noticed
the extraordinary vividness of images and emotions in the
Parleying With Charles Avison. In this respect it is rivalled
only by the *Lairesse* and parts of the *Christopher Smart*.
The whole poem seems to have been induced by a picturesque
little incident which started Browning thinking of the word
"March":

> How strange!—but, first of all, the little fact
> Which led my fancy forth. This bitter morn
> Showed me no object in the stretch forlorn
> Of garden-ground beneath my window, backed
> By yon worn wall wherefrom the creeper, tacked
> To clothe its brickwork, hangs now, rent and racked
> By five months' cruel winter . . .[60]

Into this desolation comes

> . . . a bird
> Breast-deep there, tugging at his prize, deterred
> No whit by the fast-falling snow-flake: gain
> Such prize my blackcap must by might and main—
> The cloth-shred, still a-flutter from its nail
> That fixed a spray once.[61]

Browning wonders what told the blackcap, "no townsman
but born orchard-thief," that he should find here just the
scrap of manufactured rag that would line his nest better
than any loot he might have got in the country. Off the
blackcap flies carrying in his bill "the booty sure to set his

[60] *With Charles Avison*, ll. 1-7.
[61] *Idem*, ll. 14-19.

wife's each wing greenly a-quiver." But the poet cannot help pondering the fact that the bird should fly so far this uncomfortable March for such a scrap. And yet this fact is no stranger than that the word "March" should haunt his own mind until his memory like the bird

> . . . must straight clap pinion, well nigh roam
> A century back, nor once close plume, descry
> The appropriate rag to plunder, till she pounced—
> Pray, on what relic of a brain long still?
> What old-world work proved forage for the bill
> Of memory the far-flyer? "March" announced,
> I verily believe, the dead and gone
> Name of a music-maker: one of such
> In England as did little or did much,
> But, doing, had their day once. Avison![62]

In characteristic manner Browning has overlooked "the band of majesties familiar," all the great musicians of history, to light upon the organist of Newcastle.[63] The reason for the selection is of course that Browning's feet had marched to the bold measure of Avison's tune before his "hand could stretch an octave."[64] He recalls how the *March* seemed to him to "expand and greaten up to title" and how he peopled it with dream-marchers.

His memories of music in his early days bring him next to his old music-master, to whom he pays gracious tribute:

> Great John Relfe,
> Master of mine, learned, redoubtable,
> It little needed thy consummate skill
> To fitly figure such a bass![65]

---

[62] *With Charles Avison*, ll. 40-49. The beginning of the second section of the poem is strongly reminiscent of the beginning of the second book of *Sordello*.

[63] Avison was organist at St. Nicholas' Church at Newcastle from 1736 to 1770.

[64] See *With Charles Avison*, ll. 51-52.

[65] *Idem*, ll. 81-84.

He had himself learned from the great master "not only
Thorough Bass, but the whole arcana of the science." The
March was exceedingly simple, the key C "with the Greater
Third, in Triple Time, three crotchets to a bar," with no
change except the simplest one "from Tonic down to Domi-
nant." And yet if he could only catch in rhyme the manner
of that marching! But he cannot. He can only listen to the
music and

> . . . rub eyes disentranced
> And feel that, after all the way advanced,
> Back must I foot it, I and my compeers,
> Only to reach, across a hundred years,
> The bandsman Avison whose little book
> And large tune thus had led me the long way
> (As late a rag my blackcap) from to-day
> And to-day's music-manufacture,—Brahms,
> Wagner, Dvorak, Liszt,—to where—trumpets, shawms,
> Show yourselves joyful!—Handel reigns—supreme?
> By no means! Buononcini's work is theme
> For fit laudation of the impartial few;
> (We stand in England, mind you!) Fashion too
> Favors Geminiani—of those choice
> Concertos: nor there wants a certain voice
> Raised in thy favor likewise, famed Pepusch
> Dear to our great-grandfathers! In a bush
> Of Doctor's wig, they prized thee timing beats
> While Greenway trilled "Alexis." Such were feats
> Of music in thy day—dispute who list—
> Avison, of Newcastle organist![66]

As the *Grand March* is played it seems alive once more—

[66] *With Charles Avison,* ll. 92-112. Porter and Clarke, in the Florentine
edition, give the following note upon this passage:
Handel's opera "Radamista" was so successful that a party jealous of his
ascendency was formed against him, Buononcini and Ariosti being among
them. They had been attracted to London by the Royal Academy of Music,
and each had a following. To settle the difficulty, they wrote an opera
"Muzio Scaevola" together, Ariosti writing the first act, Buononcini the
second, and Handel the third. Ariosti's was nowhere in the competition;
and though Handel's was universally declared the best, the friends of
Buononcini held by him, and they were joined by all the people Handel

at least as alive as the figures of a waxwork-show who attest
that such people as they did live once. Why must music
pass? Browning wonders. If such a fugue or such a suite
would catch a soul heavenward once, why does it fail now?
Isn't perfection always perfect?

> Hear Avison! He tenders evidence
> That music in his day as much absorbed
> Heart and soul then as Wagner's music now.
> Perfect from center to circumference—
> Orbed to the full can be but fully orbed . . .[67]

Browning is face to face with the axiom from the French
memoir of Claude le Jeune: "In Music, the Beau Ideal
changes every thirty years." In some way he must find the
human reason for that fact. Avison's music was faultless, but
it fades to nothingness when it is compared with the song to
the Evening Star from Wagner's *Tannhäuser:*

> And yet—and yet—whence comes it that "O Thou"—
> Sighed by the soul at eve to Hesperus—
> Will not again take wing and fly away
> (Since fatal Wagner fixed it fast for us) . . .[68]

Even Handel cannot surpass that! And yet, the intimation
is that Wagner too will pass; for music which once filled all
the heart in another age will only attest that such emotions
once existed.

Yet in spite of this Browning is convinced that

> There is no truer truth obtainable
> By Man than comes of music.[69]

had offended, so that fashionable London was divided into two camps.
Byrom wrote a celebrated squib on the event,—
> "Some say compared to Bononcini
> That Mynheer Handel's but a Ninny;
> Others aver that he to Handel
> Is scarcely fit to hold a candle:
> Strange all this difference should be
> 'Twixt Tweedle-dum and Tweedle-dee!"

[67] *With Charles Avison*, ll. 127-131.
[68] *Idem*, ll. 132-135.
[69] *Idem*, ll. 138-139.

The reason for this is that music deals with the deeper and more elemental things of man's nature which the other arts hardly touch—man's emotions, instincts, his hopes, fears, joys—in short, what Browning calls man's soul. For soul Browning defines as that fact which eludes description but which

> Is no less recognized the absolute
> Fact underlying that same other fact
> Concerning which no cavil can dispute
> Our nomenclature when we call it "Mind"—
> Something not Matter . . .[70]

This sharp division between mind and soul is absolutely essential to Browning's philosophical system. When the mind fails or actually impeaches Browning's faith in the goodness of God, he appeals at once to what he calls soul—that is, the instinctive blind hope in man that there is an all-loving and all-powerful God presiding over the destinies of men. The soul, then, to Browning is the unplumbed sea of human feeling:

> Hates, loves, joys, woes, hopes, fears, that rise and sink
> Ceaselessly, passion's transient flit and wink,
> A ripple's tinting or a spume-sheet's spread
> Whitening the wave . . .[71]

Over this vast and restless sea of soul, mind has laid its false and flimsy superstructure of knowledge. But it is the business of true art to catch the nature of this soul, to dredge in this sea and bring some pure passion to the light of day forever. It is art's business to translate transiency into permanency; and it is as difficult to do this, says Browning, as to run mercury into a mould and thereafter have some shape to show. What we feel can never be put into the same rigid form as what we know. This is at once the puzzle and the prize. Music, and indeed all the arts, attempt to catch the Proteus

[70] *With Charles Avison,* ll. 144–148.
[71] *Idem,* ll. 188–191.

passion; and though music goes most deeply into this sea of soul and thus comes nearer attainment, she fails as do the other arts. All try to "arrest Soul's evanescent moods":

> Each Art a-strain
> Would stay the apparition,—nor in vain:
> The Poet's word-mesh, Painter's sure and swift
> Color-and-line-throw—proud the prize they lift!
> Thus felt Man and thus looked Man,—passions caught
> I' the midway swim of sea,—not much, if aught,
> Of nether-brooding loves, hates, hopes and fears,
> Enwombed past Art's disclosure.[72]

Browning thus comes once more to the struggle of the arts for supremacy, and remembering *Abt Vogler* we cannot be long in doubt of the award. In the contest poetry offers as its best the time-honored passage from the *Iliad*,[73] the same one, incidentally, that Ruskin had chosen as representative of the highest in poetry.[74] Browning paraphrases it thus:

> Fleet the years,
> And still the Poet's page holds Helena
> At gaze from topmost Troy—"But where are they,
> My brothers, in the armament I name
> Hero by hero? Can it be that shame
> For their lost sister holds them from the war?"
> —Knowing not they already slept afar
> Each of them in his own dear native land.[75]

Painting strives for the crown, offering Michael Angelo's fresco of the creation of Eve on the ceiling of the Sistine Chapel at Rome:

> Still on the Painter's fresco, from the hand
> Of God takes Eve the life-spark whereunto
> She trembles up from nothingness.[76]

[72] *With Charles Avison*, ll. 217-224.
[73] Book III, ll. 243 ff.
[74] See Ruskin, *Modern Painters*, III, Ch. 12, *Of the Pathetic Fallacy*. Ruskin had presented a copy of this volume to Browning.
[75] *With Charles Avison*, ll. 224-231.
[76] *Idem*, ll. 232-234.

And now Browning calls upon music to outdo both of them:

> Dredging deeper yet,
> Drag into day,—by sound, thy master-net,—
> The abysmal bottom-growth, ambiguous thing
> Unbroken of a branch, palpitating
> With limbs' play and life's semblance! There it lies,
> Marvel and mystery, of mysteries
> And marvels, most to love and laud thee for![77]

But, alas, music too fails. It is more poignant than the
other arts, and more successful in apprehending the soul,
but from the point of view of permanence it falls short even
of the achievements of the other arts. If she could only give
immortality to feeling she were the queenliest of arts:

> Alas—
> As well expect the rainbow not to pass!
> "Praise 'Radaminta'—love attains therein
> To perfect utterance! Pity—what shall win
> Thy secret like 'Rinaldo'?"—so men said:
> Once all was perfume—now, the flower is dead . . .[78]

The fullness of Handel's music is gone, and little more than
the ghost of it can be summoned back to inhabit earth. The
figures of the old music,

> . . . off they steal—
> How gently, dawn-doomed phantoms! back come they
> Full-blooded with new crimson of broad day—
> Passion made palpable once more. Ye look
> Your last on Handel? Gaze your first on Gluck!
> Why wistful search, O waning ones, the chart
> Of stars for you while Haydn, while Mozart
> Occupies heaven? These also, fanned to fire,
> Flamboyant wholly,—so perfections tire,—
> Whiten to wanness, till . . . let others note
> The ever-new invasion![79]

[77] *With Charles Avison*, ll. 235-241.
[78] *Idem*, ll. 251-256. Undoubtedly Browning means Handel's two operas
Radamisto and *Rinaldo*. The reason for the choice is obvious.
[79] *Idem*, ll. 266-276.

Music has no permanence. No matter what a master attains, his achievement cannot last; for "In Music, the Beau Ideal changes every thirty years."

Let others note these changes, Browning says. For his own part, he prefers to go back to the past; and to devote what talents he has to reinfusing with momentary life the half-dead, half-asleep old masters. To help him in this he calls again upon his music-master, Relfe, to whom he was an "all unworthy pupil." From the storehouse of Relfe's learning Browning now turns "to play the enlivener."

> Bring good antique stuff!
> Was it alight once? Still lives spark enough
> For breath to quicken, run the smouldering ash
> Red right-through.[80]

Are fools so rash as to call Avison, for example, stone-dead? He, the organist and theorist of Newcastle, and composer of the *Grand March*, is not to die because he lacked modern appliance and made little use of modulation in the modern fashion. Browning could make the *March* flare up if he should pitch in a few discords and resolutions, modulate without awe of Bach, and making the most of Hudl's suggestions.[81] Browning could modernize easily any old piece for those who like new lustre:

> . . . e'en thy March,
> My Avison, which, sooth to say—(ne'er arch
> Eyebrows in anger!)—timed, in Georgian years
> The step precise of British Grenadiers
> To such a nicety,—if score I crowd,
> If rhythm I break, if beats I vary,—tap
> At bar's off-starting turns true thunder-clap,
> Ever the pace augmented till—what's here?
> Titanic striding toward Olympus![82]

[80] *With Charles Avison*, ll. 293-296.
[81] Hudl, an obscure German musician of the eighteenth century, wrote a book entitled *A Tabular View of Modulation from any one Key to all other keys, Major or Minor.*
[82] *With Charles Avison*, ll. 310-318.

But Avison need fear no such irreverent innovation.
Browning prefers him to go on in his own natural melody.
After all the poet is reconciled to the fact that

> Music's throne
> Seats somebody whom somebody unseats,
> And whom in turn—by who knows what new feats
> Of strength,—shall somebody as sure push down . . .[83]

Yet the dispossessed musicians do not entirely die. We can
bring them back to life, not by modernizing them, but by
lending them our imaginations:

> Bring
> Our life to kindle theirs, and straight each king
> Starts, you shall see, stands up, from head to foot
> No inch that is not Purcell![84]

Therefore play Avison as he is; he has his place. But to suit
the mood of what we are to say, modulate the piece from
"bold C Major" into a minor key; "gently with A, now—in
the Lesser Third!"

As the music plays Browning continues to think. The impermanence of music brings him to one of his favorite subjects, the impermanence of knowledge. In music he has found
an apt illustration for his argument, because it deals primarily with the emotions of mankind, rather than with mind.
As musicians pass and the fashion changes, Browning muses,
just so does knowledge pass and change. Man's last gain in
knowledge simply undermines all he knew before. Essentially
false, knowledge has no element of growth in it. It is not a bud
that by summer's ripening breath will develop into the fruit
of autumn. Man's discarded knowledge is a blur to be wiped
from human records. Knowledge changes and dies just as an
old tune wears out and drops away, until people will say who
hear it, "Was this the song that brought tears once to all

[83] *With Charles Avison*, ll. 323-326.
[84] *Idem*, ll. 330-333.

eyes? Did this rouse heart's rapture once?" Do not trust knowledge; it will prove the "first of our delusions." Truth comes to us in other ways.

Therefore blare forth Avison's *March* as it should be played in the bold C Major!

> Lift thy brow,
> Man, the immortal, that wast never fooled
> With gifts no gifts at all, nor ridiculed—
> Man knowing—he who nothing knew![85]

Hope, joy, fear, and grief were the first subjects of music in its dim beginnings, and man has merely decked those subjects out in novel rhythm and fresh phrase since time began. Truth is essentially the same. No generation is satisfied with another's view because

> Truths escape
> Time's insufficient garniture: they fade,
> They fall—those sheathings now grown sere, whose aid
> Was infinite to truth they wrapped, saved fine
> And free through March frost: May dews crystalline
> Nourish truth merely,—does June boast the fruit
> As—not new vesture merely but, to boot,
> Novel creation? Soon shall fade and fall
> Myth after myth—the husk-like lies I call
> New truth's corolla-safeguard: Autumn comes,
> So much the better![86]

And where is Avison's *March* in all this? The march-motive is at least a permanent thing in human affairs.

> March-motive? that's
> Truth which endures resetting. Sharps and flats,
> Lavish at need, shall dance athwart thy score
> When ophicleide and bombardon's uproar
> Mate the approaching trample, even now
> Big in the distance—or my ears deceive—

85 *With Charles Avison*, ll. 361-364.
86 *Idem*, ll. 371-381.

> Of federated England, fitly weave
> March-music for the future!
>   Or suppose
> Back, and not forward, transformation goes?
> Once more some sable-stoled procession—say,
> From Little-ease to Tyburn—wends its way,
> Out of the dungeon to the gallows-tree
> Where heading, hacking, hanging is to be
> Of half-a-dozen recusants—this day
> Three hundred years ago! How duly drones
> Elizabethan plain-song—dim antique
> Grown clarion-clear the while I humbly wreak
> A classic vengeance on thy March![87]

What could be a better link from those dark times of tyranny to this future of a federated England which Browning sees at hand, than a March-motive that calls back the stirring times of England's struggle for parliamentary freedom—the times of Strafford, Pym, Hampden, Strode, Hollis, Haselrig—those times with which Browning had been familiar since he had helped his friend Forster with the prose life of Strafford, and had written his own drama, *Strafford*, to keep Macready from going out of England.[88] So now Browning utilizes the familiar material, and sets it to the music of Avison's *March* (aided by "glorious Bach"), to make a song for the mob as they cheer their troop to Preston Pans:

>   Man's
> The cause our music champions: I were loth
> To think we cheered our troop to Preston Pans
> Ignobly . . .[89]

Since that day progress has continued, as that day marked a progress from Elizabethan days. Music marks the milestones of progress in man, if it cannot progress itself. It has aided man and championed him. So the *Parleying* closes with

---

[87] *With Charles Avison*, ll. 382-399.

[88] See Griffin and Minchin, pp. 107-108. See also Orr, *Life*, p. 82.

[89] *With Charles Avison*, ll. 405-408.

the song Browning has written to go with the music of Avison's *March*, the song the mob is to roar to Pym:

> Fife, trump, drum, sound! and singers then,
> Marching, say "Pym, the man of men!"
> Up, heads, your proudest—out, throats, your loudest—
> "Somerset's Pym!"
>
> Strafford from the block, Eliot from the den,
> Foes, friends, shout "Pym, our citizen!"
> Wail, the foes he quelled,—hail, the friends he held,
> "Tavistock's Pym!"
>
> Hearts prompt heads, hands that ply the pen
> Teach babes unborn the where and when
> —Tyrants, he braved them,—patriots, he saved them—
> "Westminster's Pym!"[90]

[90] *With Charles Avison*, ll. 422-433.

AVISON'S GRAND MARCH

THE PROLOGUE AND EPILOGUE

THE *Prologue* and the *Epilogue* which Browning attached to the *Parleyings* have very little to do with the rest of the volume or with each other. The poem *Apollo and the Fates*, which serves as prologue, is a weird and dark tale recounting the intercession of the sun-god with the *Parcae* for the life of his friend Admetus. The *Epilogue* is a grotesque and humorous description of *Fust and his Friends* at the moment when the German printer admits his friends into the secret of his craft. Both poems are dramatic in form; and each in its own way enforces a cardinal thought of the *Parleyings*. The reader does not feel that there was any inherent necessity for including these poems in the volume, except that the poet made a habit of attaching prologue and epilogue to his books.

Yet in view of the biographical significance of the volume as a whole, it is not fanciful to see a significance in the themes which Browning has chosen to treat here. The *Prologue* is perhaps the commemoration of his long love of Greece. Greek literature was in all likelihood the very earliest of his intellectual enthusiasms. His father sang him to sleep with the odes of Anacreon, and one will not soon forget the lines

> My Father was a scholar and knew Greek.
> When I was five years old, I asked him once
> "What do you read about?"
>   "The siege of Troy."
> "What is a siege, and what is Troy?"
>   Whereat
> He piled up chairs and tables for a town,
> Set me atop for Priam, called our cat
> —Helen . . .[1]

Nor does one forget that Browning mastered the *Iliad* in the

1 *Development*, ll. 1-7.

original when he was twelve.[2] A heritage of this sort could not be forgotten by the poet, even though, as we have seen in the *Parleying With Gerard de Lairesse,* his doctrine of progress made it necessary for him to forswear it.

Perhaps the theme of the *Epilogue* was chosen for a similar biographical reason. It would be only fitting that in a biography of himself Browning should somewhere acknowledge the part that books and the business of printing had played in his life. Without printing there would never have been such a person as the poet Browning. The printed word had been his life and was to be his immortality. It had been, too, the vehicle of his preachments. Had he lived in the middle ages he must have lectured, like Abelard or Paracelsus. To Browning print was the means whereby the world might be saved. He could not close his autobiography without some acknowledgment of the medium through which he had become a voice to his age.

APOLLO AND THE FATES

A PROLOGUE

APOLLO and the Fates, the *Prologue* to the *Parleyings,* would have served Browning perfectly as a prologue to *Balaustion's Adventure.* The body of *Balaustion's Adventure,* it will be remembered, is a transcript of Euripides' *Alcestis;* and the play begins as the decree comes from the *Parcae* that it is time for Admetus to die. Before the opening of the play Apollo had tricked the Fates into an agreement that Admetus, who had been his benefactor when he was banished from heaven, should live when the summons came for him to die, if someone on the earth could be found who was willing to die in his place.[3] The story which is told in the *Prologue* to the *Parleyings* is the actual tricking of the Fates by Apollo. Browning gives the sources which suggested the scene to him,

[2] *Development,* l. 51.
[3] See *Balaustion's Adventure,* ll. 370-388.

in a note at the beginning of the poem. He draws from
Aeschylus' *Eumenides:*

> XO. τοιαῦτ' ἔδρασας καὶ Φέρητος ἐν δόμοις·
> Μοίρας ἔπεισας ἀφθίτους θεῖναι βρότους

and

> XO. σύ τοι παλαιὰς διανομὰς καταφθίσας
> οἴνῳ παραπάτησας ἀρχαίας θεάς . . .⁴

from Euripides' *Alcestis:*

> παιδὸς Φέρητος, ὃν θανεῖν ἐρρυσάμην,
> Μοίρας δολώσας· ἤνεσαν δέ μοι θεαὶ
> Ἄδμητον ᾅδην τὸν παραυτίκ' ἐκφυγεῖν,
> ἄλλον διαλλάξαντα τοῖς κάτω νεκρόν.

> οὐκ ἤρκεσέ σοι μόρον Ἀδμήτου
> διακωλῦσαι, Μοίρας δολίῳ
> σφήλαντι τέχνῃ;⁵

and finally from Homer's *Hymn. in Mercurium:*

> . . . ἐντεῦθεν δὴ ἔπειτα ποτώμεναι ἄλλοτε ἄλλη
> κηρία βόσκονται καί τε κραίνουσιν ἕκαστα.
> αἱ δ' ὅτε μεν, θυίωσιν ἐδηυῖαι μέλι χλωρὸν,
> προφρονέως ε θέλουσιν ἀληθείην ἀλορεύειν· . . .⁶

----

⁴ Browning refers to ll. 693-694, 697-698 in the *Eumenides*. In modern
texts (see that of A. W. Verrall, London, 1908) these lines are 726-727, 730-
731. They are thus rendered by Verrall:

> *Erin:* Even such a part didst thou play in Pheres' house, persuading the
> Moirai to release a mortal from death!

and

> *Erin:* Thou, thou it was, who abolishing old division, didst deceive with
> wine those ancient powers.

⁵ Browning refers only to ll. 12 and 33 of the *Alcestis*. I give 11-14 and
32-34 as necessary to a clear understanding. They may be translated thus:

> The son of Pheres; him I snatched from death,
> Cozening the Fates: the Sisters promised me—
> "Admetus shall escape the imminent death
> If he for ransom gives another life."

and

> Did this not suffice thee, to thwart that doom
> Of Admetus, when, all by thy cunning beguiled
> Were the Fates . . .

The translation is that of the *Loeb Classical Library*.

⁶ Only l. 559 of the ΕΙΣ ΕΡΜΗΝ is mentioned by Browning. For clarity
ll. 558-560 are necessary. The thought is:

From their home they fly now here, now there, feeding on honeycomb and

From these hints concerning the nature of the Fates and concerning Apollo's dealing with them in the case of Admetus, Browning fashions his weird little scene.

As the drama opens Apollo descends from the sky, pauses for a moment upon the slopes of Parnassus, and then sinks down into the black pit where the Fates reside. There the three sisters are crouched, one by the other, dealing to men of earth their little lives. Clotho, the first, takes a pinch of fleece, and brays "Birth" from her bronze lip; and a man is set upon the earth to measure his little span of life. Lachesis, the second, with her "niggardly digits" measures the fleece its due length, mixing meanwhile grief and pleasure into the weave. Atropos, the third, shears the threads, and one more mortal is lost in nothingness. As Apollo arrives, the sisters are measuring the life of Admetus:

CLOTHO
I spin thee a thread. Live, Admetus! Produce him!

LACHESIS
Go,—brave, wise, good, happy! Now chequer the thread!
He is slaved for, yet loved by a god. I unloose him
    A goddess-sent plague. He has conquered, is wed,
Men crown him, he stands at the height,—

ATROPOS
He is . . .

APOLLO (*Entering: Light.*)
"Dead?"

Nay, swart spinsters![7]

The sun-god has surprised the *Parcae* at their dreadful business. He has brought light into their black pit. The sisters bid the young god go back to the upper regions, but he by a sunbeam makes them pause. Then with his eyes upon

bringing all things to pass. And when they are inspired through yellow honey, they are willing to speak truth . . .
The translation is that of the *Loeb Classical Library.*
    [7] *Apollo and the Fates,* ll. 26-31.

the horrible shears about to clip the life-thread of Admetus,
Apollo requests that his benefactor be granted a few more
years of life:

> To threescore and ten
> Extend but the years of Admetus! Disaster
> O'ertook me, and, banished by Zeus, I became
> A servant to one who forbore me though master:
> True lovers were we. Discontinue your game,
> Let him live whom I loved, then hate on, all the same.[8]

But the Fates wish to argue the point. They doubt that it
will be to Admetus' happiness to live longer. It is only hope
in man that makes life worth living, they say; and the hope
is all illusion, created by Apollo himself. Apollo, not Prometheus, has set blind hopes to inhabit the houses of men. Admetus would scorn life were it not for hope. The Fates review
the life of man:

> What's infancy? Ignorance, idleness, mischief:
> Youth ripens to arrogance, foolishness, greed:
> Age—impotence, churlishness, rancor: call *this* chief
> Of boons for the loved one? Much rather bid speed
> Our function, let live whom thou hatest indeed![9]

And after all, they conclude, Apollo's gleam produces only
the semblance of good, not good itself. When the sun goes,
the earth will be an ice-ball.

But Apollo is not willing to take the answer of the Fates.
If they say true, why do friends always wish each other long
life? And why, if death is such a relief, do men cling so to
life?

The glamor which Apollo gives to life, the Fates answer,
lures men on in a perpetual hope of better things. Apollo is
forced to admit the truth of this. He does practise illusion
upon men; he leads men on to other and higher things. Yet
Apollo believes man has in himself an independent virtue.

[8] *Apollo and the Fates,* ll. 55-60.
[9] *Idem,* ll. 76-80.

There is light in the heart of man—a small sun comparable in substance to the sun itself. As Apollo speaks he proffers to the sisters the bowl he has with him, and presses them to partake of man's invention, wine. He tells them of its history—how Bacchus, the youngest of the gods, would fain earn the worship of man by some excellent gift to him; and finding that all things had been given to man by the other gods, Bacchus prompted man to invent wine.

The sisters are persuaded to drink, and instantly become intoxicated. Under the happy influence of wine they begin to tell the truth. Clotho and Lachesis almost dance. They admit that "one could live—at a pinch"—an amazing concession for them. When Apollo presses more wine upon them, and exhorts them to see some good in the world, they all join hands and dance. Presently under the influence of the red wine, the Fates pronounce the ultimate truth concerning life, denying what they had said before:

Infancy? What if the rose-streak of morning
   Pale and depart in a passion of tears?
Once to have hoped is no matter for scorning!
   Love once—e'en love's disappointment endears!
A minute's success pays the failure of years.

Manhood—the actual? Nay, praise the potential!
   (Bound upon bound, foot it around!)
What *is?* No, what *may* be—sing! that's Man's essential!
   (Ramp, tramp, stamp and compound
Fancy with fact—the lost secret is found!)

Age? Why, fear ends there: the contest concluded,
   Man *did* live his life, *did* escape from the fray:
Not scratchless but unscathed, he somehow eluded
   Each blow fortune dealt him, and conquers to-day:
To-morrow—new chance and fresh strength,—might we say?

Laud then Man's life—no defeat but a triumph![10]

10 *Apollo and the Fates,* ll. 206-221.

The Fates have readily told the truth under the influence
of the glorious drunkenness. Wine, by which Browning intends to symbolize the imagination of mankind,[11] has been
compounded with the commonplace facts of the Fates, and
the lost secret is found. Life may be very happy and purposeful. Flesh and spirit, fact and imagination, the actual
and the hoped-for, have joined each other in man's existence,
and man's life is a triumph.

Suddenly there is an explosion from the earth's center.
The sisters are sobered at once. They break the dance, loose
hands, and start in horror at the things they have said in
their drunkenness. They admit they have conceived and
borne truth. But now they return to their swift shuttles to
decree the fates of men.

Apollo pleads once more for the life of Admetus:

> Be gracious though, blent,
> Good and ill, love and hate streak your life-gift![12]

But the Fates pronounce their decision. Admetus may live
his years out if he can find a person upon earth to die in his
place. Apollo is pleased with his triumph. He knows his
friend, and dares prophesy that Admetus will bear himself
well:

> Admetus, I know thee!
> Thou prizest the right these unwittingly give
> Thy subjects to rush, pay obedience they owe thee!
> Importunate one with another they strive
> For the glory to die that their king may survive.[13]

[11] See Orr, *Handbook,* p. 342: "The one serious idea which runs through
the poem is conveyed in its tribute to the power of wine; in other words, to
the value of imagination as supplement to and interpreter of fact. Its par-
tial, tentative, and yet efficient illumining of the dark places of life is
vividly illustrated by Apollo: and he only changes his imagery when he
speaks of Reason as doing the same work. It is the imaginative, not the
scientific 'reason' which Mr. Browning invokes as help in the perplexities
of experience; as it is the spiritual, and not scientific 'experience' on which,
in the subsequent discussions, he will so emphatically take his stand."

[12] *Apollo and the Fates,* ll. 249-250.

[13] *Idem,* ll. 256-260.

In his mind's eye Apollo sees the friends, the father, the
mother, of Admetus rushing to die for him; and he sees also
Admetus refusing their sacrifice. The young and hopeful
god sees more nobility in human nature than is really there.
The Fates, foreseeing already the selfishness of all save Alcestis, laugh in mocking fashion as the young and ignorant
god ascends back into his place in the sky. Darkness settles
again in the pit of the Fates.

Thus ends the weird and fantastic *Prologue*. What
Browning means to say by the poem is, I think, sufficiently
clear. The *Parcae*, who tell the ultimate truth about life only
when they are intoxicated, see life from infancy to age as a
progressive triumph. It is wine, or imagination, the latest
acquisition of mankind, which makes the sisters see truly.
The lost secret is rediscovered and life is seen as it truly is.
The infinite potentialities of man become apparent, and life
becomes a purposeful and progressive march. This idea that
imagination must be a supplement to and an interpreter of
fact, is one that underlies every one of the *Parleyings*. The
poem is another expression of Browning's faith.

The poem is significant in one other respect. It is Browning's characteristic idea that good and evil are inextricably
mixed. The Fates are ultimately made to admit by the outcome of the affair that the web of destiny defeats their spin-
ning. The things which they intend to be good and evil often
change place with each other. Then, too, Apollo gilds the
earth with illusory hopes. The result is that man struggles,
and as he struggles he grows, and the ultimate result is progress. Thus seeming evil is ever turned to good by the ingenuity of Browning. In this way the *Prologue* strikes several
major chords which are to be heard again in the body of the
Parleyings.

FUST AND HIS FRIENDS

AN EPILOGUE

For the *Epilogue* to the *Parleyings* Browning chose to depict the scene in which printing was first made known to the
world. It takes place in Mayence at the house of John Fust,
whom Browning conceives, either wilfully or ignorantly, to
have been the first printer. The moment is on August 14,
1457, when Fust and his helper, Peter Schoeffer of Gernsheim, are about to publish their famous *Psalter.* Here, too,
as well as in the *Prologue,* Browning seems to have fashioned
an imaginary scene from hints from several different sources.
Apparently he did not know the facts of the invention of
printing as the most reliable historians gave them. He took
quite seriously the idea that John Fust was the first printer,
and that the *Psalter* was the first printed book. These mis-
conceptions were quite common in the nineteenth century;[14]
and though Browning's tone is jocular, he nowhere suggests
that the story is not authentic. The most startling misconception Browning may have derived from his favorite *Biographie Universelle.* Where more accurate historical accounts
saw in Fust the sinister money-lender who beguiled Gutenberg out of his invention, the *Biographie* saw simply goodness of nature. Fust was an

. . . orfèvre à Maïence, au milieu du 15ᵉ siècle, l'un des citoyens
notables de cette ville, et distingué par ses richesses non moins
que par ses connaissances dans les arts, partage, avec Guttemberg et Schoeffer, la gloire d'avoir inventé l'imprimerie. . . .[15]

After mentioning the various contributors to the art of
printing, and praising the zeal of Fust, and describing the
first printed book, the *Biblia Sacra Latina*—which the *Bio-*

[14] See Sutherland Edwards, *The Faust Legend,* London, 1886, pp. 31 ff.
Browning may have consulted this volume.
[15] *Biographie Universelle,* XVI, 203.

graphie inaccurately says is undated[16]—the account goes on to say:

Des difficultés s'élevèrent, en 1455, entre Fust et Guttemberg; et par suite, ils se séparèrent (6 Novembre 1455). Fust, en remboursement des sommes qu'il répétait, resta propriétaire de l'établissement, qu'il exploita avec Schoeffer. Q'est à cette nouvelle société que l'on doit le Pasutier (*Psalmorum codex*), de 1457 (14 août), le plus ancien des ouvrages imprimés avec date . . . On a quelquefois confondu Fust avec Faust le Magicien.[17]

Browning seems also to have depended on the *Biographie* for his dates. Yet if he used the *Biographie* as his main source, he found it necessary to ignore some of the material given there, for the sake of his poetical idea.

With the material from the *Biographie*, Browning incorporated material from other sources. His description of the drinking-bout in which Fust engaged, he took outright from Goethe's *Faust*.[18] The view of Helen of Troy and the visit of friends to Fust he may have taken from Goethe's, Marlowe's, or any other version of the legend. It is interesting, too, that Browning seems to have known the account of Dr. Faustus given by Defoe, who was the first writer to spread extensively in England the idea that the printer Fust and the magician Faust were one and the same.[19] Many details in Browning's poem seem to have their origin in the description of Dr. Faustus in Paris:

Thus the famous doctors of the faculty at Paris, when John Faustus brought the first printed books that had then been seen in the world, or at least seen there, into the city and sold them for manuscripts: they were surprised at the performance, and questioned Faustus about it; but he affirming they were manu-

---

[16] The famous Gutenberg Bible is dated at Mainz, 1455.

[17] *Biographie Universelle*, XVI, 204.

[18] See Goethe, *Faust*, Part I, ll. 1720 ff. See especially ll. 1912 ff. The scene is in Auerbach's cellar in Leipzig.

[19] I state this on the authority of William A. Speck, Curator of the Collection of Classical German Literature at Yale University. Browning, it is clear from l. 29 of the *Epilogue*, did not confuse Fust with Faust, even though he used material from the Faust legends.

scripts, and that he kept a great many clerks employed to write
them, they were satisfied for awhile.

But looking farther into the work, they observed the exact
agreement of every book, one with another, that every line
stood in the same place, every page a like number of lines, every
line a like number of words; if a word was mis-spelt in one, it
was mis-spelt also in all, nay, that if there was a blot in one, it
was alike in all: they began again to muse, how this should be;
in a word, the learned divines not being able to comprehend the
thing (and that was always sufficient), concluded it must be the
Devil, that it was done by magic and witchcraft, and that in
short, poor Faustus (who was indeed nothing but a mere
printer), dealt with the Devil.[20]

Under Browning's hand the similarity between the "manuscripts" is worked up into a very effective scene.

The poem begins with the arrival at Fust's house of seven
of his friends, all divines. As the drama opens they are seen
climbing the stairs to find Fust, whom they consider as lost
to the devil. They find him in his workroom, his head sunk
upon his desk between his outspread arms. The word is about
Mayence that Fust has sold his soul to Lucifer and they
have come to save him. They demand that he answer their
questions, expecting to hear him confess to sins so enormous
that his tongue will halt in the telling.

As they speak Fust half lifts his head and denies that he
has mortgaged his soul to the devil. He grants that he may
be a lost man, but not in the manner they imagine. They
reply that the whole town says he has sold his salvation for
lust's sake:

> How else but by help of Sir Belial didst win
> That Venus-like lady, no drudge of thy sort
> Could lure to become his accomplice in sin?
> Folk nicknamed her Helen of Troy![21]

[20] Defoe, *Political and Modern History of the Devil*, in *The Novels and Miscellaneous Works of Daniel Defoe,* ed. Sir Walter Scott, Bohn Standard Library, London, 1913, III, 559.
[21] *Fust and his Friends,* ll. 62-65.

They are curious. They want Fust to tell them from start to
finish the whole story, beginning with his father, the goldsmith. Fust admits that the gold of his father has helped him
to a leman; he admits that he tricked the drinkers at the inn
and made them see grapevines growing in the tavern. But he
did it by plying them with wine, and by boring gimlet holes
through the table, and not by the aid of Satan. He admits, in
short, that his sin has been excess in all things, but nothing
more. They want to know how a goldsmith's son achieved
such honors, but Fust will not bother to explain. They want
to know what has become of Peter Genesheim (Schoeffer of
Gernsheim). Why has he been so taciturn? Why does he hint
that Fust has taught him to speak in such a manner that all
the men of the earth may hear him? The friends knew, they
say, that Fust was in league with the devil, but in the last
few days their hopes of saving him have been restored because he has seemed so despondent. But Fust turns upon
them:

Spare Fust, then, thus contrite!—who, youthful and healthy,
　　Equipped for life's struggle with culture of mind,
Sound flesh and sane soul in coherence, born wealthy,
　　Nay, wise—how he wasted endowment designed
For the glory of God and the good of mankind!

That much were misused such occasions of grace
　　Ye well may upbraid him, who bows to the rod.
But this should bid anger to pity give place—
　　He has turned from the wrong, in the right path to plod,
Makes amends to mankind and craves pardon of God.[22]

Fust hints that he has retrieved his soul by doing service to
mankind.

But the friends insist upon knowing what is behind the
closed door in the next room. With a psalm in Latin, they begin to exorcise the devil which possesses the soul of Fust, but
their Latin is so uncertain that it is unwise to guess what

[22] *Fust and his Friends*, ll. 141-150.

psalm they may have in mind. They do not agree among
themselves upon that matter. They quarrel ludicrously over
what the Latin should really be. The sixth friend admits
that he had the psalm upon a sheepskin but was tempted,
and sold it. The seventh swears that his purse would have
been empty ere he would have parted with such a prize. Fust
sees his opportunity. They have brought the conversation to
the very point he could have wished. He has found a place to
stand, and now like Archimedes he can move the world. But
as he utters the name of Archimedes the seven friends think
he is calling on one of his familiar spirits, and almost run
away. Fust has to reassure them. He bids them wait a moment. As he goes behind the closed door to the mysterious
room, the friends momentarily expect Archimedes to appear.
Five minutes later, Fust returns with the psalm they have
been attempting to repeat completely printed in black and
white. He presents to each of them a printed slip. Inspection
assures them that their slips are all alike, letter for letter,
word for word, and line for line. Fust then throws open the
mysterious door, and the printing press is seen in operation.
As he does this he tells how he has struggled through the
long years, how near he has been to failure and discouragement, how hard he has hoped. And now that he has succeeded
he begins to praise God:

> Omniscient omnipotent God, Thee I thank,
> Thee ever, Thee only!—Thy creature that shrank
>
> From no task Thou, Creator, imposedst! Creation
>   Revealed me no object, from insect to Man,
> But bore Thy hand's impress: earth glowed with salvation:
>   "Hast sinned? Be thou saved, Fust! Continue my plan,
> Who spake and earth was: with my word things began."[23]

Fust's allegiance to evil is ended. He has freed himself by his
invention:

[23] *Fust and his Friends,* ll. 279-285.

"Far and wide, North and South, East and West, have domin-
   ion
O'er thought, winged wonder, O word! Traverse world
In sun-flash and sphere-song! Each beat of thy pinion
   Bursts night, beckons day: once Truth's banner unfurled,
Where's Falsehood? Sun-smitten, to nothingness hurled!"[24]

Truth will be spread, and false tradition and loose narration
by word of mouth are done with. The slow scribe has been
replaced by a swifter and more accurate recorder. Fact can
now be fixed fast, even though "truths change by an hour's
revolution." Man need no longer depend on the distorting
processes of narration and tradition. Truth is to become the
heritage of all. In seeking for a method to spread truth
broadcast, Fust recalled how he had seen goldsmiths engrave
letters on gold. Why not letters on lead? Thus Fust explains
his invention to his friends.

Once explained, it does not seem to them such a miracle.
The possibility of such a thing had occurred to them often.
Fust admits the simplicity of the invention, but points to the
fact that time makes small things great. He begins anew to
praise God, who is everywhere at work in nature. Only a film
hides God from us as He works His wonders. Even the smallest things obey the laws of God—they grow, decline and dis-
appear. All things in nature follow their natural instincts:

In such various degree, fly and worm, ore and plant,
   All know, none is witless: round each, a wall
Encloses the portion, or ample or scant,
   Of Knowledge: beyond which one hair's breadth, for all
Lies blank—not so much as a blackness—a pall

Some sense unimagined must penetrate: plain
   Is only old license to stand, walk or sit,
Move so far and so wide in the narrow domain
   Allotted each nature for life's use: past it
How immensity spreads does he guess? Not a whit.

24 *Fust and his Friends*, ll. 291-295.

> Does he care? Just as little. Without? No, within
> Concerns him: he Knows. . . .[25]

Thus does Browning make the printer Fust preach his doctrines concerning ignorance and knowledge in man, and
again the heart is extolled at the expense of the head. Knowledge of the head is ever changing, we are reminded again,
and as soon as the new knowledge comes the old is invali-
dated. He follows God yearningly with his heart, and that is
man's salvation. It is, after all, only simple hope.

> Such, friends, is my lot:
> I am back with the world: one more step to the goal
> Thanks for reaching I render—Fust's help to Man's soul![26]

Truth will fly from the printing press like manna from God.
But the friends intrude themselves on Fust's exclamations.
Why, if he is saved now and happy, was he so dejected when
they came in? Fust turns to them with his explanation. If his
press will spread truth, it will also spread lies and falsehood.
Again his friends announce that they have already foreseen
this difficulty. Heresy can no longer be stopped by the burning of the chief heretic; the unorthodox will retort upon the
priests through the medium of the press. The divines are at a
loss as to how to meet the changed situation. They fear for
the future, and quote the prophecy of Huss:

> When, goosequill, thy reign o'er the world is abolished!
> Goose—ominous name! With a goose woe began:
> Quoth Huss—which means "goose" in his idiom unpolished—
> "Ye burn now a goose: there succeeds me a swan
> Ye shall find quench your fire!"[27]

The prophecy, of course, points to Luther; and Fust, the

---

[25] *Fust and his Friends*, ll. 401-412. I correct an obvious mispunctuation
in l. 412 by the first edition.

[26] *Idem*, ll. 428-430.

[27] *Idem*, ll. 471-475.

far-seeing, closes the *Epilogue* with his own hopeful
prophecy:

I foresee such a man.[28]

The meaning of the poem is sufficiently apparent. Again,
as in the *Prologue*, there is the suggestion that good and evil
are almost inextricably bound up together. There is too another favorite idea of Browning's, that man can never really
attain knowledge and that his salvation lies in his emotions.
What stands out most prominently, however, is the idea of
progress. In spite of Fust's fear that his invention will serve
to spread falsehood as well as truth, there is a strong suggestion of advancement, from the "blur, blunder and blot" of
the scribes to the greater accuracy of the printing-press.
Browning is repeating here once more his favorite themes.
The repetition has become a bit tedious.

Analysis of the *Prologue* and *Epilogue* has shown, I think,
how different they are in form from the body of the *Parleyings*, and yet how similar in their underlying themes. They
are decidedly inferior to the seven *Parleyings*, both in style
and in interest; and it is rather unfortunate that Browning's
autobiographical poem, in which there is so much that is excellent, should begin and end in such prosaic fashion.

Yet it should not be forgotten that while the *Prologue* and
Epilogue are prosaic and dull, they add, by dint of repetition, to Browning's delineation of his philosophy. The poet's
contribution to the myth of the *Prologue* is the interpretation of wine as imagination. Here his insistence on the greatness of man's emotional nature appears once more. It is only
by transforming the facts of life through the power of the
imagination, that man can see the vision of his potentialities.
When he has seen them, he struggles for them, and the great
result is moral progress. But, says Browning, the necessary
factor is imagination; it is through it that man catches some-

---

28 *Fust and his Friends*, l. 475.

thing of God. It is indeed fitting that the *Parleyings,* which delineate Browning's full thought, should thus begin with an insistence on the necessity for having exactly his type of philosophy.

As the *Prologue* shows how imagination "touching all that is leadlike in life turns it gold," the *Epilogue* shows an example of the working of imagination in the great cause of progress. Fust's allegiance to evil is ended when he has the idea that enables him to aid the advancement of mankind. He has invented a machine that will serve the cause of truth by spreading the winged words which are the symbols of man's visions. To be sure, his invention may serve evil as well, but Browning implies that God, through the medium of time, will glorify the whole and will work greater wonders than Fust can foresee. So the poem is one more example of Browning's optimistic philosophy, which has found utterance all through the *Parleyings.* As the song of the Fates proclaimed Browning's hopefulness, so too does Fust's praise to God.

BIBLIOGRAPHICAL NOTE

THE works most frequently referred to throughout this study are listed below:

The Life of Robert Browning With Notices of his Writings, his Family, & his Friends, by W. Hall Griffin, completed and edited by Harry Christopher Minchin. London, 1910. This is referred to as Griffin and Minchin.

Life and Letters of Robert Browning, by Mrs. Sutherland Orr. New edition, revised and in part rewritten by Frederic G. Kenyon. Boston and New York, 1908. This is referred to as Orr, *Life.*

A Handbook to the Works of Robert Browning, by Mrs. Sutherland Orr. London, 1923. Sixth edition. This is referred to as Orr, *Handbook.*

Life of Robert Browning, by William Sharp. London, 1890. This is referred to as Sharp.

Catalogue of Pictures, Drawings and Engravings; Autograph Letters and Manuscripts; Books and Works of Art, the Property of R. W. Barrett Browning, Esq. (Deceased), 1913. References to this work are given as Sotheby. The catalogue was published by the auctioneers, Sotheby, Wilkinson and Hodge.

The Letters of Robert Browning and Elizabeth Barrett Barrett, 1845-1846. In two volumes. New York and London, 1899. This is referred to as *Letters of R. B. and E. B. B.*

Letters from Robert Browning to Various Correspondents. Edited by Thomas J. Wise. Two volumes. London, 1895-1896. This is referred to as *Letters from R. B. to Various Correspondents,* 1st Series.

Letters from Robert Browning to Various Correspondents. Edited by Thomas J. Wise. Two volumes. London, 1907-1908. This is referred to as *Letters from R. B. to Various Correspondents,* 2d Series.

Letters of Robert Browning to Miss Isa Blagden. Arranged for publication by A. Joseph Armstrong. Waco, 1923. This is referred to as *Letters of R. B. to Isa Blagden.*

Publications of the Browning Society (London), 1881-1891. These papers are bound in three volumes. They are referred to as *Browning Society Papers,* by title of paper and volume.

A Guide-Book to the Poetic and Dramatic Works of Robert Browning, by George Willis Cooke. Boston and New York. This will be referred to as Cooke.

Browning as a Philosophical and Religious Teacher, by Henry Jones, M.A., LL.D. Glasgow, 1902.

Robert Browning, How to Know Him, by William Lyon Phelps. Indianapolis (n. d.).

Robert Browning's Complete Works, Florentine edition. New York, 1910. In twelve volumes. Introductions and notes by Charlotte Porter and Helen A. Clarke, with an Introductory Essay by William Lyon Phelps. The text of this edition is Browning's revised text. Line references in this study are to this edition because of its accessibility and convenience.

Parleyings With Certain People of Importance in Their Day: To wit: Bernard de Mandeville, Daniel Bartoli, Christopher Smart, George Bubb Dodington, Francis Furini, Gerard de Lairesse, and Charles Avison. Introduced by A Dialogue between Apollo and the Fates; concluded by Another between John Fust and his Friends. By Robert Browning. London, 1887. This volume is the basis of the present study.

INDEX